N

N

THE
FIRST HOLY ONE

by
MAURICE
COLLIS

FABER AND FABER
24 Russell Square
London

To

FELIKS TOPOLSKI

First published in mcmxlviii
by Faber and Faber Limited
24 Russell Square London W.C.1
Printed in Great Britain by
R. MacLehose and Company Limited
The University Press Glasgow

Contents

I. THE FIRST HOLY ONE   11

II. THE FIRST HOLY ONE AND THE VENERABLE SIR   32

III. THE ECLIPSE OF THE FIRST HOLY ONE   48

IV. THE EMINENT FOUNDER COMES   66

V. WU SEEKS TO COMMUNE WITH HEAVEN   98

VI. WU BATTLES WITH SORCERY   125

VII. A GREAT CONFUCIAN   137

VIII. WU FINDS A NEW EARTH AND OPENS A WAY TO

HEAVEN   168

IX. THE FIRST HOLY ONE WINS OUT   195

NOTES ON AUTHORITIES   216

LIST OF DATES   217

NOTES ON ILLUSTRATIONS   219

INDEX   231

Illustrations

(For details of Plates see Notes on Illustrations, page 219)

I. ATTEMPT ON THE FIRST DIVINE AUGUST ONE

facing page 80

II. (*a*) A HAN CHARIOT

(*b*) A HAN AUDIENCE   81

III. THE STANDARDS OF HSIANG YÜ   96

IV. THE EMINENT FOUNDER AT HSIEN-YANG   97

V. A TRIBAL WAR DRUM MADE DURING THE HAN
DYNASTY   112

VI. A PORTRAIT OF THE EMPEROR WEN OF THE
HAN DYNASTY   113

VII. A BATTLE BETWEEN THE CHINESE AND THE
HUNS   128

VIII. (*a*) A HAN SORCERER

(*b*) A HAN EXORCIST

(*c*) FEMALE MUSICIANS   129

IX. THE PRINCESS OF COLOURED CLOUDS   160

X. CONFUCIAN SCHOLARS COLLATING CLASSICAL

TEXTS   *facing page* 161

XI. (*a*) KING EUCRATIDES

(*b*) KING DIODOTOS

(*c*) KING MENANDER   176

XII. THE GRECO-BUDDHIST RELIQUARY OF

BIMARAN   177

XIII. A BUDDHA IN GHANDĀRA STYLE   192

XIV. A BODDISATTVA IN EARLY CHINESE STYLE   193

XV. A GHANDĀRA STYLE HEAD OF A BUDDHA   208

XVI. PORTRAIT OF THE EMPEROR WEN OF THE SUI

DYNASTY   209

Maps

CHINA AT THE TIME OF CONFUCIUS (500 B.C.)

SHOWING STATES OF THE GRAND FEUDATORIES   *page* 13

STATES CONQUERED BY CH'IN WHILE BECOMING

THE PARAMOUNT POWER DURING THIRD CENTURY

B.C.   51

HAN EMPIRE IN SECOND AND FIRST CENTURIES B.C.   66

THE HAN EMPIRE AND THE HELLENISED WEST IN

SECOND CENTURY B.C.   168

The First Holy One[1]

Confucius was not a god, or God, or a Prophet of God. Gods there were in plenty at his period; Buddha, his contemporary, later became God, as did Christ; the Jewish Prophets of God slightly preceded him, and Mohammed and Mani, also Prophets of God, appeared after him. Speaking of himself, he said: 'As to being a Divine Sage or even a Good Man, far be it from me to make any such claim.'[2] And he added: 'A Divine Sage I cannot hope ever to meet, the most I can hope for is to meet a true gentleman.'[3] As both these sentences occur in the *Analects*, one of the so-called *Four Books*, which constitute half the Confucian Canon, they must be said to reflect the orthodox view. It is true that later Emperors conferred title after splendid title upon him, among them styles intimating that he was a Divine Sage, as does the style First Holy One, and that of Universal Father conferred in the

[1]One of the posthumous titles of Confucius. The name, Confucius, is the latinised rendering of the Chinese K'ung Fu-tzu. K'ung was his surname: Fu-tzu means 'The Master' in the academic sense it carries in such a phrase as 'The Master of Balliol'. Confucius and his great follower Mencius are the only Chinese with Latin names. The explanation is that the Confucian books were translated first into Latin (c.f. the *Confucius Sinarum Philosophus* of the Jesuits published in Paris in 1687). Having become famous in Europe as Confucius, it was impossible thereafter to call him K'ung Fu-tzu.

[2]*Analects*, Book VII, 37, Arthur Waley's translation.

[3]*Analects*, Book VII, 26, same translation.

seventh century A.D. But the necessity of magnifying him in public esteem on occasions when the populace was attracted by rival systems suggests a political reason for these titles. For the educated he was and remained a man, though gifted with extraordinary powers of mind. To call him, out of profound respect, a Sage or even a Divine Sage or Holy One was not improper, though he had disclaimed the titles. But, as employed by the educated, such terms did not imply that they believed him to be a transcendent being. Had they done so, it would not have sufficed to make him a god. As the infallible author of the state cult, he would have had to be God, or at least the inspired Prophet of God.

There is no trace of this, however, in the canonical books. Speaking further of himself, he said: 'I am not one of those who have innate knowledge', i.e. like a divine person. 'I am simply one who loves the past and who is diligent in investigating it.' (*Analects* VII, 19.) And he explained that his study of it had led him to a conclusion which could be summed up in the sentence: consideration for others' feelings is the basis of society. (*Analects* XV, 2 and IV, 15). This consideration, he said, was the grand quality of the ancient rulers. If everyone showed this consideration, this 'not doing to others what you would not have them do to you', a universal reciprocity of goodness, as in the Golden Age of the Sainted Emperors, would result.

These thoughts had a very particular realness for Confucius, because he lived at a period when the old society of China was disintegrating. His dates are 550–479 B.C.[1] These fall within the Chou Dynasty which lasted from 1122–253 B.C. But from the reign of Yu Wang (780 B.C.) the Emperors had begun to fall under the power of the great feudal lords. These at first had been more numerous, since their estates were smaller than they became later on. By the time of Confucius, the Grand Feudatories had estates the size of kingdoms and ruled them with sovereign power, leaving

[1]He was therefore born nearly a hundred years before the Greek philosophers whose works have come down to us in more than fragments.

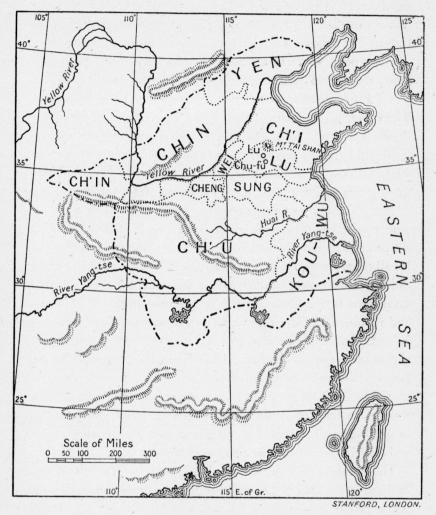

CHINA AT THE TIME OF CONFUCIUS (500 B.C.) SHOWING
STATES OF THE GRAND FEUDATORIES

to the Emperor an empty title and the ritual duty of the imperial sacrifices. His Court was at Lo-yang by the Yellow River in a small domain marked as Chou on map p. 50. China was no longer one country but a dozen, each potentially the enemy of any other.

The times to which Confucius looked back with admiration were firstly those of the early part of the Chou Dynasty, when, as he saw it, the Emperors governed a united land through loyal feudatories. There were no wars then; any fighting was the chastisement of a disobedient feudal lord. The people were content and dutiful, the lords kind and on good terms with each other. This golden age stretched into the remote past, because before the Chou Dynasty was the Shang (1766–1122 B.C.), before the Shang the Hsia (2205 –1766 B.C.), and before that again the Five Sovereigns, among whom were the Yellow Emperor (2697 B.C.), and the Sainted Emperors Yao and Shun, non-pareils whose conduct was a model for all time. Confucius thus looked back two thousand years. There did not exist a history of those ages in our sense, but there were old documents in the Chou archives at Loyang, much oral tradition and a multitude of stories. The investigation which Confucius says he made into this immense past led him to conceive that China was much better governed then than in his time. His studies were largely directed towards discovering why this was so, what principles the old Emperors had followed and how far these could be revived. In sum, he aimed at a contemporary reintegration of the original Chinese culture in its various departments of rites, music, ceremonies, etiquette under a Son of Heaven.

The details of his career are much disputed, but it is certain that he lived in the state of Lu, a part of the present Shantung; that he was a private person and spent much of his life in the aforesaid study of the past, formulating the code of behaviour he deduced from this study, and teaching it to the sons of the local nobility who were sent to him for instruction. He attempted to interest the Grand Feudatories in his system, but without success, for they did not think it workable in the altered circumstances of the day. His name is also connected with five compilations which have come down to us—evidently much altered in content since his time—under the title of *The Five Classics* (*Wu Ching*), to be distinguished from *The Four Books*, hereafter to be described. The former works contain the essence of what was deemed valuable in the records of the past and may be termed a summary of ancient Chinese culture, the culture so rapidly disintegrating under the rule of the Grand Feudatories. In exactly what manner Confucius had to do with *The Five Classics* is unknown, the great difficulty being that their texts as they exist now are in part later than his day, for they were added to by his subsequent admirers to make them more Confucian. Tradition has it that it was he who put them together; that is the reason why they have had all these centuries the standing of canonical books. But the view now taken is that they, or rather their prototypes, existed in his era, partly in a written and partly in an oral form, and that he made them the basis of his teaching to such an extent that to after writers it seemed not incorrect to ascribe their compilation to him. In a modern sense he was therefore not either their author or editor, but a man, evidently of extraordinary force of character, ability and goodness of heart, who, after making himself thoroughly acquainted with the great oral and written tradition of his country, lectured upon it unceasingly in an earnest endeavour to preserve it from neglect.

He died disappointed, because he did not live to see his doctrines put into practice. He had lectured not only in his own state of Lu, but in other adjoining states, such as Wei and Ch'i. Accompanied by men afterwards termed his disciples, who were presumably his friends and pupils, he is represented as arguing with the Grand Feudatories, to whose Courts he went, and describing to them the conditions of the old Empire when a code of behaviour prevailed under which everyone worked harmoniously in his proper sphere, the peasants cultivating, the merchants trading, the lords acting justly with their people, fairly with each other, and respectfully towards the Emperor, who, for his part, as their sage exemplar and overlord, kept Heaven well disposed by maintaining the imperial sacrifices. Confucius offered, it is said, to transform the states he visited into models of good government if he were entrusted with the office of minister. The Duke of a state that engaged him would acquire the reputation of a philosopher king, the others would copy him and so the whole Empire would be reformed. But he was never entrusted with an important ministership. The Dukes tired of his homilies, deeming them impracticable, and terminated his visits with more or less brusqueness.

During his last years, spent exclusively lecturing in his native Lu, he was surrounded by a body of admiring students and, like his successors in Europe, the fifth century Greek philosophers, was the head of a body of adherents, devoted to his doctrines and vowed to perpetuate them. But this academic position did not satisfy him; he yearned to see his ideas given practical effect, which could only have happened had he been the trusted counsellor of some Duke. At the age of 61, ten years before his death, he is stated by his first biographer, Ssu-ma Ch'ien, writing nearly four centuries later, to have said: 'I have not sought fame during my life, but would like to feel that my work would keep my memory green. But alas! my doctrines have never been tested by use, since none of the Dukes have been intelligent enough to employ me.' He was buried by his followers in a grove of scented trees about a mile north of Lu, where his tomb has remained inviolate to the present day. Neglected by the official world during his lifetime, he became eventually that world's greatest figure. By the irony of history, the doctrines of the man whose grief was that he had not been employed in the administration, were destined for two thousand years to be the compulsory reading of all students who aspired to qualify themselves for such employment.

The Five Classics, the prototypes of which, as I have said, represented the ancient culture on which Confucius founded his teaching, consist of *The Book of Changes, The Book of History, The Book of Rites, The Book of Songs*, and *The Annals of Lu*, known as *The Spring*

The First Holy One

and Autumn. The Book of Changes is a manual of augury which we cannot properly understand, *The Book of Rites* is a detailed record of various kinds of ceremonial, both imperial and other, and *The Annals of Lu*, the driest of all, is a catalogue of events in Lu state for 240 years, ending with the time of Confucius. But *The Book of Songs* and, in places, *The Book of History* are interesting for the general reader of today. The former, sometimes called *The Odes* or *The Book of Poetry*, is an anthology containing a variety of verses, about love, parting, welcome, battles, some lively, some sad, and most fresh as dew. They can be compared to our ballads. Their meaning is apparently direct, though the later commentators, in their endeavours to bring these early writings into line with Confucianism, thereby making more plausible the claim that the Master himself had edited them, give doctrinal meanings to simple or rustic sentiments. With Mr. Waley's permission I will quote one song as translated by him:

'On Mount Chung-nan what is there?
There are peach-trees, plum-trees.
My lord has come
In damask coat, in fox furs,
His face rosy as if rouged with cinnabar.
There is a lord for you indeed!

On Mount Chung-nan what is there?
The boxthorn, the wild plum-tree.
My lord has come
In brocaded coat, embroidered skirt,
The jades at his girdle tinkling.
Long may he live, long be remembered!'

There is nothing inconsistent with Confucianism in this poem, though to squeeze out a particular doctrinal meaning will have required ingenuity: but our own commentators have been as ingenious with the Song of Songs which is Solomon's.

The Book of History, which in its dusty old way is the repository of a high morality, may be described as concerned with the legendary Emperors under whose beneficent rule China enjoyed the alleged golden age. Its chapters are made to appear like documents, as if it were a collection of ancient state papers. Each of them is in the nature of a Confucian homily. Some of them may be from the Chou archives, others were composed at later periods. As the Sainted Emperors, Yao, Shun and Yü, with whom the book chiefly deals, are not known to have existed in fact, the whole takes on the form of a fiction which nevertheless enshrines the Chinese classical ideal of a humane administration. A few citations from James Legge's translation will help to evoke from their remoteness the portentous apparitions which were these Emperors.

The character of the Emperor Yao (2357 B.C.) is thus described: 'He was reverential, intelligent, accomplished and thoughtful—naturally and without effort. His courtesy was sincere and his complaisance without bound. The influence of these qualities was felt to the four quarters of the Empire. Thus the states were harmonised and the people transformed. There was universal concord.'

The Emperor Yao's resignation and how he selected Shun to succeed him is a passage rich with Confucian overtones. We see Yao presiding over the Council. There had been a discussion about floods, a subject which throughout Chinese history was always on the agenda; no one has yet discovered how to confine the Yellow River within its bounds. The names of various persons thought capable of dealing with the calamity were put forward. Yao raised objections to each. Of one he said: 'He is insincere and quarrelsome—can he do?' Of another: 'Alas! when unemployed he can talk, but when employed his actions turn out very differently. He is respectful only in appearance.' Eventually they proposed a certain K'wan. 'No, by no means,' said the Emperor emphatically, 'he is disobedient.' One of the Eminences put in: 'Well, but try him, and then you can have done with him.' Evidently K'wan was a man they wanted to be rid of. The argument appealed to the Emperor. He said to K'wan: 'Go and be reverent.' It was after this that Yao brought up the matter of his own resignation. He was very old. To whom could he yield the throne? A person present was mentioned, who protested, as was customary: 'I have not the virtue: I should only disgrace the Dragon Seat.' The Emperor unexpectedly took him at his word, and said to the Council: 'Put forward another name, and it is no matter whether he be a gentleman or not, so long as his virtue is adequate.'

At that, all cried: 'Shun is the man.'

'I have heard the name,' said Yao. 'What is his character?'

One of the Eminences replied: 'He is the son of a blind man. His father was obstinately unprincipled; his stepmother was insincere; his half-brother was arrogant. But Shun by his filial piety has been able to live in harmony and lead them gradually to good behaviour.'

When Yao heard that the Council's unanimous choice was noted for filial piety, he said: 'I will try him.' Shun was tried for three years. At the end of that period Yao summoned him to audience. Speaking from the throne he said: 'Approach, you Shun. For three years I have compared your acts with your words: you do what you say. Ascend the Dragon Seat.'

Shun protested his lack of virtue, but Yao insisted. The abdication of Yao, magnificent in his apron and hat, for he spared no expense in ritual matters, and the induction of Shun, soberly dressed as was proper, took place soon afterwards before the ancestral altar of the Yellow Emperor, the first on the long list of imperial rulers.

In his turn Shun resigned to Yü and among the admonitions he addressed to him at that time are the following: 'Sincerely hold fast to the Mean. Of all who are to be loved is not the sovereign the chief? Of all who are to be feared are not the people the chief? If the multitude were without sovereigns whom would they sustain aloft. If the sovereign had not the multitude, there would be none to guard the country for him. Be reverent. Carefully demean yourself on the throne which you will occupy, and respectfully cultivate the virtue expected of you.'

The First Holy One

Once when the Emperor Yü asked what were the nine virtues, the minister Kao-yao replied: 'Affability combined with dignity, mildness with firmness, bluntness with respectfulness, ability with reverence, docility with boldness, straightforwardness with gentleness, easiness with discrimination, vigour with sincerity, valour with goodness.' This accords with the Confucian conception of an ideal mean in behaviour.

Yü, however, seems never to have been satisfied that his virtue was adequate. The story goes that one day, when out driving with his minister, he met a man on the road wearing a chain and in the custody of a police officer. At the sight the Emperor immediately reined in and alighted from his carriage, weeping without restraint.

'My man,' he said, convulsed with grief, 'what is the nature of your crime?'

The minister, shocked by the imperial tears, here interposed: 'The fellow is a scoundrel, nor merits a glance.'

To which the Emperor made answer: 'During the reigns of my predecessors, Yao and Shun, there were no criminals, the virtue of those two great rulers being such that they spread a golden age around them. I have sought to follow their example, having performed the rites, sacrificed to Heaven, harmoniously balancing earth and sky, so there be no cause for criminals to spring. But now today in my progress through the realm I meet a criminal in the public road. Have I not bitter cause to weep? My virtue is proven insufficient.'

The minister Yi, on another occasion, gave the following advice to the Emperor Yü: 'Pay attention to the law. Let no favourites come between you and your appointed ministers. Do not go against the right to get the praise of the people. Do your work by the light of reason. Do not oppose the people for private grounds.' And the Emperor said: 'To ascertain the views of all, to give up one's own opinion and follow that of others, to refrain from oppressing the helpless and not to neglect the poor—it was only the Emperor Yao who could reach this level.' To which Yi replied that Heaven would not have granted Yü the mandate to rule had his virtue been inadequate.

Yü is listed as the first Emperor of the Hsia Dynasty (2205–1766 B.C.). It runs its course and the last of the Emperors is an evil ruler. It is the duty of subjects to overthrow such a ruler. They are led by a lord called T'ang. A few sentences from T'ang's speech to his army before the battle with the Emperor will illustrate the Chinese classical theory of the people's right to rebel. 'It is not I, the little child, that rebels; it is Heaven that has ordered me to punish this criminal dynasty of Hsia. Therefore, as I fear Heaven, I dare not but obey. Help me, the one man, to carry out this punishment.' T'ang calls himself 'little child' in relation to Heaven and is the 'one man' in distinction to the general population. He was successful and founded the Shang Dynasty, which continued until 1122 B.C. when it was superseded by the Chou and for analogous reasons.

The Book of History contains no narrative in our sense, but one of its chapters, called the Metal-bound Coffer, is a story, and, since it is the classical citation for loyalty, a most important moral attribute in the Confucian view, and, moreover, gives a vivid impression of the times, I will narrate it. The chief character in it is the Duke of Chou, whose memory Confucius held in such reverent affection that he often dreamed of him and when in later life he ceased to do so, he attributed it to his failing powers and disappointed state. The Duke was a younger brother of the first Emperor of the Chou Dynasty, Wu Wang (1122–1115 B.C.), who, two years after he had destroyed the Shang Dynasty, was taken seriously ill. He was in very low spirits and seemed to be dying. A proposal was made that a solemn service of divination should be held in the ancestral temple of the imperial House, when the spirits of the Emperor's father, grandfather, and great-grandfather, who during the Shang Dynasty had been Dukes of Chou, should be asked to state the cause of their descendant's illness. The ancestral spirits would not be heard to speak, but they would each intimate their response through a tortoise, for at a point in the service, when the music and the dancing mediums had summoned them, the Chief Diviner would apply red-hot irons to the shell of tortoises kept in the ancestral temple and the resulting cracks would, when deciphered according to rules governing the interpretation of cracks, reveal the ancestors' diagnosis.

The Duke of Chou, however, said: 'No need to trouble the imperial ancestors with such a question,' for he had already made up his mind what he should do. The proposal, accordingly, was withdrawn. Without letting it be known, beyond a circle of confidential assistants, what he was planning, he caused to be raised in an open place three altars of earth, facing the three quarters south, east and west, and a fourth altar facing north, at which he proposed himself to preside during the ceremony upon which he had secretly resolved. When all was ready he stationed himself at his altar, mace in hand; on the three other altars jade symbols proper to the Emperor's three great ancestors had been placed, for, in spite of what he had said, he intended to invoke these spirits, but for a purpose quite other than had been proposed.

When the rite, a conjuration by mediums, was sufficiently advanced, and the imperial ancestors, who were, of course, also the Duke's ancestors, were believed each to have taken his stance at the altar appropriate to him, the Duke of Chou was handed by the Grand Historiographer, who was in attendance, a tablet upon which was written a prayer, and he addressed the three spirits in its terms, saying: 'So and so, your chief descendant, is suffering from a severe and dangerous sickness. If you three pre-eminent ancestors have desired to call him to you, take me, I pray, in his stead. I am specially fitted to serve you in the abode of spirits, being noted for my filial piety. But your chief descendant is not as well endowed to serve you as he is to succour the inhabitants of the empire. The people of the four quarters hold him in reverence. Heaven set him where he is; oh! do not cause Heaven's will to be undone! I will now seek your response from the great tortoises.'

After delivering this prayer, the Duke caused the Diviner to touch with his heated irons the shells of three tortoises which stood one at each of the ancestral altars. When the cracks were examined, they portended acquiescence with his plea. To make more sure the Duke took a key and opened a book of oracular responses. These, when he had consulted them according to rule, were found to support what the tortoises had declared. Thereafter, the Duke left the place of divination and returned back, ready to meet his end whenever it might come, and confident that the Emperor, his brother, had a long reign before him under the guardianship of the aforesaid spirits. On arrival at the palace he placed the tablets upon which was written his prayer among the archives in a metal-bound coffer. All the assistants were sworn to secrecy. Next day the Emperor began to recover. But the Duke of Chou's health showed no decline. In fact, the Emperor was completely restored without the Duke suffering any ill effects. At the end of five years, however (1115 B.C.) the Emperor died and the Duke became Regent for the Heir, who was thirteen. The late Emperor's other brothers were annoyed at not being associated in the Regency, and prejudiced the Heir against the Duke, who was obliged to resign the regency and retire to a country place. Two years later, however, the young Emperor had occasion during a crisis to consult the archives kept in the metal-bound box. When it was opened, he saw the tablets which the Duke of Chou had placed there seven years before. He read the prayer and, confused, asked the Grand Historiographer to explain. That functionary replied: 'It really happened that way, but the Duke commanded us not to dare speak of it.' The young Emperor held the writing and wept: 'How loyal to our House has been the Duke! I was too young to know it at the time. Propriety requires me now to go out and call on him at his place of retirement.'

This was the kind of absolute loyalty, Confucius used to tell the Grand Feudatories, which a ruling Duke should give to the Son of Heaven. *The Book of History* devotes a good deal of space to homilies by the Duke of Chou. He was sent to govern Lu and afterwards was looked up to as the founder of its ducal house. It is in this guise that he appears in the poem in *The Book of Songs* beginning: 'Broken were our axes' and with a refrain to the effect that since he came to Lu all had been well. When Confucius speaks of him it is always in terms of the highest reverence. 'Even if a man had gifts as wonderful as those of the Duke of Chou' begins one of his dicta in *The Analects*.

The virtue of loyalty was one of the most important in the Confucian system; that of filial piety was yet more fundamental. The family was conceived of as the microcosm of society, the theory being that the son who cherished his father and mother was likely to be of sounder character than one who did not, and would grow into a good subject, considerate to others and loyal to his ruler. There is extant an old book—the date of it is uncertain—called the *Filial Piety* classic, which though not a premier classic like *The Four Books* and *The Five Classics* had great authority. It contains some stories of the filially pious, and other stories of such worthies have also been preserved. Since the essence of Confucianism is that if each individual does his duty, all will be well with the state and the world, and that the first and greatest duty is to parents, the tales that drive this home have canonical weight and one cannot understand the system without having sampled them. Take the story of Tseng Ts'an, one of Confucius's disciples. This personage once, when touring a remote part of the countryside, came at sunset to a village. Being extremely tired, hungry and thirsty, he was preparing to enter it and order at the inn the best fare the place provided, but before doing so enquired what might be its name. When they told him it was called Better-than-Mother, he immediately turned away and, though the temperature was below freezing point, camped for the night in a turnip field.

Chun Yü, another of the disciples, is also the subject of a filial piety tale. In his youth he was extremely poor. There was rice in the house, which he procured by his own exertions, but all of it at his express wish went into his parents' bowls. He himself lived on bishopwort, a common wild herb of extreme insipidity. His virtues were such that in later life he rose to high administrative office. But, as he lolled on double cushions and picked morsels from jade dishes, longing for the dear old days would assail him, and, brushing his eyes with his damask sleeve, he would murmur, to the vast edification of his guests: 'Happier then with bishopwort than now with birdsnest.'

The story of Mao Jung—a somewhat later one—has for centuries been much admired for the neat way it teaches that filial piety is more important than hospitality. A traveller one night knocks at Mao's gate and asks to be put up for the night. Mao brings him in with his usual politeness and directs his wife to kill a chicken, the only chicken, it happened, they had. In due course it is served, chopped in a bowl. Mao invited the traveller to the table. Already installed there was Mao's mother. The traveller expressed his grateful thanks for the generous fare he saw in front of him. Mao besought him not to mention it, insisting he was bound to lay before his guest the choicest food there was in the house. The traveller renewed his thanks and awaited his helping. But Mao had gone, as he conceived, as far as hospitality could go in the circumstances. A higher order of exigencies now became operative. With an expression at once pious and resigned, he passed the entire chicken to his mother, and, certain that the traveller would understand and applaud, invited him to share a dish of boiled herbs, which his wife had deftly placed between them.

My own pick of these stories is that of Han Po Yü. In childhood, when his mother beat him, he never cried, a fact which she, it will be supposed, ascribed to his conviction that she was beating him for his good. But in this she was in error, as transpired later on. Beating him one day after he had attained his fifteenth year, she perceived the tears rolling down his cheeks, and, much astonished, asked him the reason. 'Mother,' he replied with respectful earnestness, 'up till now when you whipped me it hurt and I was glad, for

I knew for certain you were strong and well; but now it hurts no longer and therefore I weep, for I know that your health and strength must be failing.'

The other half of the Confucian canon, *The Four Books*, were also, like *The Five Classics*, not written by Confucius. They were composed after his death and contain information about him, collections of his sayings and expositions of his views. There is no biographical narrative in them of the sort found in our Gospels and the sacred books of some other religions. They consist of the *Analects*, the *Works of Mencius*, *The Great Learning* and *The Doctrine of the Mean*. The last two are thought to have been written in the fourth century B.C., perhaps a hundred and fifty years after Confucius's death. Recently Mr. E. R. Hughes has edited them. Their thesis is that, if the individuals composing a state are cultivated personalities, the state will be glorious, a thesis particularly directed against the hard realism of the times, which declared that the cultivation of the individual led to disorder and weakness, and that for a state to be strong, the only real glory, the interests of the individual must be subordinated to it. This, as we shall see, was the great debate of the fourth and third centuries B.C. as it has been of the twentieth A.D.

Mencius, who was given the posthumous title of the Second Holy One, may be described as the fourth century champion of Confucianism, a movement (for after a century and a half it was still no more than a movement) which was then dangerously threatened by the real politics, referred to in the last paragraph, which eventually brought it near extinction, as will be related in its place. As the sustainer of Confucianism at a critical moment he is necessarily more a disciple than an innovator, but the book that bears his name is no mere commentary; it amounts, in fact, to the most complete and brilliant statement of the Confucian position in the whole canon.

The remaining volume of *The Four Books*, the *Analects*, is a collection of the dicta of Confucius. By reading it one gets a personal impression of that great and charming person, and, since the present chapter is concerned to give that impression to the exclusion of the many other aspects which might be raised, the best course will be to dip into the *Analects*, using Arthur Waley's translation, since by its felicities of phrasing it brings out far better than any other the sweet gentleness of the old sage.

I have already cited a few passages from this book when Confucius speaks of himself, such as when he humbly puts aside any claim to sageship, and when he laments that he dreams no longer of the great Duke. They are very revealing, as also where he declares that in any hamlet you could find someone as loyal and true to his word as he, but not anyone with such a love of learning. His longing to get nearer to his ideal of the good by ceaseless effort is beautifully suggested in the next saying: 'Once when the Master was standing by a stream, he said, could one but go on and on like this, never ceasing day or night.'

One gets almost direct sight of him from the entry: 'In his leisure hours the Master's manner was very free and easy, and his expression alert and cheerful.' How he managed to induce strangers to answer his enquiries, says one of his disciples, was by addressing them in a way that was 'cordial, frank, courteous, temperate and deferential.' Nevertheless, though affable, he was firm, a firmness that was commanding but never harsh.

Once he said: 'I have been faithful to and loved the Ancients. I have listened in silence and noted what was said, I have never grown tired of learning nor wearied of teaching others what I have learnt. These at least are merits which I can confidently claim.'

We know his admiration for the Sainted Emperors. On one occasion in the state of Ch'i he heard the Succession, a dance that mimed the coming to the throne of Shun, and for three months afterwards did not know what he was eating. 'I did not picture to myself that any music existed which could reach such perfection as this,' he said.

His conception of what a gentleman should be is touching, for one can see that he strove always to be like that himself. 'A gentleman takes as much trouble to discover what is right as lesser men take to discover what will pay.' And again: 'A true gentleman is calm and at ease; the small man is fretful and ill at ease.' One of his disciples is made to say of a gentleman: 'From every attitude, every gesture that he employs he must remove all trace of violence and arrogance; every look that he composes on his face must betoken good faith; from every word that he utters, from every intonation, he must remove all trace of coarseness and impropriety.'

Ritual was one of the elements of the old Chinese culture, as the reader himself will have argued from the fact that *The Book of Rites* is included in the canon. The word, however, had a much wider sense than it generally bears with us; it covered deportment for all occasions. The *Analects*, which is a very disjointed work, contains as its Book X a description of such deportment, but it is worded in such a way that it reads as if it were a description of Confucius's own particular style of conducting himself. Ssu-ma Ch'ien, whose second/first century biography of the Master has been referred to, understands it in that sense, and incorporates the better part of it, as if he thought that it referred exclusively to Confucius. But it seems clear that what is given is merely correct Confucian deportment in general. Nevertheless, since Confucius laid the greatest stress on ceremonial manners, in distinction to the Taoists who, as we shall see, had no manners, it can be assumed that he actually behaved as described in Book X of the *Analects* when the circumstances demanded. But as some of the other persons present will also have behaved in the same way, his deportment had not the suggested singularity. As the passage stands, it sounds to us like caricature, though this is far from being its intention. In summarising it, I must repeat again that I am not giving a description of Confucius as an eccentric poseur, but of the sort of ceremonial manners that were derived from old books of rites and which Confucius considered to be good form. The admiration by Confucians for so histrionic a deportment was made fun of by their opponents as we shall see. Just as our Puritans caricatured themselves and seemed to others ridiculous in their formal clothes, so the early Confucians were considered odd in manner and because of the gowns and hats they wore.

The passage in the *Analects* goes as follows: 'At Court in the first ante-chamber, where were gathered officials of a lower grade, Confucius spoke out freely, like a frank and affable person. Passing into the second or inner waiting room, where the dignitaries were of higher standing, he adopted a degree of blandness, combined with precision, a formality at once polite and correct. When the Duke came in, he managed to get his features to suggest a respectful wariness, an uneasiness that was complimentary, and a gravity that was composed but not too cramped.

'If, instead of being a client in an ante-chamber, he were acting on the Duke's staff, his studied manner was further elaborated. On receiving instructions, for instance, to go and receive a guest, he became as it were confused and as though his knees were giving under him, the suggestion being that the honour was more than he could support. Nevertheless, he was sufficiently collected to excuse himself to the colleagues with whom he might happen to be in converse, making them the correctest of inclinations, the while being careful that the folds of his robe remained evenly adjusted both before and behind. Hastening, then, upon his errand, his walk would be a blending of briskness with dignity, his long sleeves thrust out like a huge bird's wings.

'If at any time he passed the ruler's empty chair, he would visibly change countenance, and, if he then spoke, it appeared to be with difficulty, as though his heart were beating violently. Again, when mounting the steps in the audience hall towards the dais where the Duke was sitting, he would lift his robe with both hands, bend double and hold his breath, like one overcome with reverential emotion. On his return he would ease the tension gradually; after descending one step his face relaxed and he allowed satisfaction and relief to appear on it; at the bottom of the steps, he righted himself and, assuming the brisk step with sleeves like wings, went to his place, sat down, and resumed his attitude of respectful wariness.

'When presenting gifts on behalf of the ruler, he made a point of looking placid, as though to suggest the Duke's condescension and his own profound concurrence in the same.

'At home, to appear modest and unassuming, he put on the look of a person incapable of an opinion. But he could also be particular. At meals he would not touch what was over- or under-done nor anything that was out of season. This insistence that detail was of great importance and that all should be exactly right, led to his refusing meat that was jaggedly cut. If they forgot the salt or spices he was offended. Sweetness of breath occupied him, too; he had a rule so to mix meat and rice that his breath smelt of the second, not the first. And if his mat was crooked, he had it put straight.'

The sum of what I have cited here about early Confucianism amounts to a statement that it was not a religious system but rather a way of life. Confucius and his coadjutors took for granted the existence of Heaven, a term less anthropomorphic than our God. Heaven was goodness; to live in harmony with Heaven was to be good; and in human nature was an innate inclination to goodness, for civilisation could not otherwise have arisen. These were assumptions not in dispute. To probe into the mystery of Heaven was fruitless. It was believed that after death a man's spirit existed somewhere, but of happiness, divine compassion, an eternal home, a paradise of love, nothing was said. No assurance of future recompense was held out to the oppressed; the suffering were offered no consolation; the terror of death was not abated by promises of bliss. Hardly a peep beyond the veil was vouchsafed; 'Heaven does not speak' were the words in which Mencius summed it all up.

This extent of information, declared the Confucians, was sufficient to sustain a man on the right road through life, and since to behave properly in life was fundamental to their system, which was politico-social rather than metaphysical, no more information was essentially necessary.

Though this modicum became the state cult, it never sufficed the Chinese. Their minds ranged like those of any other nation. The uneducated sought communion with every sort of god or spirit and by every conceivable means, by magic, by mediums and by sorcery; the speculations of the educated were without limit. But the particularity of China is that no god ever managed to become officially recognised as God and that no speculation became accepted dogma. Having complete freedom to believe anything, a majority of educated persons eventually found the cautious and practical Confucian attitude more congenial than any kind of transcendence. An Emperor whose temperament drove him to seek more definite answers to the eternal questions was not likely to be admired for such a search. That a good ruler could only be a Confucian ruler was an opinion which, when accepted in the second century B.C., thousands of years failed to modify. In the next chapter some observations will be made on a body of thought that ridiculed this plodding middle way.

The First Holy One and the
Venerable Sir

In his recent book, *The Perennial Philosophy*, Aldous Huxley brings together the chief varieties of mysticism, the Hindu metaphysic, the Mahayanist metaphysic, Taoism, Neo-Platonism and the writings of the European contemplatives. His approach is not academic; he does not attempt any tight classification; but he gives ample reason to perceive close affinities in these several systems of transcendent thought. And his general conclusion is that always and in every civilisation there have been thinkers who held that perfection on earth consisted in the passive and continuous contemplation of the divine source of all things, a source called God or the Logos or, by some Chinese sages, Tao. Taoism, therefore, with its conception of divinity as the pervasive essence of the cosmos, is in no way foreign to us or hard to estimate. We can perceive it without difficulty to be right outside Confucianism. The Taoist was unlikely to be a typical civil servant, obedient to restraint and respectful to rank. Rather, he resembled our idea of the artist, the recluse, the bohemian and the visionary. For the Taoists, reason, honest work, loyal service, good behaviour were less important than the cultivation of a state of awareness towards divine reality, that unchanging unity behind changing appearance, that sum of all things and the power that moved them. The reply of the old anchorite, Chang Chih-ho, whose style was the Old Fisherman of the Mists and Waters, to the man who asked him why he went roaming alone through the countryside, phrases this awareness most felicitously: 'With the sky as my home, the lighted moon as my constant friend, and the four seas my inseparable companions, what do you mean by roaming alone?' he replied. His habit was to tour endlessly the rivers in his boat. To one who offered to give him a house, he said: 'I prefer to follow the gulls into cloud-land rather than bury my ethereal self beneath the dust of the world.'

No one knows when Taoism made its appearance in China, nor whether it arose spontaneously or in result of an influx of Indian ideas, though how Indian ideas could have penetrated ancient China is difficult to conceive. It has no historical founder like Confucianism. In default of one, the Chinese invented a personage called Lao Tzu, a name which may be translated as the Venerable Sir. He is placed at the head of the school and appears in their chief classic, the *Chaung Tzu Book*, which is now thought to have been written in the third century B.C. The Venerable Sir is represented as a sage who had apprehended the ultimate truth, the oneness in plurality which was Tao. As the supposed contemporary of Confucius, he is made to meet him and, of course, to put him in his place. Their colloquy took place at P'ei, a town 150 miles south of Lu, to which Confucius is described as having travelled in order to pay his respects and hear the great Taoist expound.

Lao Tzu received him thus: 'So you have come, sir, have you? I hear you are considered a wise man up north. Have you succeeded in finding Tao?'

'Not yet,' Confucius replied.

'In what direction,' enquired Lao Tzu, 'have you sought for it?'

'For five years,' said Confucius, 'I tried to extract it from the science of numbers, but without success.'

'And then?' asked Lao Tzu.

'Then for twelve years I made efforts to hunt it down in the theory of the opposites.'

'Was that any good?'

'I am obliged to admit that it was not.'

'I am not surprised,' said Lao Tzu, 'for Tao cannot be apprehended by such dodges.' And he proceeded to lecture Confucius at length on the ineffable nature of the secret light. After a final admonishment, he dismissed him.

On his return home to Lu, Confucius did not speak for three days. His disciples were longing to know what had transpired at the great meeting, and at last one of them ventured to ask: 'When you saw the Venerable Sir, in what direction did you admonish him?'

Confucius replied in a heartfelt tone: 'As the apparition of him was like a dragon in an azure cloud, whence radiated the great secrets of creation, I could only gaze with my mouth wide open. How do you think I was able to admonish him?'

In this way the Taoists represented Confucius as dazzled by their doctrines. And they liked to turn him into a figure of fun, as in the following lampoon from the same *Chuang Tzu Book*.

A certain Chih was a notorious bandit. His elder brother Hui met Confucius one day. The conversation turned on Chih and his misdeeds.

'Why do you not reprimand him?' asked Confucius.

'He would not listen to me if I did,' replied Hui.

'Then I shall go and admonish him myself,' replied Confucius.

'If I were you, I should not try that,' protested Hui. 'He is an awkward man of a passionate disposition, and has never been known to take advice.'

'For all that, I will go,' returned Confucius, and he set off in his carriage, Yen Hui, his favourite disciple, driving, and Tzu Kung, another intimate, on the seat beside him.

Chih's encampment was on the south side of T'ai-shan, one of the sacred mountains of China, where Taoist hermits liked to settle. In theory Chih was also a Taoist, though his practice hardly accorded thereto, for at the head of his nine thousand partisans he would sally forth and worry the Grand Feudatories.

On arrival at the camp Confucius got out, and, leaving his disciples with his carriage, went alone to the gate of the stockade. The sentries were there, cooking their supper. Addressing their sergeant, Confucius introduced himself. 'What do you want?' the sergeant demanded. Confucius put on the appropriate expression. 'I have heard,' he said, 'of the high character of your General. Please say that I am here and request the honour of an interview.' And with every appearance of affable respect he saluted the sergeant, who, impressed, immediately went to convey the message.

While he was gone, Confucius in an effort to be pleasant enquired of the sentries what they had cooking. One of them, a low-browed, horrid creature, replied facetiously that it was minced human livers. At a loss how to continue the conversation, Confucius turned and tidied himself.

Presently the sergeant returned in a hurry. His manner was greatly changed for the worse. 'You there!' he called. Confucius looked round. The sergeant advanced upon him threateningly. 'The General wants to know what you mean by coming here,' he said with truculence. 'You are to go at once. He won't see you.'

'Come, come,' said Confucius, all conciliation. 'Did you say who I was? Did you give my name correctly?'

'I did,' said the sergeant. 'That is what made him angry.'

'Angry?' exclaimed the Sage, with assumed surprise. 'How can that be? I am received everywhere. I have stayed with all the Grand Feudatories. I am most popular at the leading courts. What precisely did he say? You are probably mistaken.'

'There is no mistake about the rage he is in,' said the sergeant. 'As soon as he heard your name he bawled: "That's the man who lives by talking, who wears the most extraordinary hat and whose belt is at least three sizes too large for him. Tell him to get out of here," he roared at me. "Tell him I won't have him hanging about.

He goes round the Courts pretending to preach piety, but really licking the boots of the rulers to induce them to give him a salaried appointment. I suppose he has come here on the same errand, to preach me a sermon and beg for a job. I will not see him! Go and tell him so!" That is the message his Honour sent.'

But Confucius was not unaccustomed to messages of this sort: they had been sent to him so often by the Feudatories. He knew what to do and put on another face, that of a man who takes you fully into his confidence. 'Sergeant,' he said in a low voice, 'listen attentively while I tell you a secret. The General's brother, his Honour Hui, has sent me to make an advantageous offer.'

'Is that so? His Honour, Hui? An offer, an advantageous one?' The sergeant's determination seemed to waver. Then he remembered the General's rage. 'You must go,' he said. 'You should have told me this first.'

'As you like,' replied Confucius, 'but when your master learns that his brother's emissary was turned away and a good offer along with him, perhaps he will blame you and that might be unpleasant.'

'Very unpleasant,' agreed the sergeant wryly, and hastened back into the camp. He returned again in a few minutes. 'Follow me,' he said, 'The General summons you.'

Confucius had not to be told twice. He followed the sergeant through the gate of the stockade and, perceiving ahead the bandit on his mat, advanced towards him at a trot, or amble, a gait which, indicating eager compliance to command, he considered suitable to the occasion. On reaching the mat, which he was careful not to tread on, he went backwards five steps, and prostrated himself twice.

Chih was seated with his sword across his knees and seemed to be feeling the sharpness of the blade. The sergeant had not misrepresented his mood; he received his caller with a harsh guffaw. 'I was right; you are wearing that forked hat of yours and the belt as broad as the side of a bull.' And he bellowed disagreeably: he was a typical bandit.

The First Holy One and the Venerable Sir

'My hat and belt,' explained Confucius, 'conform to the old fashions which, if men followed them today, would bring us all prosperity and content.'

'There you go, sermonising the moment you open your mouth,' cried the bandit. 'Stop that and tell me what you want. And I warn you, that if you annoy me, I shall do what the Feudatories nearly did to you, and have you put out of the way.'

'Annoy you? Am I the sort of man who annoys Grandees?' replied Confucius in the mellow tone of reasonableness which he had perfected. 'On the contrary, I feel bound at once to say that I have never met a ruler of finer presence than yourself, no, nor one whose face reflected greater qualities of mind or a more steadfast soul. That, distinguished by these excellencies, any one of which would suffice to make you a Superior Man, you should nevertheless follow the career of banditry, is very astonishing. And this brings me to the offer, of which I trust your Lieutenant apprised you, and which has the concurrence, I am glad to say, of his Honour Hui, your respected brother.'

This opening gambit of lavish compliment had often sufficed to gain a Duke's ear, but the bandit Chih found it merely tiresome. 'Go on,' he said grimly through his teeth. 'Let me hear your offer, and be quick about it.'

Quite undeterred, Confucius continued: 'The most handsome offer I could make to any man is to offer him my services. That offer I now make to you. Take me as your consellor and I will change all this.' He made a wide gesture over the encampment. 'Instead of this poor stockade, you shall have a walled city; instead of these hutments, high tiled roofs; instead of this rabble, prosperous citizens. I will be your ambassador to the Grand Feudatories. They will applaud when I tell them of you, of your resolve never to fight, always to compromise, to appease the strong, protect the weak, sacrifice to the ancestors, follow the rites, copy the ancients, establish harmony. You will become a Sage, a Superior Man, your lofty countenance facing south, the worthy descendant of the Anterior Sainted Ones, the Emperors Yao and Shun and Yü, whose Golden Age you shall restore.'

'I thought so,' exclaimed Chih, 'word for word the same old story! Now listen to me. I said if you annoyed me I would have you put away. Yet you make me an offer that assumes that I am a simpleton!'

'How so?' asked Confucius, regulating his expression till it radiated innocence, candour and enthusiasm tempered by reverence, modesty and regard. 'Am I not putting true greatness in your grasp? Have I not pointed the road to a happiness that the whole world longs to regain?'

'You have not,' said the bandit flatly. 'Yao, Shun and Yü, all the old Emperors, were a pack of ruffians, who waged wars, massacred thousands; had venial ministers, evil counsellors; who oppressed the weak, maltreated the virtuous, circumscribed freedom, made the laws harsher. There was no Golden Age after government was set up, for the one is not compatible with the other. No, the Golden Age was before the first Emperor, when men lived in perfect amity, as in a garden where the eye is pleased with beauty, the ear with music, the mouth with sweets. Such is the era we want to return to, but you go round, dressed up as a mountebank, preaching your rubbish and misleading the public, not because you believe the humbug you propagate, but because you hope to better yourself. That is brigandage, if you like! You, not I, are the brigand of the age; for while you would rivet tighter the chains of rule, I stand for freedom, the fulfilment of dreams. Now, not a word more. Out of this you march! And count yourself lucky I am letting you go.'

Confucius made a double prostration, retired backwards, then took to his heels. On reaching his carriage he was so flustered that three times the mounting-rope slipped through his hands. His friends got him up and he leant on the rail, panting, a mist in front of his eyes, his head hanging down, his face like a sheet. 'Home, Yen Hui,' he uttered, 'drive for your life.'

On reaching Lu, the first person he met was Hui, the bandit's honourable brother. 'Haven't seen you for days,' exclaimed that gentleman, 'and your horses look tired. What have you been up to?'

'Oh,' said Confucius, 'I have been on tour.'

Hui smiled. 'Not in my brother's direction, I suppose?'

'Well, yes,' admitted Confucius, 'I did drop in on him.'

'And he was not more amenable than I predicted,' suggested the honourable Hui slyly.

'I cannot exactly say that he was,' confessed the other. 'In fact, to be candid, I hardly escaped the fate of the hairdresser who offered to plait the tiger's whiskers.'

Since, as is supposed, this lampoon was written in the third century B.C., it was directed against a school of thought which was not to become the official cult for another century. What is strange to our eyes is that, when Confucianism did become the official cult, the story was not suppressed and the whole *Chuang Tzu Book* with it. But that did not happen; the book never fell into disrepute, even though the several passages in it which caricatured Confucius must gravely have offended the whole official hierarchy. For two millennia it has continued to be read unexpurgated, and is regarded as one of the classics of the language. This curious fact allows us to gauge the profound difference between the position of Confucius and that of the founder of a cult who is a divinity. In Europe, where the founder was God, such a skit would have been impossible, as it would also have been in Arabia, where the founder was the Prophet of God.

The Confucians' greater tolerance may partly be attributed to the fact that Taoism as a quietist philosophy supplemented Confucianism. It was quite feasible to be a staunch upholder of the Confucian way of life and at the same time to let the mind wander with the gulls into cloudland; indeed, for some characters such an outlet was essential. And there was another reason why Confucians were never moved to go to lengths against Taoism; the Taoists had no coherent political system with which to displace Confucianism and, therefore, were not a real danger. Since the Chinese demanded of a philosophy that it should be applicable to politics, the Taoists made some attempt to argue politically. But Taoism as politics was anarchy. Here is what the Venerable Sir says about ideal sovereigns in the *Chuang Tzu Book*: 'Their government was one of achievements which covered the whole Great Society, but which did not appear to come from them. They just made everything pleased with itself, while they maintained their poise in the incommensurable and wandered in the non-existent.'

Since this kind of magical inactivity was the Taoists' conception of good government, they liked to laugh at the Sainted Emperors, so admired by the Confucians for their solid kindness. In the fable which follows, that wonderful old worthy, the Emperor Yao, is shown as obliged by his own doctrine of virtue and responsibility for the people's welfare to offer his throne to certain Taoist sages, since they were reputed to be his superiors. Its point is that the duties of day-to-day administration, all important for the Confucian, were for the true Taoist a soiling of the soul.

The fable can be related in the following free way: the Emperor Yao, informed that on the Miao-ku-shê mountain lived recluses of extraordinary virtue, called his ministers and propounded this question: 'Since on the said mountain the recluses there resident have a more perfect virtue than mine, which, though I try my best to mend it, is but a cracked imperfect vessel, should I not resign my throne to one of them so that the country be the gainer?'

This enquiry the ministers answered as they might, and, though what they said is not on record, we can be sure they strove to dissuade the Emperor, in part because the elevation of a hermit to the throne was an expedient without precedent, in part because a Taoist at the head would prove an unworkable arrangement, and in part because the proposal was unnecessary, seeing that Yao's virtue was transcendent. But Yao had already made up his mind. He dismissed the Council, ordered his red carriage and, attended by an abbreviated suite, set out for the mountain Miao-ku-shê.

On reaching the first slopes he called a halt to consult the secretary in attendance. 'Which recluse shall I visit first?' he asked that gentleman, who replied: 'Sir, the one most likely to accept.'

'You think,' said Yao, rather surprised, 'that my offer of the throne may be refused?'

'Oh, no!' the secretary hastened to assure him, 'but, as Your Majesty will agree, these mountain hermits are somewhat brusque. Living alone or with one servant, wandering at will, watching the mists, writing verse, listening to the wind, their wits are often rapt away, so that to bring them down to earth and get a plain answer is not easy.'

'Ah, is that so?' said Yao, reflecting. 'Consider, therefore, which of these here is reputed to be the most approachable.'

The secretary paused, and then replied: 'I submit that Your Majesty first tries Ch'ao Fu. He lives a trifle higher in the mountain than, for instance, does Hsü Yu, but from all accounts is more amenable. Should he refuse, though that is unlikely or, at least, likely to be unlikely, we can consider calling on Hsü Yu.'

'I notice,' said Yao, 'you remain doubtful.'

'Not at all,' protested the Secretary, 'but it is my duty to suggest a plan to meet contingencies that may arise.'

'Well, let us get on. Where is Ch'ao Fu's cottage?'

The secretary pointed up the slope: 'Yonder, Your Majesty, in that clump of pines.' They ascended and, skirting where Hsü Yu lived, presently came to Ch'ao Fu's fence and to the gate that led into his garden. When the carriage was stopped, Yao alighted, looked through the gate, saw lettuce plants, butterflies hovering, a chuckling brook, a convolvulus trailing its flowers on a porch: silence and peace in an afternoon sun.

'Where is Ch'ao Fu, do you think?' he asked.

'Probably indoors,' replied the secretary.

'Announce me, will you,' Yao commanded.

The secretary drew back the stanchions of the gate and advanced up the path to the house. His approach was observed by Ch'ao

Fu's servant, who came out and asked him his business in a tone
that was barely civil.

'Be careful,' said the secretary, a hush in his voice. 'The Emperor
is here. That is his carriage. He wants to have a word with your
master. You may say that he has a proposal to make, and one that
is highly advantageous, too.'

The servant's manner changed on the instant. 'The Emperor!
And an advantageous offer!' He ran into the house.

Yao meanwhile had entered the garden and seated himself on a
stone bench. His idea was that, when Ch'ao Fu appeared and prostrated himself according to custom, he would raise him up, cause
him to sit by him, explain the visit and resign to him the throne.
Now he summoned the secretary to stand behind him, and so
awaited Ch'ao Fu's coming.

Half an hour passed in this way. Yao was in no hurry. He had
had a fatiguing drive; an old man, he was glad of a rest. But it was
strange Ch'ao Fu delayed. 'Did his man say he was definitely in
the house?' he enquired at last, though without impatience.

'By the prompt manner of his re-entry he suggested that such
might be the case,' replied the secretary, choosing his words, for
he never committed himself exactly.

But now they saw the servant approaching. He came forward,
made the prostration. 'Lord,' he said, 'I gave the message, but my
master has refused to come out. When I said it would be to his
advantage, that only made it worse.'

'Worse?' said Yao, 'how worse?'

'He was angry, and he got angrier.'

Yao turned and eyed his secretary. 'I cannot understand why he
has taken umbrage. What would you advise for the next step?'

'Your Majesty might order him to come out,' the secretary submitted with a faint smile.

'No, no, impossible,' pronounced Yao. 'I am here to offer him
the throne on the ground that his virtue exceeds mine; how can I
order him into my presence?'

'Your Majesty will remember I hinted at difficulties,' the secretary answered with a trace of smugness.

The servant was now showing signs of excitement. 'Did your Highness speak of an offer of the throne?' he asked hoarsely, and as if incredulous.

'That is so,' responded Yao. 'My reason in calling was precisely with that object. But you seem amazed. Let me particularise. The accounts that came to hand of your master convinced me that, to remain Emperor, would be for me an act lacking in propriety, when so superior a man was available for the post. Accordingly I gave all the necessary instructions. On Ch'ao Fu's arrival at the palace he will be suitably welcomed by the council, inducted, robed, installed on the Dragon Seat, entertained by the Empress and Imperial Concubines. All await his coming with respectful joy. I place my carriage at his disposal. For myself, I will either walk home or stay here until such time as the modest retreat I have planned to build is ready for occupation!'

'Will your Worship let me tell my master all this?' The servant's eyes were starting out of his head.

'I would have preferred to tell him myself,' said Yao, 'but since, as it seems, he is disinclined to come out, occupied no doubt with his meditations on earth and heaven and how to conjoin them, I raise you to the rank of Imperial Envoy and authorise you, on special mission, to lay these matters before your master, soon I trust to be mine and the world's.'

The servant, curtailing the obligatory prostrations, rushed into the house, and there was silence, save for the bubbling of the brook and the mild plaint of the wind in the pines.

'He will come out now, do you agree?' said the Emperor, adjusting the tassels on his hat.

'Oh, very much so,' replied the secretary, but in a voice without conviction.

'When he does appear,' went on Yao, 'I have decided to dispense with the prostrations. Rather, I shall rise from my seat and meet

43

him, lead him to this bench, cause him to sit down, myself thereafter sitting on his left. After a short exchange of compliments, I
shall come to the matter, explain it at large, and urge him not to
delay his concurrence. When he has accepted, as, I opine, he will
do after thrice protesting his unworthiness, a formality he is unlikely to omit and which I shall meet with more eulogy of his
character, I shall vacate my place on his left and on the ground
prostrate myself to him. Does it occur to you that I have omitted
anything which might lend greater propriety to the proceedings?'

The secretary seemed genuinely moved at these words, though
they did not cause him to abate his caution. 'Far be it from me,' he
answered, 'to suggest by putting forward emendations that the pro-
gramme, which Your Majesty has sketched with such grace and
pristine virtue, could by any means be improved. When the said
recluse emerges, if he intends to, and time goes on, the proceedings
of Your Majesty will stand forever as the prototype of how such
renouncements should be conducted.'

It is possible that this conversation might have continued still
further had not a man burst from the cottage. There could be no
doubt it was Ch'ao Fu, for he wore a bark hat, widely spreading, a
cotton robe, and carried a gnarled walking-stick. He did not, however, go towards the Emperor, nor even take a look at him, but,
followed by his acolyte, who had emerged at his heels and who by
his gestures seemed trying to stop him, stalked at a rapid pace to
the brook-side. There he removed his hat and bending down rinsed
his ears again and again.

'If that is Ch'ao Fu, what is he doing?' enquired the Emperor,
with a noticeable degree of apprehension.

'I am afraid he is washing his ears,' said the secretary, though
without the smallest trace of surprise.

Yao had now risen, and watched Ch'ao Fu, who continued to
cleanse his ears, now one, now the other, now plunging his head
under water and scrubbing, while his servant stood by, chagrin on
his face, a green despair in his tilted eyes.

At last Yao said: 'No use waiting longer.'

'No use, I fear,' concurred the secretary.

The Emperor sighed: 'Who would have thought that the mere fact of hearing my offer of the throne would require so very drastic a lustration?'

The secretary sighed also: 'Recluses are odd.'

At last Yao said: 'Conduct me to my carriage.'

When they were back in it, the secretary asked: 'Shall I tell the coachman to drive straight home?'

'You are forgetting Hsü Yu,' Yao reminded him. 'We arranged, you remember, to call there second.'

'But is there not danger of loss of face, going thus from one recluse to another and running the risk of a further refusal?'

'Virtue cannot lose face,' said Yao.

'It cannot, I know,' admitted the secretary, 'though the ill-disposed might allege that it could.'

But Yao refused to consider this. 'Whip up,' he gave his order to the coachman, 'and drive me at once to Hsü Yu's cottage.' It lay immediately below, and though a slight detour was necessary owing to the steepness of the hill, they did not take long to get there. Looking through the gate as before, they saw a kitchen-garden and a yard, beside which was a stream, the same stream that ran through Ch'ao Fu's property. In the yard were several calves. As they looked, an elderly person, also in a bark hat, and leaning on a thorn stick, entered the yard and called his servant.

'Keep the calves away from the stream,' he ordered in a shrill voice. 'They are not to drink; the water is contaminated.'

'It looks clean enough to me,' answered back the man.

'It is contaminated, I tell you,' shouted Hsü Yu, for it was he. 'Ch'ao Fu has had to wash his ears in it. He is still washing them. It was very bad what he heard.' The servant seemed to grumble, but he drove the calves into a pen.

Yao turned away, looking sad. 'News seems to spread fast here,' he said. And, speaking for the first time with a touch of asperity, added: 'Ch'ao Fu's washing of his ears was at least intelligible as a demonstration of principle, but for this Hsü Yu to pretend that his calves would get stomach-ache from drinking water sullied by the offer which his colleague has laundered out of his ears, is zeal amounting to a lapse of propriety.'

'It may be just rivalry,' suggested his secretary. 'He wants to go one better than the other.'

'I did not ask for your opinion,' replied the Emperor more than stiffly. 'A lapse of propriety is what I said, and surely that is the end of the matter?'

'Indeed, it is,' quickly uttered the secretary. 'A gross lapse, if Your Majesty will sanction the emendation.'

The Emperor, whose dignity was beyond conception, rapidly regained his former calm. 'What next?' he said. 'Who is the next hermit?'

'Do I understand Your Majesty correctly? Your Majesty proposes to make the offer a third time? I beg Your Majesty to consider the facts. The persons who represented that the recluses on this mountain were men of supernormal virtue have been proved deplorably misinformed, for the two we have met are but ideologues. Sir, I submit it is time to go home.' The secretary trembled when he said this, so anxious was he about his master's face.

But the Emperor was not satisfied that he had done all that was possible to find a ruler more virtuous than himself. 'My informants,' he said, 'may have been mistaken twice, but it does not follow they will be on a third occasion.'

To this the secretary dared to make the following submission: 'With great respect I beg to say that though there is no logical presumption of their continued error, ground for it amply exists in the fact that the one remaining recluse on the mountain by repute has a fervour greater than his colleagues.'

'Be more particular,' Yao admonished him, 'since, as it appears, you are so well posted on this subject.'

'I thank Your Majesty,' said the secretary with a crouching gesture, and, taking breath, continued thus: 'The name of the personage I refer to escapes me, but that is no matter since only his character is in point. Your Majesty will deduce it from what I shall relate of him. He lives in a very mean hut by that shoulder,' and he pointed upwards to a spur, 'without servant or the smallest amenities, even drinking at the brook from the hollow of his hand. Remarking this last and supposing it his poverty, not his choice, a charitable person gave him a gourd, which he, despising such a convenience, did not make use of, but hung on a tree. One day of wind he heard a musical note that delighted his ear, and, seeking the cause of it, found it in the wind as it sounded in the gourd. That the gourd should thus have pleased him, he accounted a weakness and immediately flung it far down the slope. Such being the third hermit's extremity of mood, it is impossible that he will accept Your Majesty's offer, the most pleasing that any man could receive.'

To this Yao had no reply, for, though impulsive, he was eminently reasonable, and turning to the coachman, he cried: 'Turn back home!'

But the Taoists were not all mountain contemplatives; the word Taoism covered more than a quietist philosophy. Had it been only that, its following would have been very small. But it also included the imaginations of men, who were not mystical but who loved marvels. They interpreted such passages in the *Chuang Tzu Book* as 'they maintained their poise in the incommensurable and wandered in the non-existent' as referring to sages who had become Immortals or Genii and by their discovery of the Elixir had overcome death. The Elixir, in fact, stood in popular idea for the philosopher's union with divinity. A vast region of such unreason was given respectability by being called Taoism; numberless magicians, sorcerers and mediums were dignified by the name of Taoist priests. It was this kind of Taoism, not the splendid sweep of its higher philosophy, that was in conflict with the Confucian ideal of sane behaviour, as will be illustrated at length further on.

The Eclipse of the First Holy One

Before Confucianism was established as the national cult in the second century B.C. it suffered a total eclipse. This was not due to Taoism, but to the momentary triumph of a totally different order of ideas.

To understand this, a short recapitulation will be found convenient. The China of the Chou Dynasty was an area about 800 miles broad and 600 miles long between the Yellow River and the Yangtse, governed by an Emperor through feudal Lords. It was cut off from the rest of civilised mankind, and its inhabitants thought of it as the world. By 800 B.C., some Lords had begun to increase their territories at their neighbour's expense, contrary to the established rules of the Empire. By 500 B.C., the time of Confucius, there were some ten Grand Feudatories. Each of these was in practice the king of an independent state, and regarded the others as foreign sovereigns. The Emperor had no political power, though as the Son of Heaven he was maintained as an institution. The years from 500 B.C. onwards were distracted by wars between the states, wars as ruinous as those between the states of classical Greece at approximately the same period. Like the Greek states, the Chinese were the scene of a vast politico-philosophical discussion. How to end the wars was one of the great topics. By what means could the Grand Feudatories, the rulers of ten kingdoms, be induced to give up war as an instrument of policy? It was lunacy that the inhabitants of a once feudal empire whose various parts had lived together in harmony under one Emperor, should now be destroying each other. Together they had created a civilisation: divided they were ending it. There was no reasonable cause for their mutual enmity; that they had become dispersed in states under particular sovereigns had, as was inevitable, given rise to jealousy, rivalry, ambition and greed. Every thinker agreed that these causes of disunity must be eliminated by a grand union. But how to achieve it? How could an agreement embracing all of the states be drafted? Was it possible to conceive of the Chou Emperor, so feeble and discredited, as the head of their united nations?

There were only two possible answers to that harrowing question. Confucianism provided one of them. The union of the states could be effected by a great moral renaissance and could be maintained by the practice of that morality. If rulers and people were kind and humane, truthful and loyal, agreements advantageous to all parties could be made and would be kept. The powers which had been taken from the Emperor would be restored to him; he would preside over a council of rulers; war would be impossible, since all the world would have agreed to work under one sovereign.

The other answer was that China would only get peace when one state, having conquered all the rest, imposed it by force. If union had to await a moral reformation it would never come. But let one state by superior discipline and armament destroy its rivals in battle and it would be recognised as paramount over the rest. All the world would be united under its sovereign, and there could never be war again.

Which answer was right? Could the world be saved by reason or must it be saved by force?

As we are today confronted by the same question, though this time on a real, not a fictitious, basis of world sovereignty, the answer given by the Chinese at this early date is full of interest.

It may be set out by relating what happened in the state of Ch'in. Ch'in was the most northwesterly of the kingdoms. About 600 miles from the sea the Yellow River takes a great sweep north-wards. At this turn it is joined by the Wei River. The state of Ch'in lay on the Wei River. Its position was very strong because between it and its eastern neighbours, the states of Wei and Ch'u, were high mountains. The passes across them were held to be im-pregnable. While it was most difficult to attack, its armies were well placed to debouch from the passes. By marching down the Yellow River to the sea they could cut the Empire in two. There-after, to dispose in detail of the northern and southern states would be easy. Such were the possibilities inherent in Ch'in's strategical position. But since it was the most backward of all the states, there appeared small likelihood of its being intelligent enough to make use of its advantages. To march on a career of world conquest, it must have a cleverer government, a better trained army, a superior supply system, and a more controlled people than existed in the other states, or any combination of them. How it did acquire all these essentials by adopting a political system the opposite of the old civilisation codified by the Confucians will now be narrated.

The story begins with the coming of one, Yang, to Ch'in in about the year 359 B.C. Yang's biography was written two and a half centuries later by Ssu-ma Ch'ien, the great historian of the Han Dynasty, of whom much is to be related further on. In it we first see Yang as a tutor at the Court of the Wei state. He was a brilliant and ambitious young man, but his appointment gave him little scope, being purely academic. He had been trained in the law, and the theory of government interested him intensely. From time to time he was encouraged to air his views by the Chancellor of Wei, the man to whom he owed his appointment as tutor. The Chancellor was so impressed by some of his proposals for the strengthening of the Wei state as a military power that he promised

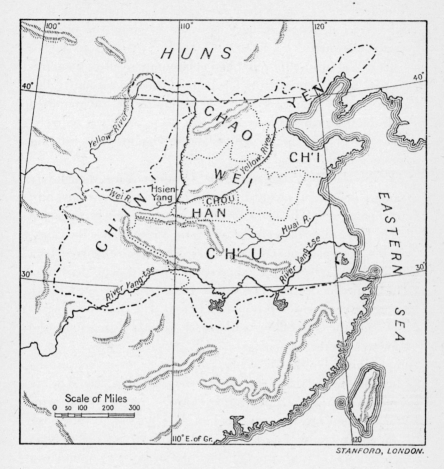

Scale of Miles
0   50 100   200   300

110° E. of Gr.

STANFORD, LONDON.

STATES CONQUERED BY CH'IN WHILE BECOMING THE
PARAMOUNT POWER DURING 3RD CENTURY B.C.

to introduce him to the Duke of Wei.[1] What Yang wanted was a Ministership or a seat on the Council and he had hinted that if he did not get it, sooner or later he would be obliged to offer his services elsewhere.

Before the Chancellor could find opportunity to effect the introduction, he fell seriously ill. The Duke, anxious about him, called at his house. 'Your Excellency,' he said, after he had conversed with the sick man and ascertained that his recovery was unlikely, 'the state of your health obliges me to enquire, who, in your opinion, should succeed you in your office?'

To this the Chancellor answered: 'The tutor, Yang, though very young, is remarkably talented. Your Grace would be wise to give him the appointment. His advice on affairs of state would be valuable.'

The Duke made no reply, because Yang's youth made the Chancellor's proposal seem very fanciful. He continued to converse for a little time on other topics and presently rose to take his departure. The Chancellor detained him with a gesture. 'Before you go, I have a word for your Grace's private ear,' he said. The Duke's staff withdrew, and the Chancellor continued: 'It would be dangerous were Yang to leave the country, as he might do were Your Grace not to employ him.' On the Duke enquiring what he meant by this, the Chancellor hinted that Yang's talents were such that, should he become adviser to some other ruling House, it might go hard with Wei. 'If your Grace has no use for him, have him put to death. That is my advice as a loyal minister.' The Duke, who took this to be an ingenious way of further recommending Yang, gave a soothing nod and left the house.

As soon as he was gone, the Chancellor sent for Yang. 'When the Duke was here just now,' he said, 'he sounded me on the subject of my successor. I mentioned your name, but I could see from his face that he did not take the suggestion seriously. I therefore felt bound to give him certain advice.' He paused.

[1]Really the King of Wei, but the state rulers still maintained the fiction that they were the feudal Dukes of the Son of Heaven, the Chou Emperor.

'May I enquire what that was?' said Yang.

'I told him that should he not employ you, one day you would go to some other Duke, which would embarrass us here if you advised him as you are able. To prevent that you should be put to death, I said.'

'And did he agree?' asked Yang calmly.

'Yes.'

'Why did you tell him this?'

'It was my duty as his Minister.'

'Then why have you warned me?'

'It is my duty as your friend. And I beseech you to fly at once or you will be arrested.'

But Yang replied: 'Since the Duke did not accept your advice to appoint me, he will not accept it to put me to death. For by rejecting my services he has adjudged me incapable, and so will not care where I may go to.' The coolness and logic of this reply was characteristic of Yang. He stayed where he was.

As was anticipated, the Chancellor died, and the Duke filled his place, but not by nominating Yang. It happened at this time that the Duke of Ch'in gave out that he had vacancies on his council for men of proved administrative ability. This Duke was known to be ambitious and to harbour the secret desire of forcing Wei to return a slice of former Ch'in territory west of the bend of the Yellow River. That an ambitious ruler wanted a counsellor was exactly the news that Yang had long hoped to hear. Accordingly, he departed discreetly from Wei and crossed the border into Ch'in. Through one of the Duke's favourites, with whom he was acquainted, he obtained an audience soon afterwards.

In this first meeting with the Duke he proceeded with great caution. It seems that his Grace asked him a number of questions about foreign policy. Instead of giving his real opinions and perhaps meeting with a fatal rebuff, Yang sought to probe the Duke's mind, and find out how determined he was and how resolute might be his character. So in answer to the questions he began by talking in a conventional manner about the Sainted Emperors and the customs of the old feudal empire, and to describe the way a Duke might set about rectifying his frontier legally by inducing the Son of Heaven to sanction its extension. During this discourse the Duke of Ch'in repeatedly dozed. That the Duke was bored by the moral maxims of antiquity told Yang what he wanted to know, but at that interview he did not disclose his own mind. Afterwards, in conversation with his favourite, the Duke complained about having been afflicted with so tiresome a fellow. 'What made you think,' he asked, 'that I should find that dull friend of yours a job?'

'He is not so dull as might appear,' replied the favourite, 'as your Grace will find if you accord him a further interview.'

Even in the second audience, which the Duke granted five days later, Yang did not deem it prudent to reveal his full thought before he had explored further the Duke's intentions, but though he still confined his remarks to the customary procedure which was supposed to govern the actions of feudatories, he let drop some hints about alternatives. The Duke's opinion of him rose somewhat, though when speaking to his favourite later he was still inclined to be sarcastic. However, his interest was sufficiently aroused for him to keep Yang in mind, for this tutor from Wei was evidently very erudite and in spite of the apparent conventionality of his views made a forceful impression.

By this time Yang was convinced that the Duke was really consumed with ambition, but, lacking expert advice, was at a loss how to realise it. In the next interview he abandoned all pretence and, speaking in a confidential manner, began to give such absorbing information that the Duke did not notice how, oblivious of etiquette, he had moved up so near that his knees were actually on the ducal mat.

This intimate conversation was a long one and caused much speculation at Court. As Yang was coming away, the aforesaid favourite detained him by the sleeve. 'You have evidently succeeded in capturing his Grace's attention this time,' said he. 'May I know what transpired?'

'I gave up talking about the Sainted Emperors,' replied Yang, 'for his Grace on a previous occasion had observed that, though he much admired them, their methods were very slow at producing results, while he, so he said, was too impatient to wait. "What I want," he told me, "is a policy that will make me powerful at once." So today I suggested how that might be accomplished.'

'He seems to have been absorbed by what you told him.'

'He was,' said Yang, 'though of course the morality of the methods I sketched for him hardly bore comparison with the Sainted Emperors'.'

It is not recorded that Yang smiled sardonically when he said this, but it will be taking no liberties with history to assume that he did.

For the Duke of Ch'in to realise his ambition and become a powerful sovereign, he had to amend the customary laws of the Dukedom. To amend customary laws by special enactments is always denounced as tampering with the liberty of the subject. The Duke knew well the objections he would have to counter both from the nobility and the people if he followed the advice which Yang had given him. One finds Yang reassuring him when he wavered because of opposition in the Council. 'Your Grace,' said he, 'should reflect that men of great and original talent are always disliked and misunderstood. If your Grace hesitates now, you will never realise your aims.'

A Councillor called Ken-lung had spoken against the new proposals. His views were those of a Confucian, whether he called himself so or not. 'A wise sovereign,' he said, 'governs not by making laws and forcing the people to obey them, but by interpreting the people's wishes in accordance with old-established customs.'

To which Yang had retorted that, while the average sovereign should rule in this conservative manner, the really great man was above precedent, and shaped his policy with the sole object of bringing his plans to fruition.

The Eclipse of the First Holy One

It was after this debate that the Duke made up his mind to promulgate the revolutionary measures designed to transform the happy-go-lucky old form of his government through landed seigneurs and vassals into what we should now call a centralised bureaucratic state with an army at direct call, a reliable supply system, and a secret police resting on a network of spies. This would mean retrenching the privileges of the nobility by empowering central officials to give orders in the fiefs, which, as feudal tenures, had been hitherto administered solely by the landed lords. It would also entail bringing direct pressure on the people over the heads of their lords, a pressure to take the form of harsh punishments. Feudal quarrels and disorders would be made capital offences; the people would be obliged to cultivate more land, so as to build up supplies for the army, to do forced labour on government projects such as roads and fortifications, and would be always liable to military service. They would be forbidden to leave the state, and their education, in place of a study of antiquity, would be to make themselves thoroughly acquainted with the new laws and their application. Their duty would be, not to think, but to obey. A government which could thus dispose of the whole force of its people and launch an army upon the other states with their loose feudal forces, diversity of command, laxity of discipline and inadequate supply, would be certain to win, and its sovereign would become, not only the most powerful of the Grand Feudatories, but their master and, so, would displace the Chou Emperor and found a real dynasty, a most desirable end, for universal peace would obtain ever after.

With Yang to advise him, the Duke of Ch'in set out to centralise his realm in this realistic way, which was the exact opposite of the Confucian belief that a careful attention to the moral doctrines of antiquity would suffice to bring a state to renown and the whole Empire to tranquillity. His policy, therefore, has a double interest —as a political theory which was put into practice with the astonishing results which we shall see, and as a moral theory which, by the sensational nature of its political achievement, effected the eclipse of Confucianism. But since Confucianism survived its eclipse and came to power, it is easy to understand that Yang, the Duke of Ch'in's mentor, has always been regarded in China as one of the greatest rogues in its history.

First the Duke published as mandates the new laws and enforced them with the utmost severity. To effect this, Yang must have succeeded in organising a body of fanatical adherents, strong enough to overawe both the landed lords and the people. The Duke's heir, indeed, resisted at the head of his partisans, but Yang was able to insist on his punishment, his tutor being made scapegoat and having his nose amputated. So thorough was the new police, that feudal quarrels, banditry, and violent crime became rare. No discussion of the new laws was allowed. Even people who came forward to praise them were snubbed. With insufferable arrogance, Yang is reported to have said of some men of the kind: 'It is an impertinence for these fellows to approve. They are no better than disorderly persons who oppose. Let them be banished to the frontiers.'

As soon as he felt strong enough, the Duke decided to force Wei to give back the piece of Ch'in territory west of the Yellow River. He made Yang commander-in-chief of the new army. Wei was defeated and the land restored. This territory had great strategic importance, being the first objective to be secured if a future campaign to subjugate all the Feudatories were to be successful.

Returning victorious, Yang was enfeoffed as Lord of Shang, the name which appears as the author's in the *Book of Shang*, a volume which, whether written personally by Yang himself, or not, contains a detailed exposition of his views. It has been compared to Machiavelli's *Prince* and, though the comparison is not exact, it has aptness, for the aim of both writers was to demonstrate how a Prince, by disregarding traditional morality, could climb to the top.

In spite of Yang's prodigious success and the glory he had won for Ch'in arms, he was much hated, by the nobility for his entrenchment on their privileges, by the people for his oppression, and by the literati for his discouragement of the study of antiquity. He became Chancellor after the victory over Wei and so continued for ten years, when the Duke was seen to be dying. This was the event which the nobility had been waiting for.

The Ssu-ma Ch'ien biography of Lord Shang, from which I have been quoting, has preserved a scene which occurred shortly before the Duke's death. A certain Chao Liang, a gentleman of the conservative or Confucian type, calls on Lord Shang, and dares to speak out because he knows that the Chancellor's time is nearly up.

The interview begins with a display of elaborate politeness by his Lordship. 'I had the privilege on a former occasion,' he says, 'of being introduced to you. May I now have the further privilege of offering you a post in the government?'

Chao Liang replies with sarcastic innuendo that he is not virtuous enough to serve a state whose government is so famous for its morality. Lord Shang, nettled by his tone, enquires whether he approves of him as Chancellor. Chao Liang parries this by saying that if his Lordship modelled himself humbly on the Sainted Emperor Shun there would be no need to ask such a question.

There follows from Chao Liang a harangue in which he denounces the Lord of Shang to his face. He compares him unfavourably to a famous councillor of Duke Mu of Ch'in of the seventh century B.C. who, though he made Ch'in a famous state 'did not sit in a carriage when he was tired, did not have a sunshade held over his head in summer, and when touring the country dispensed with ox-carts and horses and went without a bodyguard. But when your Lordship tours, you are escorted by armed men picked for their strength who stand in chariots that keep pace with your Lordship's carriage, while tens of vehicles follow behind. Without these precautions your Lordship would not dare go out.' And he continues with increasing invective: 'Your Lordship's peril is like that of the morning dew. Why do you not resign, while still you can? Why not go back to your fief and quietly water your vegetable garden? For if the Duke of Ch'in should of a morning leave his guests, and no longer stand in Court but depart utterly, how would it be with your Lordship? Would the state continue to sustain you? I fear your Lordship would perish in no more time than it takes to lift the foot.'

Having uttered these menaces, Chao Liang withdrew. Like many another adventurer since, Lord Shang deferred his retreat until it was too late. The Duke died, and the Heir succeeded, who had been so gravely insulted by the outrage to his tutor. The police were sent to arrest Lord Shang on a charge of plotting against the state. He fled towards Wei, his old home. En route he drew rein at a hotel on the mountain pass and demanded a room for the night. The manager asked him to register in accordance with the rules, for one of the police regulations, which Lord Shang himself had been responsible for, enjoined the registration of all travellers. He refused angrily to comply, not wishing to disclose his identity. The manager expressed regret but refused to admit him; he did not dare to do it, he said. The Lord Shang sighed: 'I never thought,' he muttered bitterly, 'that one of my laws would be proved so demonstrably ill-conceived.' Driving on, he came to Wei. His welcome there was very chilly. The government regarded him as a renegade, who had left Wei to serve a rival state and at the head of its army had marched against his own countrymen. 'If you refuse to have me back, let me pass through to Chao or Ch'i,' he urged. But the authorities would not afford him any facilities. On the contrary, perceiving in the affair an opportunity of ingratiating themselves with the government of Ch'in, of which they were much afraid, they ordered Lord Shang to return the way he had come.

But Shang had one shot left. He did not go back to the capital, Hsien-yang, but to his fief of Shang, some hundred miles to the south-east of it. There he rallied his partisans and broke out into open rebellion. But the new Duke's forces were too strong for him, and he was defeated and killed in a pitched battle near Cheng on the Wei river. To demonstrate the detestation in which he was held by the new government of Ch'in, he was posthumously dismembered, his body being torn asunder between galloping war-cars. So ended this 'hard and cruel man' as Ssu-ma Ch'ien, his biographer, calls him.

The fall of Lord Shang from power did not mean the reversal of his realist policy. During the twenty years between his arrival in 359 and his death in 338 B.C., Ch'in had become a unified military state, more modern than any of the other states, and therefore stronger. The new Duke had no intention of throwing away his chances of wider power by any return to old-fashioned thinking. His overturning of Lord Shang was an act of private revenge; but he would foster the laws which had made his realm so strong. Ch'in was already officially recognised as the leading state, for the Son of Heaven five years before had conferred upon his predecessor the title of Leader, and sent him a portion of sacrificial meat, an act of solemn confirmation of the title. As Leader of the States, he would continue. To do so, he must maintain his power and increase it.

What happened can be succinctly stated in a series of dates. The succeeding Dukes of Ch'in, seeing that it was within their capacity, not only to lead, but also to overcome the other states, proceeded methodically to do so. At this time the Empire, for it was still so-called, consisted of seven states, Ch'in up the Yellow River, Wei, Chao, Yen and Ch'i, north of the river, and Han and Ch'u south of the river, with the imperial domain of Chou in the centre. From the death of Lord Shang in 338 B.C. until 253 B.C. a series of ferocious invasions of these states by Ch'in armies took place, enormous casualties being inflicted. In 253, the then Duke of Ch'in overran the imperial domain, extinguished the Chou dynasty, seized the imperial palladia, the nine bronze ritual vessels supposed to have belonged to the Sainted Emperor Yü, and offered the imperial sacrifice to Heaven; but he did not at this time take the title of Emperor and Son of Heaven. In 230 B.C. the succeeding Duke, now called the King of Ch'in, felt strong enough to strike the final blow. He annexed Han in 229, Chao in 228, Yen in 226,

Wei in 225, Ch'u in 223 and Ch'i in 222. In 221, having possession of all China, he took the imperial title, styling himself the First Emperor of the Ch'in dynasty, or, more literally, the Ch'in First Divine August One.[1] Thus, in a little over a hundred years, Ch'in, from being a backward tract beyond the passes to the north-west, became master of the Empire, as Lord Shang promised would be so if it abandoned feudalism, ceased to admire antiquity, centralised its administration, reorganised its army, built up its supply, and drove on its people. It had given the answer to the great debates of the fourth century on how to achieve unity and abolish war. As master of all the states, it unified them, and gave them peace. The whole world had been given peace, not by moral suasion, the Confucian ideal, but by a display of main force.

During the course of these political events, the ideas, first advanced by Lord Shang and subsequently developed by several other eminent jurists, became a school whose thought, tested by events, had triumphed. Its jurists could claim that they, not the Confucians, had given practical solution to the fundamental problems by rejecting antiquity as a guide for conduct and substituting a current expediency instead.

Against the jurists it was argued that if the Ch'in revolution had required during its continuance expedients of a special kind, these were now too oppressive and harsh since universal peace has been established. It would be good policy, some urged, for the new Ch'in lords to liberalise their ideas. The army was no longer required for there was no one to fight. The military organisation could be reduced and a large measure of freedom restored to the public. But the Ch'in did not see things in this light. The states they had conquered had to be held down. Accordingly, they continued their military government, the whole of China being divided into commanderies and administered by military police. Fortifica-

[1] The style Divine August One (Huang Ti) was the Yellow Emperor's style. The taking of it with the addition of the word First was tantamount to the claim that Chinese history began, not with the Yellow Emperor, but with the Emperor of the Ch'in.

tions of a far greater size and involving an enormous labour force were projected; for it was argued that, though the world was at peace, there remained the steppe; and the barbarians of the steppe must be kept out. The vast labour of constructing the Great Wall was thus undertaken.

The continuance of so arduous and oppressive a policy was the Ch'in Dynasty's great mistake. Even so, they might have maintained themselves had they not made mortal enemies of the educated class by an act of particular enormity. This class was composed mostly of Confucianists, but among them were also general readers of the mass of literature which had been produced by the numerous minor schools of thought of the fifth and fourth centuries B.C. Though the Ch'in had accomplished by unifying the Empire what Confucius had always advocated, the unification had been done in so non-Confucian a way and was being administered so despotically, that the Master's adherents were necessarily in opposition. For the bulk of the gentlemen of the realm to be opposed to the government was highly dangerous. Sooner or later they would lead the people against it. But instead of conciliating them, it was decided to strike at the root of their being, and suppress the culture of which they were the mouthpiece. The Ch'in Emperor's Minister of the Left was a fanatic called Li Ssu. His memorial to the Throne, dated 213 B.C., which is given in Ssu-ma Ch'ien's History, describes what was proposed to be done.

Even in a Ch'in document it was impossible to dispense altogether with the Sainted Emperors, and, accordingly, Li Ssu begins by saying that the Yellow One, and Yao, Shun and Yü, did not just copy each other—they were too big for that—but enunciated policies suited to their several situations. On the principle of *autres temps, autres mœurs,* all rulers of eminence were obliged to do that. How much more so, then, the First Divine August One, whose achievement was without precedent. 'This is what narrow scholars cannot understand,' Li Ssu goes on. 'The Empire has been pacified. Laws and mandates emanate from a single authority. The common people are engaged in agriculture and industry. The upper classes study law and administrative procedures. But the erudite gentry have not accommodated themselves to the new way; they study the past in order to deny the present, citing precedents from remote antiquity with the object of showing Your Majesty to be wrong. As soon as they hear of a new edict, they proceed to criticise it from this viewpoint. At Court, no doubt, they are all propriety, but they talk at random in the public streets and induce the people to believe their calumnies. This must be stopped and there is a way to stop it. Let the histories of the States, with the exception of the state of Ch'in, be burnt. Let all the erudite gentlemen (with the exception of the seventy licensed State Scholars) who possess copies of *The Book of History* and *The Book of Songs* and the other numerous publications of the Schools of Political Philosophy, take their books to the magistrates to be burnt. Let death be the penalty for writing any further commentaries on the so-called classics. Let all discussions of these books be punishable with death. Let any officials who abet such discussions be put to death. And let the death penalty extend to the families of those who are so condemned. After thirty days' grace, every person in whose possession a copy of any of the said works is found, may be branded and sent to forced labour on the Great Wall. Scientific works, such as those on medicine, divination, agriculture or forestry, may be exempted. Those who wish to read can read them, though they are advised rather to give their time to the study of the Ch'in laws and administration and to go for instruction to the high government officials.'

The Emperor perused this memorial and, taking his Vermilion Brush, wrote below the word 'approved', thereby turning it into law, the most infamous law, in Chinese opinion, which has ever disgraced their statute book. In sum it abolished education. It was put into operation, and there followed the Burning of the Books, an attempt—for such a project could not be wholly effective—to wipe out the literary heritage of China. In this way the Confucians were deprived of the sources of their learning. They, and all they stood for, suffered for a time total eclipse.

This was the worst moment in all the long history of Confucianism. The Master was rejected, his followers were proscribed, his classics reduced to ashes. But the ordeal was short. Four years later the First Ch'in Divine August One was dead, and his successor, after a reign of three years, was murdered in the course of a rebellion. To say that the attempt to destroy Confucianism was the cause of the fall of the dynasty would be to state the case too sharply, but it can be said that in going against the deepest convictions of the Chinese race, convictions which had been given their most complete expression in the Confucian classics, the Ch'in Emperor raised a storm of anger that overwhelmed his House. Furthermore, to say that the people who rose in rebellion did so in order to set up Confucianism would be an oversimplification; they rose against tyranny and inhuman laws, and gave the Empire to a soldier of peasant origin, who promised to abolish what had made the Ch'in so hateful. But the reversal of the Ch'in political philosophy led logically to Confucianism becoming the state cult and that event was therefore one of the results of this great counter-revolution.

In the next chapter is recounted the biography of the Eminent Founder, the peasant leader of the counter-revolution, who established the Han Dynasty. But we cannot leave the First Ch'in Divine August One without a valediction. He was a fabulous monster of a sort that these latter days have made us familiar with, of whom it was said that 'he had a high-bridged nose, long narrow eyes, the breast of a bird of prey, and the voice of a jackal.' He believed that he had conquered the whole civilised world, holding there to be beyond his borders only a waste of barbarism, for he was without knowledge of Alexander, who, at the very time that the Lord Shang came to Ch'in, was over-running the western civilised world, and who shared the delusion that he had no more to conquer. Stranger and more secret than the Caesars, the Divine August One captivates us for all his cruelty, for when he became Emperor, and had built the Great Wall and a multitude of palaces in the metropolitan region, pavilions to which he passed by covered passages, so that none but his close intimates knew where he slept, he conceived the mad desire to live for ever, and sought to find the secret of immortality. In this search for the elixir he spent his last years.

The Eminent Founder Comes

Liu was the surname of the personage through whom the Chinese re-established their civilisation after it had been in eclipse from 221 B.C., the year the King of Ch'in seized the Empire and established his despotism, until 207 B.C., when the Second Ch'in Emperor was killed in the course of the rebellion against his dynasty. It is interesting and significant that they bore this negation of their fundamental morality only for fifteen years.

In spite of the mists of two millennia, the figure of Liu emerges with startling clarity from the chapter which the historian Pan Ku (first century A.D.) devotes to him in his *History of the Former Han*. When the rebellions against the Ch'in began in 209 B.C., Liu was about forty years of age. His father was a farmer whose land was near Feng in the prefecture of P'ei, the town a hundred and fifty miles south of Lu where the Venerable Sir was supposed to have admonished Confucius. But Liu, unlike his brothers, had no taste for agriculture. Instead of helping on the family farm, as his father would have liked, he sought a minor post in the rural administration and, successfully passing the tests, which were not of a literary character, he was appointed Headman of a group of hamlets.

In the East a man destined to be great is always given some intimations of his coming fortune. To the western reader this may sound an odd statement, but anyone, whose familiarity with the

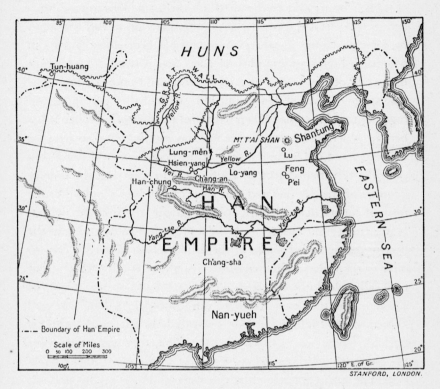

HAN EMPIRE IN 2ND AND 1ST CENTURIES B.C.

orient is close, will know it to be a commonplace. In the deep countryside are to this day astrologers, clairvoyants, and students of signs, who are ever on the watch for the future lord to pass. Such beings had already formed their opinion of Liu, as Pan Ku shows by some charming instances. A certain old gentleman called Lü, who had a high standing in those parts, was obliged to take refuge in the city of P'ei from a man who threatened to murder him. The magistrate of P'ei offered to put him up, and they got on so well together that Lü settled down with him permanently. When it be-became generally known that he was staying there, P'ei society was interested and the leading people of the neighbourhood decided to call. Though their object, of course, was to meet Lü, the code of manners of the day dictated that their call on him should take the form of congratulation to his host for having so important a guest. It was further the custom to bring a present of money to help the host to defray the expenses of the drinks which he would have to offer to the callers. The magistrate's steward let it be known that each caller would be expected to give a thousand cash if he wanted a seat in the reception room. In due course, Liu, who was well known for his bluffing humour, presented himself, and sent in his card on which was written: 'I have come to congratulate your Honour with ten thousand cash.' Really, he did not bring even one cash. The steward, however, without demanding to see his present, let him in. As soon as the old gentleman Lü caught sight of him, he was much struck by his appearance, and rising from his mat escorted him to the place of honour at the table where the drinks were laid. Liu promptly accepted the seat that was offered and though, as only Headman of a hamlet group, he was far junior to several of the callers, he showed not the slightest shyness or em-barrassment. When the party was over and people began moving off home, the old gentleman Lü detained him. 'Since I was a boy,' he said, 'I have amused myself by reading fortunes from the feat-ures of the face. I have read in my time a great number of faces, but none of them were as auspicious as I conceive yours to be. So certain am I of your future celebrity that I offer you my daughter in marriage.' Afterwards, the old gentleman's wife was angry with him. 'You have always talked of giving our girl to some really important person. You did not even think the magistrate of P'ei high enough up, because when he asked you for her, you refused him. Now you offer her to this small village official.' The old gentleman replied: 'There are some things which are above the heads of women.' This daughter it was who became the Empress Lü, and was the mother of the second Emperor of the Han.

Later, when his wife had born Liu two children, another prophecy was made. The family were staying on the ancestral estate. While his wife and children were weeding one day, an old man came by and asked for a drink. When he had refreshed himself, he said to the future Empress: 'Madam will be the most honourable person in the world.' 'How can you tell that?' she asked. 'I have long studied physiognomy,' he replied, 'and can read your fortune in your face.' 'Please read also my children's fortunes,' she begged him. He looked at the boy destined to be the second Emperor and replied: 'The reason that Madam will be such an honourable personage is this boy,' and looking at the girl, the future Princess Yüan, he added: 'She also will be an honourable personage.' Soon after the old man had gone, Liu, who had been in a neighbouring house, came out and joined his family. When his wife told him what had happened, he was excited and ran after the old man and caught him up. 'You have foretold greatness for my wife and children. Read, also, I beg the signs in my case,' he said. 'The signs are the same,' replied the old man. 'Your physiognomy, sir, is honourable beyond all telling.' Much moved, Liu thanked him, exclaiming: 'If what you have foretold really takes place, I shall never forget what you have done for me,' for he felt strengthened and animated in the depths of his soul. When eventually Liu became Emperor, the Royal Founder of the Han, he remembered the old man and made enquiries, but was unable to trace him.

His biographer suggests that Liu cherished a secret ambition from this time, the wild ambition of rising from the position of rural Headman to the headmanship of the world. From time to time he made visits to the capital, Hsien-yang, in charge of labourers sent to work there on some imperial building or road, and it is related that one day, seeing the Ch'in First Divine August One pass in his cortège of carriages and horsemen, he sighed deeply in envy and aspiration, saying: 'Ah! that is the way a real man should seem!'

Of Liu's appearance at this period of his life we read that his nose was prominent and that he had what in those days was called a dragon forehead, a term whose precise significance is lost, but which, one may suppose, denoted whatever is commanding and auspicious. His beard was beautiful, and on his left thigh were moles, seventy-two it is alleged, a mystic number. As if to dramatise his singularity of appearance and mark him off from the common run, he made himself a hat of bamboo skin, which is a thin papery bark, and sent it to town to be perfected, an errand he entrusted to his sergeant of police. This hat he wore on occasions when he desired to be remembered. On becoming Emperor he wore it constantly. It became a famous hat, and was known to everybody as the Hat of the House of Liu.

From an early date people had believed they saw rays above him. Emanations of light of this kind were thought of as indicating sublime attributes. Two women who kept a wineshop where he used to drink were so certain they saw these rays that they would rarely present him with his bill. The Ch'in Emperor, who, as we know, was deeply interested in the occult, heard there was an emanation that rose heavenwards in the south-east at a time when Liu, as will be related, had become a fugitive in the mountains of Mang, a region lying south-east of the capital. In the Emperor's library was a book on astronomy containing a passage on emanations, where it was stated that the emanation of a future Son of Heaven was red within and yellow without. On occasion such an emanation might also take the form of a man in black clothes without hands, there

being visible behind him in a vapour the gates of a city; on other
occasions a dragon-horse, a most auspicious sign, might be observed, either with or without the man in black. The Ch'in Emperor's information led him to believe that an emanation of such
forms and colours was to be seen in the south-east. Since his book
was most emphatic that the phenomenon denoted the presence
there of an embryo Son of Heaven, he became alarmed and travelled south-east in his train of sorcerers, magicians, astrologers and
mediums, with intent to take counter measures of magic. No harm,
however, came to Liu. His wife, who used to visit him in his retreat in the mountains, where he had become a bandit, said that no
matter in what place he might be hidden she could find him by the
misty light rising from him. Till this time, it is said, he did not
know that he had an emanation, and his wife's words cheered and
gave him added confidence, confirming his inner vision of his future glory. She told the people of P'ei what she had seen, and some
of the young men, convinced of his great future, went out and
joined him. They were the germ of the army with which eventually he took possession of the world. The belief in emanations that
denote the coming or presence of a saviour or transcendent being
persists in the orient till this day, as I myself have observed in remote places where the passing of two thousand years brings little
change.

How Liu lost his appointment of rural Headman and became a
fugitive and a bandit is simply told. He was in charge of a gang of
convict labourers whom he had to escort to the place of their work.
On the way there several of them escaped. By the harsh laws of the
Ch'in the penalty for allowing convict labourers to escape was
death or enslavement. There was nothing for Liu but to go into
hiding. He set free the rest of the convicts, some ten of whom followed him into the mountains of Mang.

Soon after this the Ch'in First Emperor died, and in 209 B.C.
the first year of his son's reign, the revolts presaging the rebellion
began. They took the form of the re-establishment of the old king-

doms which the Ch'in had overthrown. One of the first to massacre the Ch'in imperial officials and restore a scion of its royal house was Ch'u state, in which P'ei was situated. When the news of what had happened reached P'ei, the magistrate of that town, who was, of course, a Ch'in official, decided to join the revolution. He was advised, however, by the Chief Jailor and a man called the Superintendent of Officials that it was extremely doubtful whether he could get the townsfolk to rise, as they would be too timid to take the risk. 'Your best course,' they said, 'will be to summon back the several hundred men who have taken to the mountains through fear of the laws. You can be sure that they will support you wholeheartedly. And by using them you can coerce the rest.'

The magistrate agreed. Many of the absconders in question had joined Liu, and a man was sent to invite him back. In due course, he arrived with a large following. In the interval, however, the magistrate had changed his mind. The risk was too great, he thought; it would be better to wait till events declared themselves more clearly. He, therefore, closed the city gates and refused to let Liu and his people in. The Chief Jailor and the Superintendent, afraid that the magistrate might now arrest them, escaped over the wall and joined Liu.

Liu now took the first step in the career that was to carry him to the Dragon Seat. He wrote a letter to the elders of P'ei and, attaching it to an arrow, shot it into the town. Its contents were to this effect: 'The world has long groaned under the Ch'in. The nobles have risen against the tyrant and if they hear that you, the citizens of P'ei, are defending that city for the Emperor, they will come and slaughter you. It will, therefore, be better for you to kill your magistrate. Thereafter, you should select a leader and make common cause with the nobles. Any course else will be most dangerous for you.'

The emanations had given Liu great authority. The elders took his advice, killed the magistrate, opened the gates and welcomed him in. Be our magistrate, they begged him. He replied modestly, as was the custom: 'You must have a capable man as your leader. The times are dangerous; there is fighting ahead. Even one defeat may have fatal results. I am not qualified enough for the post. Not that I fear for my own safety, but am truly not sure that I can keep you safe.' No one else, however, dared to lead the rebellion. Even the Jailor and the Superintendent had not the nerve. The elders turned again to Liu: 'For a long time,' they said, 'we have heard of the signs that attend you. Surely you are destined to be an honourable personage. Accept the office of our leader. With such prognostics you cannot fail.'

Liu did not deem it necessary to refuse again. A meeting was convened in the great hall of the prefecture and the title of Lord of P'ei was accorded him. That day he sacrificed to the Yellow Emperor and solemnly anointed his drums with blood. His pennons were red. Three thousand more of the young men of P'ei joined his force at once. Besides his attraction as a man for whom so much glory had been foretold, his personality inspired trust and affection. It is recorded that he was naturally kind and generous. In spite of a certain brusqueness, his disposition was to like people. And he had a great talent for getting able men to serve under him, perhaps of all gifts the most certain to bring one to the top.

The steps by which Liu, or, as I shall now call him, the Lord of P'ei, rose to the imperial throne, can be clearly traced from Pan Ku's narrative. In sum the reason for his success was that, as a commander of troops, he was cleverer, more enduring, and more popular than his rivals, and, as a man, he bore a higher reputation. His chief rival was an impoverished gentleman called Hsiang Yü, also an adventurer like himself, who seemed at one stage of the rebellion far more likely to become Emperor than the Lord of P'ei. The period covered by the summary of events that follows is from October 209 to February 202 B.C.

The rebellion had three aspects: the fighting against the imperial troops; the fighting among the rebels who, after re-establishing the feudal kingdoms, quarrelled over their boundaries; and, later, the fighting of the Lord of P'ei against Hsiang Yü for the throne of the world. As an example of the second, Feng, which was near the village where the Lord of P'ei was born, revolted from him and elected to go in with a neighbouring lord. He felt this defection of his home town very much, and it took him some time to recapture it. To begin with, the operations against the imperialists were directed, at least nominally, by the newly restored King of Ch'u. After defeating their efforts to suppress the rebellion, he found himself strong enough to contemplate an attack on Hsien-yang, the imperial capital. The Lord of P'ei and Hsiang Yü, who were co-operating at this stage and had distinguished themselves more than any other of his commanders, were the obvious choice for this important expedition, but he decided to entrust it to the Lord of P'ei alone, on the ground that he had a name for fairness and moderation which might induce the holders of the Ch'in stronghold to surrender, while Hsiang Yü's reputation for ferocity would drive them into a despairing resistance. In deputing the Lord of P'ei to the sole command, he promised that if he were successful he would be made King of the state of Ch'in. Hsiang Yü was not informed of this. The King created him Duke of Lu and he went campaigning in the opposite direction.

After several battles, the Lord of P'ei entered the passes and took the imperial capital in November 207 B.C. The Second Emperor had been assassinated by his Chief Eunuch before the fall of the city, and a new sovereign was in charge. This ruler surrendered and his life was spared. The riches accumulated in the palace by the First Divine August One were astonishing. When the Lord of P'ei inspected the treasuries and storehouses he found them full of gold and jade. Later histories describe the curious rarities he also saw; the blue jade lamp, seven feet high, each of its five lights being held in the mouth of a hornless dragon, whose scales moved when the lights were lit; the bronze group of musicians, two feet high, which were made to play organs when an attendant blew into a tube below; the jade flute two feet long, on which were engraved

74

the words, 'The Flute of Bright Flowers', and which, when blown, caused an enchantment, those present seeing carriages, horses, mountains and forests; and a magic mirror, in which you beheld yourself upside down and which, in the case of women, revealed whether they had evil intentions: the Divine August One had made his women look into it and killed those whose innocence it put in doubt. All these marvels and precious objects the Lord of P'ei sealed up carefully; his troops were forbidden to loot and the inhabitants were not molested. In this course he was not only carrying out the orders of his King, but also winning the goodwill of the Ch'in people, a valuable asset when he should become, as he had been promised, their ruler.

When Duke Hsiang Yü heard that Hsien-yang had fallen to the Lord of P'ei he was very angry. At the head of 400,000 men he came up by forced marches, entered the passes and headed for the capital. Its citizens, who had been quite won over by their conqueror's kind behaviour, and were terrified by the prospect of the fierce Duke's arrival, hastened to warn P'ei and beg his protection against what looked like a second conquest.

In fact, the Duke's intention was to attack his rival. One of his counsellors had said: 'The extreme moderation shown by the Lord of P'ei is a highly suspicious circumstance, and shows that his plans are dark and vast. I sent a man recently to have a look at his emanation, of which we have all heard so much. Sure enough, it had the form of a dragon with the five colours of the five points of the compass. As that is the emanation of a Son of Heaven, your Grace should destroy him, now that you have him in your power, since his army is only a hundred thousand to our four hundred thousand.' The Duke agreed, and that night feasted his soldiers in preparation for the morrow's battle.

The Lord of P'ei perceived it was a moment for the greatest discretion. He knew how to bend; his peasant origin, no doubt, helped him in this; and he had both subtlety and intuition, an awareness that is the great man of action's ever present safeguard. He was

75

lucky too; at no time can one become Master of the World without luck. In this case the luck was that the Duke's uncle, who was a close friend of one of his colleagues, came to his camp to warn the friend of the Duke's intentions. The Lord of P'ei was apprised of his visit and asked him to take a message to the Duke and explain that in capturing Hsien-yang he had merely come on ahead and acted on the Duke's behalf, of which the proof was that none of the treasures had been touched. 'Tell the Duke,' he added, 'that day and night I have been hoping he would come.' The Duke's uncle promised to convey this message, provided that the Lord of P'ei called in person next day and apologised. 'I guarantee your safety,' he assured him. On his return to the Duke's camp, he made excuses for P'ei, saying also: 'Had he not first crushed the imperial troops and opened the passes, your Grace would have had a difficult time in forcing them.' The Duke was somewhat mollified.

Next day P'ei, with an escort of only a hundred cavalry, came to call on Hsiang Yü and make his excuses. 'Your servant,' he said in the frank pleasing manner he could so well adopt, 'has been working throughout in co-operation with your Grace. Your Grace's operations took you in one direction, mine happened to take me in this. In point of fact, it never occurred to me that I should be able alone to capure the Ch'in stronghold. That I did so was just a piece of luck. It is a great happiness now to deliver it to your Grace. Evil-disposed persons have sought to give a dubious meaning to my actions, but your Grace is too intelligent to be deceived by such talk.' This agile explanation convinced the Duke; he asked the Lord of P'ei to stay to supper.

But the Duke's intimate advisers were far from pleased. At the supper party one of them, called Fan, kept on urging the Duke by signs to stab his guest, who was sitting close by. When the Duke did nothing, Fan left the table and spoke to a nobleman outside: 'Our Duke is too soft. The Lord of P'ei must be done away with. If not, one day we shall all be his captives. Do you go in and offer to dance a sword-dance. In the course of it take an opportunity to cut him down.'

The nobleman entered and called a toast in the guest's honour. After it had been drunk, he said: 'As there are no professional entertainers in the camp, have I your Grace's leave to dance a sword-dance?' When this was granted, he drew his sword and danced. His demeanour, as he swung his sword and edged up towards his quarry, roused the suspicions of the Duke's uncle, who felt himself bound in honour to protect a man to whom he had given a guarantee of safety. Accordingly, he himself rose from his place and danced, swinging his sword so as to cover P'ei.

One of P'ei's captains was outside and, on being told that his lord was in danger, he forced his way in past the guards in a fury. 'What is this?' exclaimed the Duke, annoyed; but, unable to withhold admiration for the intruder's magnificent physique and bold loyal heart, he offered him a cup of wine. The Lord of P'ei, well aware of the mortal danger he was in, took advantage of this interruption to slip out on the excuse that he wished to relieve himself. He managed to make a covert sign to his intimates and they too slipped out and followed him to the door. His carriage with its escort was waiting there, but instead of entering it he threw himself on a horse and galloped by side paths back to his headquarters. This was one of the Eminent Founder's narrowest escapes.

The Duke, calmed by his uncle and by a present of two antique jade disques, did not pursue and attack the Lord of P'ei, but contented himself with marching into Hsien-yang. One may suppose that he did not take the emanations as seriously as did his staff. Since the Lord of P'ei had surrendered his conquest without a fight, to fight him on the ground that his emanation was dangerous would be ridiculous. On entering the city, the Duke did what the Ch'in people had been so grateful to the Lord of P'ei for not doing: he looted the treasuries and palaces, and set fire to them; he fired the city and massacred the inhabitants. In this fire was consumed the imperial library of Ch'in. Since it contained copies of the Confucian classics, which along with the other texts of the so-called Hundred Schools of the fourth century had been preserved there for the use of the seventy certificated scholars above-mentioned after the Burning of the Books seven years earlier, its destruction amplified that burning and made the subsequent reconstruction of the Confucian texts a still more difficult matter. The Duke also broke open and looted the Ch'in First Emperor's tomb, which was on Li-shan, a mountain of those parts. This tomb was the proto-type of all subsequent imperial tombs, though it far exceeded them in magnificence and in the cruel circumstances in which the corpse was laid in it. At the foot of Li-shan the masons first dug down till water was reached. As a base for the stone sarcophagus a bronze platform was built. On this was laid out a raised map of the empire, the palaces, ministries, towns and villages being shown in miniature. The main rivers and their tributaries were made of mercury, as was the sea, into which by a mechanical con-trivance the rivers flowed. The vault of the tomb was painted to represent the firmament. The whole was lit by lamps fed by tanks of fish-oil and calculated to remain alight for many years. A great treasure of gold, jewels, jade and silks was deposited. All the de-ceased's wives who had borne no children were buried with him, as well as a full staff of servants. After the funeral ceremonies were over, the workmen closed the inner gate of the tomb and entered the subterranean passage leading to the outer gate. But that gate was shut against them and they were immured in the passage, on the principle that dead men give away no secrets. As a further pro-vision against the possibility of violation, crossbows which would loose their arrows if a thread were broken had been fixed to com-mand all conceivable points of ingress. Finally, the mound was planted with bushes and trees in such a way that the entrance to the passage was hidden by them.

But these precautions protected the tomb for only three years. Duke Hsiang Yü had no difficulty in breaking in and took every-thing of value. When he reported to the King of Ch'u what he had done at Hsien-yang, the King said bluntly that the Lord of P'ei had been promised the Ch'in state. But the Duke was now all powerful. 'My family set the King where he is,' he said, 'and I am not bound by what he may have promised.' Next month he gave the King the title of Emperor out of feigned respect, and made himself King Lord Protector of Ch'u. In that capacity he passed orders on all important matters without reference to the so-called Emperor. One of his first orders was to create the Lord of P'ei King of Han,[1] an appointment which was tantamount to a banishment on the extreme western frontier. Later in the year he had the Emperor assassinated. Thus by November 206 he was *de facto* master of the empire.

But the Lord of P'ei, or rather the King of Han, as we must now call Liu, had not given up. He still believed in his great destiny. His father, generally referred to as the T'ai Kung or Revered Parent, and his wife and children, remained at P'ei, eight hundred miles away on the opposite side of China and directly in Hsiang Yü's power. This worried him, but though he tried to get them, he was unsuccessful; they were held as hostages for his good behaviour. Nevertheless, he did not remain quiet. Both nobles and troops joined him in Han and later in the same year he broke out, entered the former Ch'in state and made himself master of the passes. This gave him the same strategic advantage over the King Lord Protector as the Ch'in power originally had had over the other states. Hsiang Yü had been unable to prevent this happening because his forces were dissipated in fighting against those who resisted his authority at all points of the compass.

In April 205 B.C. the King of Han received some advice in the old tradition from a person called the Great Excellency Tung, whom he met at Lo-yang,[2] a city east of the passes to which he had advanced. Tung was what was then called a 'cultivated personality' and as such had a title and an advisory position in the administra-

---

[1] With capital at Han-chung, see map p. 66.
[2] The metropolis of the Chou Emperors.

tion. He may be described as a savant in the Confucian sense. The King, now past forty, had remained during his metamorphoses as rural Headman, bandit, Lord of P'ei, and King of Han, the illiterate peasant Liu he was born. He knew nothing of the classics or of any books. But his moral outlook, without his defining it, was Confucian, and when the Great Excellency spoke to him of the grand tradition of conduct which the classics held up, he was deeply impressed. First Tung quoted six lines in rhymed verse to the effect that virtuous conduct paid and wicked conduct led to disaster. If you make clear, therefore, that your enemy is in the wrong, he can be defeated, he said, and added: 'Hsiang Yü has acted in an inhuman fashion; he has murdered his lord, the King of Ch'u who became Emperor. Make this clear, so that all can understand it, by ordering every man in your army to wear mourning for the Emperor. So also will it be clear that your sole purpose is the chastisement of his murderer. Then the nobility of the realm will join you and march eastwards against the wrong-doer. Your virtue will be admired by all within the Four Seas. Thus acted Yao, Shun and Yü, the Sainted Emperors of antiquity.'

To which the King of Han humbly replied: 'Good, good! But for you, my master, I should never have heard such sage advice.' And he immediately took the advice and proclaimed to the nobles and people everywhere that the object of his fight with Hsiang Yü was not to settle a quarrel or wrest from him the chief power, but to punish a disloyal subject and a criminal usurper. In May, at the head of a large army, he advanced eastwards and made a sudden swoop upon P'eng-ch'eng, a city not far from P'ei, which Hsiang Yü had made his capital. Hsiang Yü was absent and he captured the city, took prisoner the Court Beauties (such being the official style at that date of the Court Ladies), seized what valuables were to hand and gave a grand banquet. But the King Lord Protector was not far away. On hearing the news he hastened up with some thirty thousand picked troops, and in a battle outside the city routed the army of Han. There was great slaughter, the river being

I. ATTEMPT ON THE FIRST DIVINE AUGUST ONE

IIA. A HAN CHARIOT

B. A HAN AUDIENCE

blocked with corpses. It looked as if the King of Han would be taken prisoner or killed, but his luck saved him, for a cyclone suddenly broke over the battlefield, uprooting trees and overturning houses. Such a cloud of sand and dust was raised that it grew dark, and in this darkness and wind and confusion he evaded the troops which surrounded him and, putting the four horses of his war-car into a gallop, escaped from the field with some fifty of his guard. He drove by P'ei to rescue his family, but was told that they had already fled. As he drove on at full speed, he overtook his son and daughter and gathered them up into his war-car. The Han chariot, though it had a canopy, was not unlike the Roman chariot; one stood in it and held on to a bar, and it was by no means easy when going at a gallop over rough country roads to keep one's balance. At a certain point a squadron of Hsiang Yü's appeared in pursuit. At sight of them, the King of Han in his excitement jostled the children; they lost their hold and fell out. He had to stop and get them in again. In spite of this delay he threw off his pursuers and managed to escape. But his wife and father, who were fleeing by side roads, were captured.

Hsiang Yü was not strong enough to pursue him very far. He rallied further westwards, was reinforced from beyond the passes, and continued the struggle. During the rest of 204 B.C. the two great protagonists thrust and parried. At the turn of the year the armies were encamped over against each other and a parley was arranged in the valley that separated them. At one side of the stream was the King of Han and he spoke across it to Hsiang Yü on the other. Both armies were exhausted by the unending campaign. 'Let us settle it by a duel,' shouted Hsiang Yü. 'I will not fight a duel with a man like you,' Han shouted back. 'You have cheated me and murdered your lord. You have done what the world cannot endure. Your deeds amount to treason and inhuman conduct. At the head of the nobility I am punishing a brigand. If you want a duel, sir, I will send a convict to fight you.'

In a fury Hsaing Yü loosed an arrow at him from a hidden crossbow. It wounded him in the chest, but he had the presence of mind to grasp his foot and cry out: 'The scoundrel has hit me in the toe!'

Though he was destined to die of an arrow-wound, Han's time was not yet, and he recovered. The marches and counter-marches continued through 203 B.C. but Hsiang Yü was weakening, for he had been unable to maintain his supplies, which depended ultimately upon the people being willing to go on working for him. In October of this year he proposed to Han a settlement. Let them divide the world. As an inducement he sent back Han's wife and the Revered Parent.

While Han was willing to agree to this settlement, at least for the time being, his council was against it. They argued that Hsiang Yü would not have offered to divide the world had he not been in grave danger of losing his half of it. 'The troops of Ch'u are at the end of their tether,' they said, 'and their food is gone. This is the time when Heaven will destroy them. If you do not profit by this opporunity and finally defeat Hsiang Yü, it will be like rearing a tiger that presently eats you.' The King of Han followed their counsel and two months later, January 202 B.C., he invaded Ch'u and surrounded the place where the King Lord Protector was encamped, about a hundred miles south of P'ei.

So far we have been following the historian Pan Ku, but for this scene will found the narrative on Chapter VII of Ssu-ma Ch'ien's *Historical Memoirs*, one of this historian's most famous passages. It is night. Hsiang Yü is lying in his tent, his half-starved and exhausted troops about him. Presently there came to his ears the sound of singing, many voices in a vast chorus singing the songs of Ch'u. 'What is this?' he cried, startled, 'Who is singing our songs?' They told him, the enemy. 'How can that be?' he asked. 'It is as if the whole population of Ch'u were singing. Has Han won them to his side?' And he was in despair, for it seemed to him that his subjects had deserted him. That it was a ruse to make him lose heart, he did not guess. The singing stopped, but he could not sleep. Presently he got up, and calling his sweetheart, Yu, a Beauty who always followed him in his campaigns, asked her for wine. She filled his cup and when he had drunk he composed a lament and sang it to her:

> *Once I was strong enough to pull up mountains;*
> *My energy sufficed to rule the world;*
> *But now the times have turned against me.*
> *What can I do? What can I do?*
> *Tsui, my old charger, will gallop no more.*
> *And Yu, Yu, what will become of her?*

So he sang, the tears coursing down his cheeks, and continued to sing other verses, Yu accompanying him. Those present could not restrain their grief, nor could anyone raise his eyes to look at him. But his despairing melancholy passed and suddenly he declared that he would escape through the enemy's lines while it was still dark. He mounted his charger and, along with eight hundred guardsmen, broke out and galloped south until the sun rose. His escape had been detected and five thousand Han riders were in pursuit. On reaching the mountains he lost his way and, enquiring of a peasant, was directed to go left. But that road took him into a marsh. By the time he had extricated himself the Han riders were close. Soon afterwards he was brought to bay on an eminence. When he saw that he could not escape, he said to his followers, now much reduced in numbers: 'Eight years I have been fighting. I have been in seventy battles and have never been defeated. I took the world and made myself master of it. See the extremity to which I am now reduced. It is not that my military dispositions have been wrong, but that Heaven has turned against me. But I shall die in a manner worthy of you, my friends. I shall burst into the Han lines, I will cut down a General, I will break a standard. And you shall testify that, not lack of valour, but Heaven's despite has brought me to my end.'

Then, telling his companions to split up and make their way to three points which he indicated and to one of which he would come, if he survived, he charged into the ranks of Han shouting a battle-cry. His onrush was so violent and unexpected that he succeeded in reaching a General and killing him. There followed a fierce mêlée, from which he fought his way out and rejoined a party of his men. This was near a river, and he hailed a boatman whom he saw on the bank. The fellow brought his boat and invited him to embark. But now Hsiang Yü seemed to have changed his mind; he turned away from the river.

'Let me take your Honour over,' the boatman urged. 'The country on the other side is small, but not too small to have a King. I am the only man here with a boat. If I take your Honour now, the men of Han cannot cross.'

But Hsiang Yü laughed a bitter laugh. 'Heaven has decided upon my death,' he said, 'What use therefore to cross the river? Besides, I have no heart to cross. It was from the country beyond that I drew eight thousand young men for my campaigns, and now not one of them remains alive. If their fathers and elder brothers should, out of pity, make me their King, how could I look them in the face? Even if they uttered not a word of reproach, nevertheless I should be overwhelmed with shame.'

The boatman had no answer; he was much moved. Addressing him again, Hsiang Yü said: 'I perceive that you are a man of feeling. See this horse of mine. I have ridden him these five years. There is no horse like him in the world. He has done as much as three hundred miles in a day. I have not the heart to kill him. You shall have him.' He dismounted and gave the boatman the rein. His companions also dismounted, and all now stood shoulder to shoulder, their swords in their hands, awaiting their pursuers. These were not long in coming, led by the Commander of the Han cavalry. Hsiang Yü recognised him, and said: 'Long ago you and I were acquainted.' The Commander looked closely at him and exclaimed to his Adjutant: 'It is Hsiang Yü himself, the King Lord Protector!'

'Yes, it is indeed he,' said Hsiang Yü. 'And since I know there is a great price upon my head, no less than an estate of ten thousand tenants and ten thousand pieces of silver, I wish you to have it for old sake's sake.' As he said this, with a sudden movement he cut his throat and fell dying. When he had expired, the Commander decapitated him. There followed an unseemly wrangle for his limbs, for a price had been set upon each one of them also.

After thus describing Hsiang Yü's last stand and death, already become a romantic episode of the heroic past, for a hundred years separated the event and the record, Ssu-ma Ch'ien comments on the character of Hsiang Yü in a more sober strain. 'I have heard it said,' he writes, 'that Hsiang Yü had double pupils to his eyes. How sudden was his elevation! At the outbreak of the rebellion against the Ch'in he had not a foot, not an inch of land of his own. Seizing his opportunity, he rose up from the very furrows of the fields. After three years, five great nobles were serving under his command; in four, he was dividing the Empire among his nominee Kings. In all antiquity no private individual has ever wielded such authority. But he became drunk with success and thought he was a man of such unparalleled brilliance that he had no need to look up to antiquity. Instead of modelling himself on the Sainted Emperors, he sought to impose his will by force. In the fifth year after he had seized power he lost everything. Nor did he understand why, but declared that through no fault of his Heaven had turned against him. Was there ever such blindness!'

The reader will readily appreciate the historian's point: the rebellion had been against a despot, but Hsiang Yü himself had become a despot: its aim had been to re-establish the moral values upon which rested the ancient civilisation of China, but Hsiang Yü, by his murders and ill-faith, had shown himself unfitted to bring in such a reformation.

As soon as his death was known, all the states of the empire submitted to the King of Han except Lu, of which Hsiang Yü had been Duke. Now, Lu was the homeland of Confucius, the locality where the movement he had started was kept alive by his followers, the hub, in fact, of the Confucian world. To find it faithful to a Duke whose character was so lacking in Confucian virtue would be surprising were it not that loyalty to the head of a state was one of the principal virtues of that code. Electing to stand on this virtue, the leaders of Lu sent a defiant message to the King of Han. In the ordinary way, the answer would have been an attack on Lu and the massacre of its inhabitants. But the King, sensible of the motive which inspired the refusal to submit, and moreover impressed by the upright and humane conduct which had characterised the inhabitants of Lu during the rebellion, decided to give them an opportunity for reflection. Before attacking, he ordered the head of Hsiang Yü to be held up outside the walls in sight of the Lu elders. On this they surrendered. Resolved to be no less correct than they, he gave the body of Hsiang Yü a state funeral, which he attended in person and at which, with an extraordinary sense of propriety, he wept. Continuing his gentlemanly behaviour, he ennobled four of Hsiang Yü's relatives with the title of Marquis. One of these, however, was the uncle who had danced in his defence on the occasion when they tried to kill him at the supper party. His next act was to proclaim an amnesty for all except capital crimes, declaring: 'The troops have not had rest for eight years. All the people have suffered severely. But at last I have brought the world under control and to peace.'

The sequel was a foregone conclusion. The nobility presented a petition begging him to ascend the throne of the world, not because he had conquered the world, but because his virtue was transcendent. They said: 'The Ch'in dynasty acted contrary to principle and the world punished it. You, illustrious King, were the first to capture the King of Ch'in. Your achievements have been abundant and your virtue is great. You have preserved the perishing and given repose to those in danger, have rescued the ruined and bestowed tranquillity on the people. Risking death and making repeated obeisances, we offer to our superior the honourable title of Emperor.' (The first part of the last sentence was an official phrase used in memorials and did not imply the abject respect it suggests.)

There follows a correspondence, founded on the precedents of the ancient Empire of which the reader has had a glimpse in *The Book of History*. In reply to the petition, the King of Han stated: 'I have heard that pre-eminence in talent and virtue qualifies a man for the title of Emperor. As a person of little virtue, I am unfitted to receive such a title.'

To which he received this reply: 'We are unable to find words adequate to express Your Majesty's virtue. For you to take the position of Emperor would be most appropriate. We hope that the illustrious King will favour the world, and do so.'

Following precedent, the King refused again; was asked a third time, refused a third time; and then said: 'Since the nobility consider that my acceptance would be advantageous to the people of the world, I accept.'

A propitious day was chosen, 28th February, 202 B.C., and at a place on the bank of the river Szu not far from where the final victory over Hsiang Yü was won, the King of Han ascended the imperial throne, and thereafter became known as Kao-tzu, the Eminent Founder, the first Emperor of the Han dynasty. His wife, the daughter of the old gentleman Lü, who had followed him from the farm, became Empress, and her son the Imperial Heir-Apparent. His mother was not forgotten; he gave her the posthumous title of Lady. Of his father, the T'ai-kung or Revered Parent, more will be told below.

To begin with, the imperial capital was fixed at Lo-yang, the city below the passes about 150 miles east of the Ch'in capital. The capital of the Chou dynasty had been there. Indeed, on a general view, the rebellion had restored the old empire, Grand Feudatories and all, for Kao-tzu parcelled out all the states among nobles. But the time had gone when a feudal society and universal peace were compatible. There was a lesson to be learnt from the Ch'in dynasty. It was not to be followed in its theory of government: the amoral political philosophy of Lord Shang had been discredited; but it was right in holding a strong central government to be essential. Now the conception took shape of an Emperor ruling through a civil service staffed by men educated by a study of antiquity. The

Emperor would be strong enough to govern efficiently because he would have reliable persons to carry out his orders, but both he and his agents would be restrained from injustice and oppression by the maxims contained in the books they studied. These books would be raised to the status of classics, less literary expositions of high merit than infallible guides to rightful behaviour. No other books so well supplied these requirements as the five which Confucius was supposed to have edited and the four which contained his comments and dicta. In sum, it may be said that once Kao-tzu had established a new dynasty on the discredited ruins of the Ch'in, Confucianism, by the very logic of events, was likely to become the state cult. Several elements helped to that end—the reaction from the Ch'in tyranny, the vital necessity of finding a formula which would ensure peace, and the personal character of the new sovereign who, though he was illiterate, was in a curious way a sort of natural gentleman. Probably, however, the final determining factor was the people; they wanted Confucianism because it was identified with benevolent administration. But Confucianism as meaning rule through officials was irreconcilable with a privileged nobility. It became essential eventually to reduce and finally to abolish the nobles, substituting for them the official administrator trained to behave like a gentleman. The nobles did not foresee this when they offered the imperial throne to Kao-tzu. In his short reign of seven years he laid the first stones in this new edifice of society. What follows here are some more biographical details which illustrate his character and show how he became the vehicle by which the ideas which the First Holy One despaired of ever seeing adopted were at last taken up. It had been a long wait (283 years) before a great enough ruler was at hand. But when the desired ruler came he was very great, for Kao-tzu is one of the huge figures of history, certainly the greatest man of action alive at his time, not only in the eastern, but in the western civilised world, where the two leading men (his exact contemporaries) were Hannibal and Scipio Africanus, over both of whom he towers in importance.

The Eminent Founder Comes

In June 202 B.C. the Emperor gave a banquet at Lo-yang in the Southern Palace. It was not very formal, because no palace etiquette had been worked out, and was more like a feast given by a victorious commander to his companions in arms. At a certain point, the Emperor said: 'Marquises and Generals, I want you to tell me the unvarnished truth. How was it that I gained the world? What were the reasons that caused Hsiang Yü to lose? Do not mince words. Speak out plain.'

An old campaigner replied: 'Your Majesty has always been noted for a brusqueness of manner, amounting almost to rudeness, while Hsiang Yü was all suavity and respect. But while Your Majesty gave a man credit for what he did, so that he could be sure of his fair share, Hsiang Yü was jealous of his subordinates and the more able they were the more he was suspicious of them. His best men were not properly rewarded and that is the reason he lost the world.'

Said the Emperor: 'Gentlemen, that is part of the truth but not the whole of it. Not only did I reward my able lieutenants, but I took their advice. Hsiang Yü's fatal mistake was that he did not take advice.'

Everyone agreed that this was so.

Soon after the banquet, the Emperor was given a piece of advice. A certain man said to him in a private interview what amounted to this: 'While the reason put forward by the nobles for the offer of the throne was Your Majesty's virtue, a more realistic view would be that you won it on the field of battle. It will be safer therefore for you to depend on the fact of your strength rather than upon the excellence of your reputation. Lo-yang is outside the passes. I advise Your Majesty to make your capital inside them. There you cannot be attacked, but can advance upon rebels wherever they may be.'

Kao-tzu took this advice at once and established his capital at Ch'ang-an, a city in the old state of Ch'in about five miles southeast of Hsien-yang. Indeed, he thought the advice so good that the man who gave it was created a Baronet and, more astonishing, was allowed to adopt the Emperor's family name of Liu. After this change of capital a certain T'ien K'en presented a memorial of congratulations in which he used the following striking phrase to illustrate the strategical potentialities of the new site: 'When Ch'ang-an sends down from the passes its troops on the nobles, it will be like a person on the top of a high building upsetting water into a tile gutter.' It is not too much to say that the Han sovereigns could not have introduced Confucianism, with its corollary of a learned civil service in place of an hereditary nobility, unless their capital had had these military advantages.

We have seen how Kao-tzu's wife, son and mother received titles, but that the T'ai-kung, his father, remained the T'ai-kung. This was not because the Eminent Founder was lacking in filial piety. In fact, he carried his piety very far. He used, when not on tour, to visit the T'ai-kung every five days and, on entering his presence, would perform the kowtow. The Household Steward of the T'ai-kung found this improper and one day in June 200 B.C. said to his master: 'Heaven has not two sons; the world has not two sovereigns. Although the Emperor is your son, he is the Lord of all mankind; although you are his father, you are also his subject. It is not right that you should be the cause of his so exhibiting himself that he and authority are disassociated.'

The T'ai-kung took this admonition to heart. We cannot say why he had not already begged his fabulous son to desist from kowtowing. Maybe, it did not occur to him; maybe, Kao-tzu still seemed to him the boy he had ordered about in the fields; or it may have been that, old and confused by such a tremendous change in fortune, everything was inexplicable and to be accepted with a simple smile. Now he perceived that he had been guilty of a solecism and resolved that on his son's next visit he would indicate beyond question the admiration and respect which were his true feelings. So, in a day or so, when they announced that the Emperor's carriage was outside his courtyard, he took a broom, went to the gate and then walked backwards sweeping the path. The Emperor was greatly startled at the sight of this unusual behaviour. He got out of his carriage and, hastening to his father, supported him. 'You must not sweep a path for me,' he said. 'It is more proper,' replied the T'ai-kung, 'that I should sweep than that you should undermine the foundations of the world.'

Though the Emperor continued to protest, it is stated that he was secretly glad his father had swept the path for him. When he learnt that he owed this to the Household Steward, he gave him a substantial gratuity.

After this episode the question of his father's style began to preoccupy him. The title of Revered Parent had been appropriate as long as the kowtowing continued. But now that this had been discontinued, some compensating mark of filial piety was required. On 5 July he issued the following edict: 'Lately the world was much disturbed, there was fighting everywhere and the people suffered great calamities. We Ourself wore armour, wielded a weapon with a point and in the van of Our troops braved every difficulty and danger in order to set a term to tyranny. Now We have ended the war and the world enjoys a great peace. That We have accomplished these things is entirely due to the example and admonishments of Our Father, the T'ai-kung. The kings, the marquises, the generals, the grandees and the ministers of state have already honoured Us with the title of Emperor; but the T'ai-kung has not yet had any title. Now We confer upon him the style of Grand Emperor.'

From beginning to end nothing could be more Chinese classical (and more essentially Confucian) than this matter of the T'ai-kung. It clearly denotes the trend of ideas.

The Grand Emperor is mentioned once or twice again. At a banquet in the Front Hall of the new Palace at Ch'ang-an we see Kao-tzu raising his jade wine cup and drinking his health, while he says to the old gentleman: 'When I was a boy you thought me no good because I refused to take up farming like my industrious brother

Chung. Now which of us has gone further, Chung or I?' There was loud laughter among the guests. Merry badinage of this sort would have been quite impossible later at an imperial banquet. This successful peasant revolutionary had little idea how a Court should be conducted. He had given general orders for a palace to be built at Ch'ang-an, but, on returning there after an absence, when he saw the imposing buildings that were going up, the Eastern Portal, the Northern Portal, the Front Hall, the Arsenal, and the Great Granary, he thought it all too grand and expensive. 'The world is full of tumultuous cries,' he said angrily, 'I have toiled and suffered for many years and even yet I cannot be certain I have won outright. Why are you building such halls beyond measure?' They had to explain that a great sovereign must have a splendid abode. 'The Son of Heaven has the Four Seas for his household. Without elegant pavilions how will he show his authority?' He was delighted with this answer, as if he had never pictured himself as a real Emperor, the head of a brilliant Court. Now he began to think that some sort of Court ceremonial must be fixed. Not that he cared for ceremonial. But it was impossible for his boon companions of revolutionary days, become grandees, marquises and ministers of state, to continue to behave as if they were still in camp. When drunk, which was often the case, they would shout in his presence, quarrel, play tricks and even hack the wooden pillars with their swords, to prove their keen edge, or just out of high spirits. So he asked a certain Shu-sun, who had been an official savant both to the Ch'in Second Emperor and to Hsiang-Yü, to draw up a ceremonial. 'Make it as easy as you can,' he told him. Shu-sun summoned thirty Confucian savants from Lu and concocted a Court ritual of gestures, poses, and expressions, which we may suppose resembled that ascribed above to Confucius when at the Court of a Grand Feudatory. After a dress rehearsal out in the country, when the Emperor gave it his approval, it was made obligatory at Court. On the first occasion when it was used, he was deeply impressed. 'Today I have understood for the first time in what consists the greatness of being an Emperor,' he remarked. Simplicity was always the Kao-tzu's chief characteristic.

Nevertheless, the Court remained rough and ready. Kao-tzu might get Confucian savants to draw up a ceremonial, but he was not interested in Confucian books, or any books. On one occasion a certain diplomat quoted to him *The Book of Songs* and *The Book of History*. This irritated him and he cried: 'I got the world on horseback. Why should I bother with your *Songs* and your *History*?' To which the diplomat replied: 'You got it on horseback, but can you rule it from horseback?'

As always when he received advice, Kao-tzu thought over it. He had had a deal of trouble with the vassal kings, and had been obliged to descend from his eyrie of Ch'ang-an time and again to punish them. In their place he had put members of his family, till eventually all the states of the empire were so ruled. To these royal nominees he did not give authority to appoint their senior officials. That power he reserved for himself, and the officials he appointed were also his agents. Their duty was to watch, advise and report, like our Residents in native states. For work of this kind he required first class men, honest, loyal and educated, and now he began to think that he was not drawing on the best class available; gentry, who made a study of the old books, had not been recruited for this service. He must somehow attract these sort of people. In April 196 B.C. we find him issuing an edict for that end. 'In the world,' he says, 'there are plenty of capable and educated men, but as things are I never meet them. There is no way by which a gentleman can come and speak to me. By the dispensation of Heaven I subjugated the world and in that task it is true that I had the aid of some notable gentlemen, who have also shared with me in its pacification. But I know that there are others of equal qualifications whose help would be very useful in furthering a settled administration. Now I call upon these gentlemen to come forward. If they are willing to follow and be friends with me, I can promote them to honour and make them illustrious. Let the vassal kings and other officials of the states see to this and urge gentlemen of reputation to come to the capital. A four-horse carriage should be provided for each. On arrival the Chancellor will interview them and made a note of their bearing and accomplishments.'

This was done; the notables sent up were for the most part Confucian scholars, because Confucianism was the best organised and most widespread of the schools of thought which had survived from the great era of the fourth century B.C. Though they were selected after an interview and not by examination, this action of bringing into the administration Confucian scholars was the first step towards founding a civil service, each member of which had passed an examination in the Confucian classics.

Thus, more by intuition, by an undefined natural inclination, and by bending to events as they arose, rather than by any thought-out policy,[1] Kao-tzu prepared the way for the coming of the Confucian state.

The last glimpse that we get of the Kao-tzu is the most personal and delightful of any. The Grand Emperor, the former T'ai-kung, his quaint old father, had died in June 198 B.C. Before his demise he became homesick for his native town, the far away Feng in the prefecture of P'ei, and Kao-tzu had gone to the length of building a replica of it near the capital and bringing to it some of the inhabitants of the real Feng. Now in the winter of 196 B.C. he himself felt a longing to visit the scenes of his youth and, on his way back from an expedition against a disobedient vassal king, he turned aside to P'ei, of which, thirteen years ago he had been the Lord. Putting up at the local palace, he issued invitations to all his old friends to attend a grand dinner, and caused a choir of a hundred and twenty children to be sent for, who before the dinner were to be taught a song which he had composed.

It was not known exactly what his intentions were about the

[1] Pan Ku states that in December 196 B.C., when Kao-tzu passed through Lu, he sacrificed at the tomb of Confucius, but this is generally interpreted as meaning, not that he thereby gave imperial countenance to Confucianism, but only that he wished to please the inhabitants of Lu by honouring their great man.

song, but, when the dinner was half through and the drinking was at its height, he suddenly struck a five-stringed lute. Whereupon, he sang his song, accompanying himself.

> *Raged a wild wind,*
> *the clouds rose and flew.*
> *At last was imposed*
> *my rule on the world.*
> *When all was achieved*
> *I came back to my village.*
> *How to find valiant men*
> *to stand guard at the four quarters?*[1]

So he sang, and now, ordering the children's choir to sing the song, he rose from his mat and danced. As he danced, he seemed overwhelmed with feeling, and the tears rolled down his cheeks. He said to the elders of P'ei: 'I am crying because the wanderer is always touched to tears by the sight of his old home. Though obliged to make my capital inside the passes, I did not forget P'ei; even after death my spirit will think of it with delight. It was while Lord of P'ei that I took the Ch'in stronghold and ended that tyranny. So now I would have P'ei as the town which provides hot water for washing my hair, my own private town, that shall be exempted for ever from paying taxes to the government.'

The festivities did not end with the one dinner. Rejoicing and drinking went on for days. The population was in the highest spirits. The old people, smiling happily, told stories of the Emperor as they had known him as a child, and amid shouts of laughter recounted his youthful exploits. At the end of ten days he announced that he would have to leave. They begged him to stay, but he said: 'My suite is very large; it is a drain on your resources.' Next morning he left the palace and set out. According to custom, the citizens

[1]This song was engraved in seal characters on a stone 350 years later, and set up at the building called 'The Terrace where the Kao-tzu sang about the Wind'. The inscription is still shown at P'ei, which is now served by a motor road from T'ung-shan junction on the Nanking-Peking railway.

had collected in a great crowd at the west gate to bid him farewell and make him a parting gift of cattle and wine. When he saw them thus, bowing and smiling humbly, and saying what a happiness it would have been could he have stayed longer, he was unable to tear himself away from them, and called a halt, pitching his tents on the open space outside the walls. There the festivities continued for another three days.

On the last evening, the elders of P'ei knelt to him and knocked their heads on the ground: 'Happy is P'ei,' they said, 'that has been given exemption from the taxes. But Feng has had nothing, Feng beside which is the hamlet the Son of Heaven was born in. If only Your Majesty would take pity on it!'

The Emperor was embarrassed. 'Feng is my home town,' he admitted. 'I was born and bred there, and it lies on my heart and can never be forgotten. Nevertheless, I cannot exempt it. At the beginning of the rebellion, when I had become Lord of P'ei and looked to Feng for loyalty, it turned away from me and joined a rival state. I have not forgiven that desertion nor ever will.'

But the elders begged him: 'Please take pity on Feng. Please, oh! please, exempt it!' They repeated this many times till at last he did exempt it. Then he started on his long drive of five hundred miles to the passes and Ch'ang-an.

In six months he was dead. Hsiang Yü had shot an arrow at him ten years before, and inflicted a wound from which he recovered; now, before he reached his palace, he was hit by a stray arrow in a skirmish with the forces of a vassal lord. His temperature rose and he became dangerously ill as he was driven along. On his arrival at Ch'ang-an the Empress immediately sent for the court doctor. But Kao-tzu would not let him treat his wound. 'Can you cure me?' he had asked, and the doctor had said he could, but Kao-tzu exclaimed, as if he believed his hurt to be mortal: 'I, a plain man, armed with a short sword, took possession of the world. That could I never have done had not Heaven decreed it. Now only Heaven can cure me of my wound. Not if Pien Ch'io, the greatest physi-

III. THE STANDARDS OF HSIANG YÜ

(see page 75)

IV. THE EMINENT FOUNDER AT HSIEN-YANG

(see page 75)

cian of all antiquity, were here, could he do anything.' And he dismissed the Court doctor, though kindly for he gave him a large present of gold.

Heaven did not cure him. His wound would not heal. Lingering till summer, he died on the 1st June, 195 B.C. But his work was finished. He had done enough to secure the future for the First Holy One.

Wu Seeks to Commune with Heaven

The fifty-four years which elapsed between the death of the Emperor Kao-tzu and the accession of his great-grandson, the Emperor Wu, in 141 B.C., were a time of peace and plenty. Two of Kao-tzu's sons reigned; his Empress reigned during a minority; and a grandson reigned. The second of the two sons, Wen, who was Emperor for twenty-three years (180–157 B.C.), was a model sovereign in the Confucian sense. He accepted the doctrine that the ruler exists for the benefit of his subjects; he reduced the taxes, abolished the punishment of mutilation and granted old-age pensions; he bore criticism and took advice; his frontier policy was one of appeasement; he selected for the administration men of the best character and tested their culture by a written examination. He could not have been a more complete Confucian Emperor even had the cult been officially established. It was not entirely so, but the Confucian element led at Court, and began to have that predominance which it maintained with few breaks for two thousand years.

The reign of the Emperor Wu, whose length was more than half a century, since it lasted from 141 B.C. to 88 B.C., is a great era in Chinese history. Matters of moment and variety took place. The object of the present chapter, however, and the one which follows, is not to give an account of the reign, but to present only that aspect of it which has relevance to the theme of this book. First will be stated how the Emperor Wu officially established Confucianism as the state cult. Then will be disclosed how the moderation of the true Confucian was alien to his character; he was more visionary than a Confucian should be. He sought the marvellous, an aberration in Confucius's opinion. Mencius had said: 'Heaven does not speak,' but he longed to hear Heaven's voice. Confucius had discouraged speculation about death, but death and its circumvention fascinated him. In fine, his mental outlook was more that of the poet than of the intellectual. Moral and intellectual integrity was the essence of true Confucianism, but that was too dry and narrow for Wu. How he, though convinced that the doctrine of the First Holy One was supreme wisdom, nevertheless could not resist the attraction of the immemorial beliefs and dreams of old Asia, will be related in detail. Some of these ancient practices and speculations had a Taoist character, not the Taoism of the philosophers, but the Taoism of the deep countryside and of the alchemist. Others were derived from the indigenous paganism that lingered on under the surface of society. And others were plain sorcery. In this welter of fairytale and dark superstition Wu became immeshed, though a highly educated man; a poet whose verses have been so much admired that some are still preserved and two have been translated into English; an administrator of talent and a soldier of eminence. That he was all this and yet was deceived by mystery-mongers and charlatans makes very extraordinary reading. The narrative demonstrates that higher Confucianism was a tiny island of sense in a vast sea of unreason, as was ancient Greek philosophy. Both represented civilisation striving to maintain itself in the midst of barbarism. As we follow Wu's extraordinary researches to their tragic sequel, we understand why Confucius firmly refused to discuss marvels: it was a dangerous thing to do in the world of that date.

First to state shortly what Wu did to establish Confucianism as the official philosophy. At his accession in 141 B.C. he was only fifteen. The Confucians, as the strongest party, memorialised that all the official Erudites at Court other than Confucians, particularly the students of the realist politics of Lord Shang,[1] should be dismissed from their posts, a course which even the Emperor Wen had considered too extreme. Their request was granted, the effect of which was that only the Confucian canon was to be officially studied. By this time the text of the books prescribed and burnt by order of the Ch'in Emperor had been reconstituted, partly from hidden copies and partly from memory. In 124 B.C. the Emperor founded an Imperial University. This was conducted by the resident Confucian Erudites and their assistants. The gentlemen of high moral character and some learning from the country towns, who had previously been examined on arrival, were now ordered to study the Five Classics of the Confucian Canon under the Erudites for a year at the University. Then they sat for an examination and the successful candidates were appointed to official posts. From that time on most of the officials in the ministerial departments were Confucian scholars. As they became more senior, they gradually were posted to all the offices of government. In that manner Confucianism was established as the official cult. So was created China's cultural unity, that survived all the many political schisms of succeeding times and the conquests by the steppe barbarians, which amounted in the thirteenth and seventeenth centuries to the domination of the whole country. By making erudition, i.e. the records of China's past, which had been preserved, collected, and edited only by Confucians, the condition of office, Confucianism was so woven into the fabric of the state that a government which was not Confucian was inconceivable, for there was no other erudition. Confucianism was Chinese civilisation. Short of changing the civilisation, Confucianism was indestructible.

[1]It may seem extraordinary that adherents of the Ch'in political philosophy should still have occupied the position of Erudites at court. The explanation must be that some elements of that philosophy were held to be useful.

Wu Seeks to Commune with Heaven

Having brought about this capital event, the Emperor Wu (for such was his character) spent the rest of his life in pursuits of an opposite tendency. Unlike later Emperors who stayed in their capital, he was continually touring over the empire and these tours brought him into close contact with the people and their beliefs. Visiting Shantung and the east coast, he became fascinated by the occultism of that area, and began to make the acquaintance of its professors of magic. Was it possible to know the ultimate secrets? They assured him it was possible. Was it possible to communicate with the dead? Yes. Was it possible to constrain Heaven to speak? Certainly. And the Elixir, could that be found, together with the secrets that went with it, the secrets of invulnerability, invincibility, immortality? All these things were possible, they assured him.

The Emperor returned to his capital after making it clear that any eminent magicians who followed him could be sure of office. There began an influx of such persons into Ch'ang-an. Occult practices, the worship of curious deities, became the vogue in the royal circle. One day in the twenties of the second century B.C. the vassal king of Shantung came to pay his respects. It was whispered that in his train was a man who knew many secrets. The Emperor, apprised of this by his intimates, expressed a desire to see the man.

This was the start of Li Shao-chun's career. When he was brought before the Emperor, there was seen an old man, very richly dressed, his expression adroit, his manner assured.

'What is your age?' the Emperor enquired.

'I always say that I am seventy,' replied Li Shao-chun. This mysterious reply had the effect intended; the Emperor earnestly demanded to know more. Gradually and as if against his will Li Shao-chun spoke of himself. 'I say that I am seventy,' he explained, 'because I look seventy. And I look seventy because it was at that age that I discovered the secret how to avoid becoming older.'

How long ago were you seventy?' asked the Emperor.

'Ah!' said he, 'a long time.'

'Will you not tell me your real age?'

'If Your Majesty will excuse me, I would rather not say.'

'Why not?' demanded the Emperor.

'Because I want to prove myself to Your Majesty rather than make claims difficult to believe. For my age is very great. It is also a long time since I have ceased to eat and drink.'

Thus, by parenthesis, he built himself up. 'Being so old,' he continued, 'I have no ambition, no wants, nor have I wife, children or dependants, who might demand provision. My happiness is only to travel about the country and impart my knowledge to such gentlemen as will listen to me.'

'Have you already imparted it?' enquired the Emperor uneasily.

'I have come first to Your Majesty,' the magician assured him. The Emperor, who on his tours had had experience of fraudulent magicians and, for all his longing for the great secrets, knew that he should proceed with caution, now decided to impose a test. He pointed to a bronze vessel in the room. 'What is that?' he asked.

Li Shao-chun, as we have said, was very adroit. His speciality was to be prepared at any time to make an observation which was both astonishing and exact. He glanced at the object, which was at some distance from him and replied in an easy tone: 'That bronze, Your Majesty, belongs to the Chou dynasty. It was placed by the Duke of Ts'ai in the Cypress Chamber above his terrace.' And he named a date corresponding to our year 676 B.C.

This answer convinced the Emperor that Li Shao-chun was a genuine magician, for there was an inscription on the bronze precisely to the effect which he had stated. The courtiers present were also profoundly impressed. It was not thought that Li Shao-chun had read the inscription by magic or by a magical intuition had become aware of the facts it recorded, but that he was alive in the Duke's time five and a half centuries before and had seen him deposit the bronze in the Cypress Chamber. The Emperor now asked Li Shao-chun to tell him how to obtain the elixir of life. The magician's statement was as follows: 'The first step is to make a sacrifice with the proper ritual to the alchemist's furnace which Your

Majesty proposes to use for your experiment. The effect of that will be to summon the spirits. As soon as they have arrived, heat cinnabar, and it will transmute into yellow gold. Use this gold for making cups and plates. By eating and drinking from them your life will be prolonged. When Your Majesty has reached the stage of established longevity, you will be able, if you station yourself on the beach of Shantung, to see the Fortunate Isles, which the Ch'in Emperor sought to find and could not, and which are inhabited by men who have the secret of eternal life. After having sight of those isles you will never die.'

The Emperor had begun to carry out this course and was busy with his experiments, when it was reported to him that Li Shao-chun had died after a short illness. But this did not convince him that the magician was an impostor. He declared that most probably he was not dead, but had changed his appearance and so departed. Orders were given to search for the Fortunate Isles and a secretary was deputed to continue the alchemical researches.

No success whatever was had; the Isles were not found nor did the furnace achieve a transmutation. The Emperor, however, did not abandon his efforts and, in addition, began to entertain the idea that if he performed sacrificial rites on the top of a sacred mountain he might induce Heaven to speak. There was the danger that Heaven might speak harshly if trespassed upon too close, though even an angry voice would be better than the empty silence with which was greeted the orthodox state liturgy. At the moment he was unable to make progress with this project.

In the year 121 B.C. an alchemist by the name of Chao Wang came to Court. He was also from Shantung and declared himself able to communicate with the dead. The Emperor at the time was distracted by grief. One of his concubines, the Lady Li, had died and left him unconsolable. It may seem strange that a man, who had residing with him many beautiful women, should feel romantic love, the passion of the heart, and should be rendered miserable by a loved one's loss. But this, it seems, is within the compass of human emotions, as any one acquainted with oriental court history is aware: potentates of Asia, in spite of their provision, suffer like the rest of mankind. On the Lady Li's death the Emperor had composed a poem, which happens to be one of the two poems of his which Mr. Waley has chosen to translate. It is very affecting. 'The sound of her silk skirt has stopped,' it begins, and goes on to lament her empty room, now dusty and chill, with drifted leaves heaped up by the door. And it ends: 'How can I bring my aching heart to rest?' Shao Wang, the new necromancer, was introduced as a person competent to bring solace to the Emperor's heart; he would raise the ghost of the Lady Li.

The séance took place after dark in one of the halls of the palace. The Emperor was placed behind a curtain through which he could see without being seen. At a distance Shao Wang began his conjurations. Presently the Emperor heard the swish of a silk skirt, and far down in the gloom he saw approaching, indistinctly, slowly, the shape of the adored Lady Li, conducted by another figure, explained to be the guardian spirit of Shao Wang's furnace. The Emperor stood staring through a chink in the curtain. Was it, indeed, his beloved? It was; there could be no doubt; she had come to him from the grave. Weeping, he waited as she drew closer, when suddenly both apparitions vanished. But this glimpse of his Lady relieved his pain. Profoundly grateful to Chao Wang, he gave him the title of Marshal of Perfect Sapience, which carried with it liberal emoluments.

This was a lucky start for the necromancer. He was now consulted on the other matter; the Emperor asked him about voices from Heaven. The Marshal of Perfect Sapience replied that a reliable way to tempt down transcendent beings was to build a pavilion decorated so as to appear like a celestial abode. With this and other contrivances he interested the Emperor and retained his favour for a time. But he failed to get manifestations and it became necessary to try a startling turn. Writing a message from Heaven on a piece of silk he induced a bull to swallow it whole, at a time when he knew the Emperor would shortly be passing. When, as expected, the Emperor arrived, Chao Wang pointed to the bull and, in the voice of a man possessed by a spirit, declared loudly that a very marvellous thing would be found in its stomach. The Emperor directed that the animal be killed and opened. The silk was found and spread out before His Majesty. The message from Heaven was of a sensational kind. But for some reason the Emperor became suspicious. He looked critically at the handwriting; it seemed uncommonly like Chao Wang's. Enquiries were made; his servants were examined, and the truth came out. The Marshal of Perfect Sapience was put secretly to death, for His Majesty did not want to publish the fact that he had been cheated.

When the news that Chao Wang had fallen from favour reached the grandees of Shantung, a lady of rank there, who had private reasons for desiring the Emperor's countenance in an intrigue in which she was then engaged, sent to the capital a eunuch called Luan Ta, a professional magician of remarkable personality in the employ of the vassal King of Shantung. A certain Marquis was persuaded to introduce him as a person whose knowledge of the occult arts was exceptional. The Emperor had begun to regret Chao Wang's execution; that he had cheated over the bull did not necessarily impugn his genuineness on other occasions; it would have been better to have tested him further; perhaps valuable secrets had died with him. So when the Marquis assured him that Luan Ta knew more than had the Marshal of Perfect Sapience, he was delighted and granted an audience.

Luan Ta was a tall man of imposing presence, a most fluent speaker, and very wily and daring. Having got into the Emperor's presence, he did not hesitate; it was the moment to make splendid promises, and he knew that the best way to create an impression and compel belief in his powers was to pitch his demands very high. ' I have travelled far,' he said in a voice of authority, 'I have sailed the seas and seen the Fortunate Isles, but was unable to obtain audience of the Immortals there.'

'What was the reason of your failure in that?' enquired the Emperor.

'The Immortals looked down on me because I was employed by a mere petty Prince,' replied Luan Ta. 'They did not think him worthy to hear their secrets.'

The Emperor was pleased. The last thing he wanted was for one of the vassal Kings to get the secret first. 'But were you not able to find out something on your own account?' he asked.

'I got assurances,' replied Luan Ta, in a guarded way calculated to make the Emperor more curious. 'Gold can be made, the drug that is the elixir can be compounded, the Fortunate Beings can be invoked.'

'But besides such assurances did you learn something definite of the great secrets?' the Emperor pressed him.

'Your Majesty will excuse me,' replied Luan Ta, 'if, while speaking otherwise with the utmost frankness, I remain circumspect about the degree of my art. The fate which overtook the late Marshal of Perfect Sapience has unnerved us magicians. We think it prudent to cover our mouths.'

'You are quite wrong about Chao Wang,' said the Emperor hurriedly. 'He died, in fact, of eating too much horse-liver.'

'Is that so?' replied Luan Ta discreetly. 'We must have been misinformed down our way.'

'You have not the smallest cause for apprehension,' went on the Emperor. 'If you can do what, had he not died, he planned to do, you will not find me stingy.'

'Since Your Majesty wishes, I will be quite open. But there are facts to be faced. The Immortals do not come to us seeking favours; it is we who must go to them. So, if Your Majesty is thinking of deputing me to revisit the Isles, I shall have to make a favourable impression. It would be useless to go in my present capacity. I suggest, therefore, that Your Majesty gives me a title and seal, thus enabling me to speak with the necessary assurance.'

'That can certainly be arranged,' said the Emperor.

'Your Majesty will know that I would not have asked were it not imperative that an Imperial Envoy should appear as convincing as possible. Even so, the Immortals may not agree to receive me. Rank alone would hardly win them, beings who never die, are incomparably rich, have ineffable powers, all conceivable happinesses. It were safer—and in a matter of such importance every precaution should be taken—to put at my disposal considerable sums, so that my retinue may be truly magnificent, my presents rare and sufficiently numerous. But if I could say I was related to Your Majesty, that would win them best of all.'

The Emperor was much excited by this address. At last, it seemed, his dream was coming true. But he held himself in check and according to his custom on a first interview called on Luan Ta to give a demonstration of his art. 'Let me see,' he said, 'a sample of your black magic.' Luan Ta was prepared for this command. One of his followers produced a chessboard and pieces. When the pieces were in position, they moved of their own accord and a battle royal was enacted, king fighting with king, queen with queen, elephant with elephant, horseman with horseman. It was all done with such dexterity that the Emperor saw no trick but only magic of the darkest potency. He was so pleased that he immediately conferred on Luan Ta the title of Marshal of the Five Vantages.

During the ensuing month Luan Ta exploited his first success and convinced the Court doubt that he would be able to perform what he had promised. So clever was he, that he induced the Emperor to confer on him three more titles with their seals, to wit, Master Magician of Heaven, Master Magician of Earth and Marshal of the Grand Communion with Heaven. These titles indicate that Luan Ta had not only persuaded the Emperor that he could get the elixir, but also had given him information or advice about the other subject, so much in his thoughts—how to invoke a voice from Heaven. At this time the Emperor addressed an Edict to the Council giving reasons why he had faith in Luan Ta: 'For twenty-eight years We have been governing the world, but latterly it has been found impossible to confine the Yellow River within its banks. Now it seems that Heaven has sent me a magician and accorded me the Grand Communion.' And he drew the Council's attention to a magical diagram, in which was a wild goose and a flying dragon. This diagram had astrological bearing at the moment, and since it could be accepted that astrologically or by the science of numbers a wild goose symbolised Luan Ta and a flying dragon communication with Heaven, he had, he said, sound reasons for what he was doing. Following this Edict we find an entry in the Court Gazette dated 22 May of the year 113 B.C. enfeoffing Luan Ta as the Marquis of Happy Communion, with the rank of General (First Class) and granting him an estate of a thousand households. From that day the said Marquis, when he went out, did not go by carriage or on horseback, but was transported in a sedan chair. A splendidly furnished palace was assigned to him with a thousand servants to do his bidding. And this was not all. So infatuated had the Emperor become that he decided to grant his outrageous request and give him a daughter in marriage, though Luan Ta, as we know, was a eunuch. Nor was some girl by a minor concubine selected, but a daughter by the Empress Wei, the Empress who had once been a famous singer, when she so captivated the Emperor that he inducted her in April 128 B.C., after the disgrace of the Empress Ch'en.[1] Her supporters were very influential and formed a clique which dominated the Court. That no opposition was raised by them to this extraordinary marriage is additional indication of the magnetic power of Luan Ta's personality. Asiatic Courts, though difficult to enter and most unsafe, have always offered unique opportunities to talented adventurers, but outside the *Arabian Nights* there can hardly be a case to equal that of the Marquis of Happy Communion. The road leading to his palace was never without imperial emissaries with despatches or presents, and the Son of Heaven himself came to call on him. The grandees could not make too much of him. The Emperor's aunt, one of the

[1] See page 126, 135, 136.

great Dowagers of the Court, invited him to a banquet, as did several Generals and Members of Council, when he was always the guest of honour and the recipient of costly presents. The Emperor added a further title, causing the style, Marshal of the Heavenly Way, to be inscribed on a jade seal and sent to him, thereby signifying his certain belief that Luan Ta would enable him to hear Heaven's voice. In this case a particular ceremony was employed, the imperial emissary, wearing a feather coat, being instructed to stand all night before Luan Ta's mansion on a mat woven of white grasses. To indicate that he was not a subject but a member of the royal family, the Marquis himself put on a feather coat and stood on a white mat to receive the seal. The reason why this action should have had that interpretation is unfortunately obscure, though to his contemporaries it was as plain as day. His sudden rise to the pinnacle of fame caused, it is said, the whole empire to tremble, as well it might, for here was a man of low birth, a eunuch, an adventurer, who had the right to use by now no less than six seals and whose power of doing harm was quite incalculable. But it made every wizard along the coast shake hands with himself, as the phrase then went, and boast that he too possessed receipts that could turn him into a sky Genius or a happy Immortal. Each night during these summer months of 113 B.C. Luan Ta conducted complicated rituals, with music, conjurations, sacrifices, and drums, calling upon Heaven to declare itself. But there was no response, though the great historian, the Duke Grand Astrologer, Ssu-ma Ch'ien, from the twelfth chapter of whose *Historical Memoirs* all these particulars are taken, declares that Luan Ta succeeded in raising a number of spirits, no less than a hundred apparitions being observed in his hall. That he was a genuine occultist need not be in doubt, but the Emperor had not made him Marshal of the Heavenly Way to raise spirits, but to carry out his promise to find the elixir and induce Heaven to speak, very much more difficult feats. Under the continual pressure of the Emperor's impatience to get into touch with the island Immortals, Luan Ta could not stay and enjoy his position at Court, but was obliged in July to set out for Shantung, a journey of over a thousand miles, off whose coast the Fortunate Isles were supposed to lie. His departure was made in great state, his retinue numbering thousands, his baggage stretching miles, a necessity, as he had explained, since he had to make a decisive impression on the Immortals. The occasion was attended by a happy augury. An ancient ritual bronze tripod was dug up by a female sorcerer at a place away down in the country. It was reported to belong either to the Chou (1122–253 B.C.) or Shang (1766–1122 B.C.) dynasty. Nowadays we do not attribute happy augury to Chou or Shang bronzes. Those who buy them—they are procurable in the West End—do so for aesthetic reasons, since with their patina, their curious shape, the stylised monsters that glare from their sides, the succinct inscriptions which adorn them, they are what the erudite collector most fancies. But the Chinese of the second century B.C. regarded them, not with a cultivated interest, but with an excited reverence, the sort of feeling we should have for Arthur's Excalibur, should it be unearthed. Just as the discovery of that sword would arouse excitement because it belonged to our first King, so the discovery in the first century B.C. of a bronze of the Chou or Shang dynasties stirred the whole country because it was a link with the old classical empire, with its sainted rulers the near descendants of Yao, Shun and Yü, and its golden age when the voice of Heaven was often heard. Such a bronze had perhaps been used at an imperial sacrifice when Heaven really communed with its Son. Therefore, its discovery augured that Heaven was about to be propitious, would give a good harvest, and restrain the Yellow River. It was also taken as a direct encouragement of the Emperor: Heaven sent him an ancient sacrificial bronze, an invitation to ask for grace and a promise to give it.

On getting the news of the sorceress's find, the Emperor set out at once for the place. The tripod was delivered to him, an attractive piece with an unctuous gloss and a patina glittering like a dragon. It had chiselled designs, but no inscription. With it packed in a cypress box he journeyed back, looking for omens as he drove. Passing a sacred hill, the weather being fine and still, he looked up and saw a cloud like a yellow dais, and at the same moment a deer went by, all well-known signs. He snatched his bow and with four arrows brought down the deer and sacrificed it on the hill. As soon as he got back to Ch'ang-an, he summoned the Inner Council to view the bronze. A discussion took place, long and learned, about where to put it, about previous discoveries, and what old Yü had once advised. In the course of it, one of the grandees drew attention to a coincidence noted in the records, that whenever a sage appeared, a bronze was sure to be unearthed. This was a reference to Luan Ta, and it did not displease the Emperor.

But in spite of this connection so flattering to the Marquis of many titles, the imperial messengers who rode to and from the coast had nothing definite to report about his progress. After reaching his destination he had sat staring out over the ocean, but had failed to detect the Fortunate Isles, they said. Even from the top of T'ai Shan, that most sacred peak, he could not perceive their outline, though he kept on assuring everybody that they certainly lay in the sea to the Eastward of it. What he expected to guide him was an emanation, a light rising from the sea and marking the exact place. But of that, too, there was no sign. On receiving this intelligence the Emperor sent a man skilled at discovering emanations; and a faint suspicion beginning to worry him, he also sent detectives to watch the Marshal of the Heavenly Way. This took time on account of the great distances involved, but by the following autumn (112 B.C.) all the facts were before him. His agents had written that nothing whatever had happened, no emanations, no signs of any kind. On the other hand he received a joyful letter from the Marshal saying that he had succeeded in getting into touch with the Immortals and soon would be able to report results. Could he have backed his letter with his mesmeric presence, perhaps the Emperor would have believed him. But he was a thousand miles away; the Emperor for some time had been growing more doubtful and now he had a revulsion of feeling. Orders went out to exterminate Luan Ta and his whole gang, including the Marquis who had originally introduced him.

This happened in November 112 B.C. The Emperor was to continue to reign until 29 March 88 B.C. It would be reasonable to suppose that after his experience with the three mountebanks, Li Shao-chun, Chao Wang and Luan Ta, he would have had enough of the Taoists of Shantung and have abandoned his search for the elixir. But this was not so. He still believed, and ascribed his ill success entirely to the fraudulent character of those particular guides. During the twenty-four years of life which remained to him he went on with his efforts to locate the Fortunate Isles, at the same time pursuing his other aim, which was complementary to the first, of inducing Heaven to speak to him on a sacred mountain-top and thereby give proof of its favour, a hope which has been entertained by other rulers, such as Moses when alone he climbed Mount Sinai. But it would be a mistake to think that these visionary preoccupations caused him to neglect his ordinary duties. He was an extremely busy man, whose policy at home was towards centralisation and abroad to extend the frontiers of the Empire. If one looks at the annalistic part of Pan Ku's *History of the Former Han* for this same year, 112 B.C., the military activity then prevailing is evident. In May, Envoys, whom the Emperor had sent to Nan-yüeh (our Canton, at that epoch the capital of an independent kingdom), were murdered. As a punishment, he resolved to extinguish that state. One finds in the same *Annals* the plan of campaign, a converging movement by a number of Generals commanding armies of criminals. The styles of these Generals enliven the picture. We have the General Who Calms the Waves approaching by one river, the General of Towered Warships by another, the General of Vessels with Dagger-axes on a third, and the General Who Can Descend Torrents on a fourth. There was also the Marquis Who Gallops to His Proper Fealty, marching by land with a force in which the criminals were stiffened by regulars. To this onslaught the

H. 66 cm

V. A TRIBAL WAR DRUM MADE DURING THE HAN DYNASTY

VI. A PORTRAIT OF THE EMPEROR WEN
OF THE HAN DYNASTY

(*see page 98*)

Nan-yüeh capital fell. In November of the following year, 111 B.C., the Emperor issued an Edict, in which he refers to this campaign, as well as to the northern frontier, and makes clear his own position as supreme commander-in-chief: 'The state of Nan-yüeh has suffered for its crimes, but We have not yet been able completely to unite the western savages and the northern barbarians under the universal sway of Our peace. We propose to travel and inspect the border. We shall hold parades and check credentials. We Ourself shall lead the army.' Immediately after promulgating this Edict, he went North against the Huns, passed through the Great Wall and mounted the steppe, the Shan-yü's Terrace, for the High King of the Huns was called the Shan-yü. Leading 180,000 cavalry, his flags and pennons streaming across the plain, he marched on another two hundred miles. When near the boundary of the Shan Yü's inner domain, he sent ahead an Envoy Clad in Embroidered Garments with the following provocative message: 'The head of the King of Nan-yüeh has already been hung upon the Northern Portal of the Han Palace. If the Shan-yü is able to fight a battle, the Son of Heaven, at the head of his troops, is waiting in person at the boundary. If he is unable to fight, let him come and submit to Us. Why should he uselessly flee and hide beyond the Gobi in the bitterly cold wastes of the North?' Pan Ku, after transcribing this message, adds: 'The Huns were breathless with fear.' But according to Ssu-ma Ch'ien, the Shan-yü was infuriated and immediately beheaded his Intendant in Charge of Guests for having introduced such a rude Envoy. Nor would he give the Envoy leave to return, and, contrary to the usages governing the treatment of ambassadors, sent him as a prisoner to the northern shore of Lake Baikal, in the present Siberia. Nevertheless, he feared to raid for some years and when he did raid he was always driven back. This note allows a glimpse of the Emperor Wu as a great military figure, but only a glimpse, for his campaigns were numerous.

In addition to them, he found time to establish a sound currency system and to control prices, to send out expeditions to explore towards Bactria, to settle Chinese emigrants in regions beyond the former boundaries, to improve the dykes of the Yellow River and to tighten the administration. These solid achievements, added to those already mentioned, concerned with the University and the training of government officials, show that his days were largely occupied with the tasks which are the usual routine of all rulers. Bearing this in mind, we may continue without danger of forming too narrow a conception of him to trace his adventures among the sacred mountains and the enchanted seas.

At this very time (112–111 B.C.) when he was so occupied with military affairs, he fell under the influence of a fourth Taoist prestidigitator, Kung-sun Ch'ing by name. This man came into notice because he spread the report of having observed the footprints of Immortals on the top of the walls of Kou-shih, a town on the way to Shantung. While he was viewing them, there flew over his head a being in the form of a pheasant, he said. When the Emperor heard of this, he was so excited that he travelled all the way to Kou-shih, upwards of two hundred miles, to inspect the traces and get sight, if he could, of the celestial pheasant. He saw nothing, however, neither footprints nor pheasant, and angrily said to Kung-sun Ch'ing, whom he had summoned to his presence: 'Are you not trying to imitate the Marquis of Perfect Sapience and his successor, the Marquis of the Five Vantages?'

'Far from it,' Kung-sun Ch'ing assured him. And he spoke earnestly about the nature of Immortals, and how one should not pester or bustle them. 'Your Majesty is always in such a hurry,' he went on. 'Results cannot be expected all in a minute. Give the Immortals time, let them take their own way. Do not prescribe for them this course or the other. Your Majesty will never get the secret like that. And do not offend them by suspicions. If they have chosen to obliterate the traces of their footsteps, if they refuse sight of themselves flying as pheasants, they have reasons for so doing, and we must have patience. Patience, Your Majesty, is the sovereign receipt. Only by consecrating years to the great quest can you hope to have speech with such as they.'

So persuasive, so reasonable, was Kung-sun Ch'ing that the Emperor was impressed and against his judgment believed it possible that this new magician had really seen footprints and could show him the way to the communion he so desired. But he had grown more cautious. He did not at once confer on Kung-sun Ch'ing a title. Nevertheless, he kept him by his side, and frequently consulted him. For instance, in the last month of the year 111 B.C., when he was returning from his expedition against the Shan-yü of the Huns, he halted at Mount Ch'iao, which was about three hundred miles due north of the capital, to pay his respects at the tomb of the Yellow Emperor. After conducting the sacrifice, he said: 'I always understood that the Yellow Emperor discovered the Elixir, and that he never died, but was transported to the Great Other in a dragon-carriage. How comes it then that his tomb is here?'

His new guide in these matters had his answer pat: 'Before the Yellow Lord left for Heaven,' he said, with the right tone of authority, 'he bequeathed to his faithful subjects his clothes and his hat. These with proper reverence they interred at this spot.'

The Emperor was satisfied. On his return to the capital he began to prepare for what he long had been resolving, the attempt to draw from Heaven a sign or voice by sacrificing on the top of T'ai Shan, the five thousand foot peak in Shantung. T'ai Shan was the most holy of the five sacred mountains. The Yellow Lord had sacrificed there, and there learnt, maybe, the secret of the elixir. But what ceremonial did he use? The Emperor was convinced that it was a ritual called the Fêng. That the Fêng was an ancient ritual no one doubted, but so many centuries had elapsed since it was last used that all record of how to conduct it had been lost. No mention of it was to be found in the classical books. The more the Emperor pondered on the Fêng, the more certain he became that if he were to succeed he must employ it on T'ai Shan. But by what means to discover the rules of that old sacrifice? In such a matter he was obliged to consult the Confucian Erudites. But they were at a loss, for they had no documents upon which to found an opinion. The safest course, they said eventually, was to observe the same ceremonial as was used every winter solstice when the Imperial sacrifice was made at the great altar of Heaven. But the Emperor was convinced that the real Fêng rites were indispensable; if he did not employ them on T'ai Shan his oblation would be of another sort, and, so, of no use. The Erudites were deliberately discouraging, the project being too unorthodox for their taste. A Venerable called Ting, who at the time was over ninety, begged him to be careful, reminding him that the abominable First Emperor of the Ch'in had planned to do this very thing, but halfway up T'ai Shan had been caught in a storm, so clear a sign of Heaven's displeasure that he had turned back at once. Better to sacrifice at the bottom, urged the Venerable, or to venture only a short way up, though, of course, if the weather were specially fine it might be safe to proceed further. The Emperor was put out by all this and especially irritated because the scholars declared the sacrificial utensils he had already had made to be of a design not sanctioned by antiquity. Indeed, so out of temper was he that he deprived two of them of their university appointments and sent the rest home in disgrace.

Obliged to postpone the T'ai Shan sacrifice, he went back in February 110 B.C. to Kou-shih where Kung-sun Ch'ing had seen the footprints. Nearby was the sacred mountain of Sung-kao. This he climbed and had an experience which much encouraged him. When his staff officers were half way up they heard as it were a voice that wished the Emperor ten thousand years of life. Enquiry was made. Those of his suite higher up swore that none of them had called out, as did those further down. The Emperor was not quite certain what voice had spoken, but that it was some celestial voice he was sure. After descending he gave orders that three hundred families living round the foot should be exempted from taxation if they undertook to maintain regular sacrifices on the mountain.

So heartened was he by the voice on Sung-kao, that he believed it to be Heaven's sign approving his intention to sacrifice on T'ai Shan. To regain favour the Erudites had submitted suggestions about the staging of the sacrifice, such as the measurements of the altar, and the position of its site; and the magicians, led by Kung-sun Ch'ing, had for their part advised the use of the novel ceremonials introduced earlier in his reign for special sacrifices which he had inaugurated. Working on the problem himself, he now made up a ritual which he believed corresponded with the authentic Fêng. But he remained nervous, for it would be a disastrous end to his ambitions were he to meet with the sign of displeasure which had turned back the Ch'in First Emperor.

In March 110 B.C. he set out for T'ai Shan, a journey of about eight hundred miles. He had an immense train of secretaries, officials of the Household, troops and servants. Among the numerous animals which he brought with him to sacrifice were elephants and rhinoceroses, which had been procured from the south-west after the Nan-yüeh (Canton) campaign.

Two thousand years ago T'ai Shan was a wilder and more lonely place than now. Today it is a pilgrim and tourist centre, covered with buildings associated with Taoism. A road of 6,700 steps leads to the summit (5069 feet) and as one climbs by it a panorama of Taoist legend is unfolded to the eye. A recital of the names of the chief objects of interest must suffice here to suggest its atmosphere of fairy-tale. At the bottom of the mountain is the walled city of Tai-an with the railway station outside to the West. On leaving the station, which is near the Temple of the Heavenly Book and the Arch of the Fairy Lu, the visitor has to make his way to the North Gate of Tai-an, since it is from there that the stairway begins. On an easy gradient, he mounts between the Temple of the Three Sovereigns and the Jade Emperor's Tower, and starting to climb in earnest reaches the First Heavenly Gate. Halting there to get his breath, he sees below him the Temple of the Military Sage and on foothills to his right and left the Eastern and the Western Halls of Bright Vision. Resuming his climb and entering a rocky gorge, he passes under the Red Gate and under the Tower of Ten Thousand Fairies, and skirting the Temple of the Mother of the Great Bear, turns left at the Temple of the Three Functionaries. He is now faced with the Peach Orchard Glen, a very steep and exhausting climb, at the top of which is an archway called Where Horses Turn Back. A little further on is the Half Way House, adjacent to the Second Heavenly Gate. Taking a view from there, he sees to the East the Mountain Which Touches Heaven and the Cliff of Quails, and above it the Cliff of the Love of Life. Westwards, though these enchanted spots he cannot see, are the Temple of the Bamboo Forest, the Thousand Foot Falls, the Black Dragon Pool, and the Fairy Shadow. Refreshments are to be had at the Half Way House, and the visitor (become a pilgrim converted to belief by the power of beauty) renews his climb, fortified and eager. The road curls left round a shoulder and is level for a short distance. But twisting up again it crosses the Snowflake Bridge over the Flying Cascade, a mountain torrent in a deep gully. There follows a steady climb. On the left is passed the Nine Maidens' Rock, on the right the Pine Tree of Fifth Degree and the Tablet of a Hundred Thousand Feet, with the Lotus Flower Peak above, at whose base is the Temple of Fairy Dreams. The pilgrim is now approaching the Dragon's Throat, the most precipitous section of the whole. This gorge begins steeply with the Slow Eighteen Flights, but their steepness is exceeded by the Sudden Eighteen Flights. There are here altogether a thousand steps, an ascent to be compared with that of a skyscraper when the lift is out of order. Besides good legs, a good head is wanted or else it is prudent not to look down. At last the South Heavenly Gate is reached, which commands a magnificent view of Shantung in the North, South and West quarters. The summit lies to the Eastward. Pilgrims' Way has now become Heavenly Way. As far as the Palace of the Princess it is fairly level. That passed, the final climb begins to the Temple of the Jade Emperor on the top, whence the sea, a hundred and fifty miles away to the East, is faintly visible on a clear day.

Wu Seeks to Commune with Heaven

Behind each of these fairytale names is a story, and these stories strung together would amount to a history of popular Taoism from the Emperor Wu's time to the present. When he was there, the mountain was thickly wooded and, though there were probably some hermitages upon it, neither the stairway nor any of the buildings existed nor had legend yet given its fancy titles to the cliffs, the cascades, the glens or the gorges. Rearing from the plain in its pristine majesty, T'ai Shan was as dread a mount as Olympus. Here, to its foot, with his elephants and rhinos, he came on 5 May 110 B.C.

Mindful of the advice of the Venerable Ting that it would be safer to feel his way, he decided first to make the Fêng sacrifice at the foot of the mountain, and then watch to see if the signs were favourable. Accordingly, he had a mound erected on the eastern side, twelve feet broad and nine feet high, with a flight of steps to its flat top. Earth of four colours, symbolising the Four Quarters, was mingled with the earth of the mound. And a mat for the Emperor to sit on was made of grasses of a particular kind. These details were taken from the procedure followed by the sainted Emperors, Yao, Shun and Yü, who were believed also to have performed the Fêng at T'ai Shan. When the sacrificial vessels of bronze, containing dark wine and raw fish, were in position on the mound, the Emperor mounted the steps, robed in yellow, and took up a position on the mat. The orchestra played and he made the sacrifice, employing the ritual which he had adapted for the purpose. He did not sacrifice the rhinos and elephants, but sent them back, though he used certain white pheasants, birds of good augury. Part of the ceremony was the sealing of a letter addressed to Heaven, for the word Fêng meant seal. This letter, the contents of which were secret, was written on gold and enclosed in an envelope, the underneath of which was stone, and the top jade.

During the ceremony, which seems to have taken place at night, a watch was kept for auspicious signs. A glow was seen in the sky, and in the morning a white cloud hung directly above the mound.

These signs assured the Emperor that Heaven was not adverse. He resolved to venture to the top of the mountain and at the summit conduct the Fêng a second time. But he would go alone or accompanied by only one person.

The utensils required for the ceremony were taken up by a party which returned to the base. Then the Emperor, selecting as attendant his coachman, who had the rank of Marquis, made the ascent, though whether by the route afterwards to become the Pilgrims' Way or by some other is not clear. What transpired on the summit was never made known, though the Emperor issued an Edict which will be given further down. The coachman was the only spectator of the event and this cost him his life, for he died soon afterwards in circumstances that suggested that the Emperor had had him poisoned.

After descending the mountain, the Emperor took his seat in a ritual pavilion and there received the congratulations of his suite. The Edict which he indited was to this effect: 'Though an insignificant person We have received the most exalted post. We have striven to be circumspect and have pondered on the smallness of Our virtue, in that We are little conversant with the rules of propriety and Our knowledge of music is disgracefully inadequate.' After this Confucian prologue he mentioned the voice that he had heard previously on Mount Sung-kao, and now the auspicious signs of the glow and the cloud. 'We were terrified by these prodigies,' the Edict continues, 'and wished to stop where We were, but did not dare to do so.' In conclusion he states baldly that he performed the Fêng sacrifice at the top of T'ai Shan. He makes no claim that Heaven vouchsafed to notice him. Of sign or voice or revelation there is not a word.

But though he disclosed nothing—perhaps he had nothing to disclose—he considered the occasion a great one and proceeded to mark it by various benefactions. The people living in the five prefectures round the mountain were to have both land revenue and capitation tax remitted. Those of them who were over seventy, and orphans and widows, were to receive two bolts of silk each. To each woman in every hundred households throughout the whole Empire an ox and wine were granted. And all the common people were to have a step in rank, whatever precisely that honour may have meant. And he said: 'We will renew Ourself, and Our congratulations to the Grandees and gentlemen of Our suite will take the form of enabling them also to make a new beginning.' He explained that the new beginning would be a new reign period, called after the sacrifice, a device which is strange to us.

Further to commemorate his ascent of T'ai Shan, he gave orders that an inscribed stone thirty-one feet high should be set up on the summit. It would be reasonable to suppose that this inscription contained at least a hint that the communion he had sought with such persistence had been achieved and that Heaven had lifted up the light of its countenance upon him. But the supposition would be wrong. The inscription was as Confucian in tone as if he had never had to do with magicians, never sought the Fortunate Isles, never tampered with the state rituals, never hankered after celestial voices. It was to this effect: 'We have served Heaven with what rites are proper and ordered Ourselves by moral principles. We have tended Our parents with Filial Piety and nurtured the people with rightful benevolence. We have organised the administration, both civil and military, and caused the Barbarians to pay us tribute. Our Empire is the world, and, with Heaven, is boundless, and Our people are safe and live in perfect peace therein. Looking down, Heaven will bless Us everlastingly.'

What could be more dignified, more bland, more succinct, more jejune, than this document, which rested squarely on ancient precedent and was itself precedent for all such utterances thereafter? The most Confucian of Emperors never bettered it. Having read so far in this book, we are well qualified to relish its lack of reality. Nothing could be further from what any one of us would have inscribed had we, in the mood of the Emperor Wu, climbed to the summit of a sacred mountain in the firm hope of meeting with deity. Had our hope been dashed, something of our disappointment would have shown; and had it been realised our style would have lifted into a paean of thankfulness. That the inscription was a routine statement of sentiments proper to an Emperor may be conceded, but one cannot exclude the suspicion that it was also, along with his Edict, calculated to save this Emperor's face. It cloaked the facts, since the truth was that he had failed in his grand emprise. He had seen nothing on the top of T'ai Shan but the view, heard nothing but the rush of wind past his ears. That was why he had no option but to poison his coachman.

For some time afterwards, though with less enthusiasm, he went on with his attempts to see behind the veil. He did not sacrifice again on the top of T'ai Shan, but his search continued for the Immortals and the Fortunate Isles. If a rumour reached him of some celestial appearance which might possibly be authentic, he often journeyed to the place and made a personal investigation. On Kung-sun Ch'ing's advice he put up high towers like observatories so that, should Immortals be flying past, they could alight; and he built a new and magnificent palace at Chien-chang, a mile west of the capital, in the grounds of which was a lake, wherein were constructed imitations of the Fortunate Isles, in order to tempt travelling Immortals to settle there. That they had once paid him a visit, he was sure, as the Edict he published in August 109 B.C. reveals. It states that a fungus was discovered in an inner room of the Kan-ch'üan Palace, his summer residence in the metropolitan area. This fungus was an orange coloured plant with nine stalks and interconnected leaves, and was called the Fungus of Immortality. The Edict went on: 'The Lords on High visit widely and do not disdain the inferior rooms; they have granted Us an eminent favour.' An amnesty was promulgated and rewards, and a special song was composed.

But gradually the Emperor tired of the quest, as he never got any results. Kung-sun Ch'ing ceased to hold his interest, though he did not dismiss him, and, indeed, gave him a title. Ssu-ma Ch'ien, who in his capacity as Grand Astrologer was in continual attendance, notes all this with his cautious smile. 'The Son of Heaven,' he says at the end of the chapter of his History from which I have been quoting, 'became more and more tired of the strange advice of the magicians, though the cord that bound him to them was not completely severed and he never lost hope altogether of finding what they promised. In result, ever more magicians came forward, but the success of their devices is patent for all to see.' And he continues wearily: 'I accompanied the Emperor on his immense tours throughout the country, when he went sacrificing upon the sacred mountains. I was with him in the Temple of Longevity[1] when the medium was possessed by the princess and I heard the voices of the ancestral ghosts. I have made a careful study of what his magicians claimed, from every angle, from the outside and the inside, and the facts which I have set down here will enable future historians to draw their conclusions.' The Grand Astrologer dared not say more —and for very particular reasons, as will later be recounted—but what he does say in the course of his narrative is ample to show how preposterous he found the Emperor's trust in his four magician favourites, and what an aberration the mountain sacrifices seemed to this scholar of great intelligence. If there was one person at the Han Court with such a developed critical faculty, no doubt others as clear-headed resided there also. The most eminent of the Confucian Erudites will certainly have shared the historian's view.

The Emperor Wu had all the culture of his day. Pan Ku, in the relevant chapter of his *Annals*, says of him: 'His writings and literary compositions are splended and will be transmitted to posterity.' Nevertheless, he could not resist the excitement of the occult. You cannot surrender yourself to such studies without weakening your judgment and eventually unseating it. The Emperor touring among the villages and listening to the legends makes a charming picture. His longing for divine revelation is touching. I know myself what it is to go roving an Asian landscape, hearing of white birds, eman-

[1]See page 126, 127.

ations from sacred shrines, of haunted mountains where a sweet scent blows, for the remoter places are still as they always were; and I know if your tastes lie in these fancies, how they presently will possess you until, responding to a pervasive prompting, you begin to see sylvan apparitions, watch the signs, listen for words in the air of dawn, and expect a miracle or a grand enlightenment. Such promenades in Arcady are the pleasures of the poets. But if you pursue them too long, you cannot withdraw yourself and end by yielding wholly to them, when you become ensorcelled, for mingled with celestial voices are cries that frighten. And to grow frightened at the occult is fatally to surrender your reason. To this state of dread the Emperor descended. As he grew older and was less sure of the heavenly powers, he became more convinced of the infernal, and from being a happy seeker became a haunted man.

Wu Battles with Sorcery

From remote antiquity there had existed in China a priest-hood called the *wu*, whose practice resembled those of the African witch doctors, as we know them, and who can be compared with the shamans of the steppe, the dervishes of Persia, and the nat-kadaws of Burma and the wewalin of Bali; who, in short, were the Chinese rendering of the Asiatic sorcerer. Such persons, needless to say, had no place in a Confucian Court, but, with the capital full of Taoist magicians favoured by the Emperor, the *wu* priestesses (they were more numerous than the priests) were able to insinuate themselves into the palace, especially into the women's apartments. No doubt these witches had always had their clients among the Beauties, but they were more openly in demand at this time than during the previous reigns of the Han sovereigns, because the head of the state had made a vogue of the occult. How the countenancing of this rabble led to the so-called *ku* witchcraft case, a *cause célèbre* which, in the commotion it caused and the grandees it ruined, was without precedent, is an extraordinary story.[1] It is related here in detail, since there could be no better example of how essential to China's well-being was the legacy of Confucius.

In 131 B.C., when the Emperor, who was twenty-six, had been

[1] What follows is founded on the ample transcripts from Chinese histories given in De Groot's *Religious History of China*, volume 5, pp. 828–841.

ten years on the throne, *wu* witches already had a hold in the palace, for in the summer of that year the Empress Ch'en, the Empress Wei's predecessor, was dismissed for being mixed up with them. The Emperor had become alarmed when it was discovered that the Empress's daughter, hardly more than a child, had used *wu* sorcery against him. The Princess was executed along with three hundred others, some of them *wu* priestesses, some courtiers, and their heads were exposed in the market place.

This happened at the period when the Emperor was establishing Confucianism as the state cult. That he objected to the *wu* priesthood was natural, but it is also clear he believed in their power to hurt him. From the first, therefore, his attitude to witchcraft was not guided by reason. Probably few people at that period were entirely without fear of sorcery. But the Emperor's fear, after he had himself dabbled in the occult, became an insane terror. The first record of his dealings with the *wu* priesthood comes in the year 119 B.C., when he resorted to them, not with the object of causing harm, but to obtain a cure. At the time he was lying ill in one of his country palaces and, hearing that a *wu* priestess lived nearby and that she was possessed by the spirit of a deceased princess, he asked the priestess to come so that he could consult her familiar about his health. A séance took place, accompanied by the usual drunken dancing to drums, and presently the princess spoke through the mouth of her medium: 'The Son of Heaven need not worry. As soon as he is better he should get in touch with me at the capital.' The Emperor soon afterwards felt better and moved to Kan-ch'üan, his summer palace in the metropolitan neighbourhood. There he recovered completely and, as he attributed his cure to the *wu* priestess and her familiar, he went to the extraordinary length of giving them a banquet in the Temple of Longevity, and marked the occasion by proclaiming a general amnesty for all prisoners except murderers. Thereafter, he continued to consult the spirit, and on these occasions he allowed the *wu* priestess to officiate in the Temple of Longevity as if she were its resident priest.

Wu Battles with Sorcery

Sometimes when she passed into her trance, there would be curious occurrences, for the spirit of the princess would arrive accompanied by other ghostly beings. They were invisible but their voices could be heard, and what they said was intelligible. As they arrived, a sound like wind sighing would be heard. They would seem to settle behind the curtains, and their voices appeared to come from there. The Emperor was so much impressed by these séances that he built a special temple for the princess where her *wu* medium was installed with free rations and drink. Everything the princess said was carefully taken down in writing. But as she never said anything of real interest and all her remarks were of the sort which an ordinary person would make, at last he grew tired of her, though he ordered that the records of her conversation should be marked secret and preserved.

With the Emperor himself patronising the *wu*, their position in the palace was much strengthened, and they were kept busy compounding love philtres, and by spells, incantations, and sympathetic magic helping ladies-in-waiting in intrigues against rivals. Nevertheless, it was not until 92 B.C., nearly forty years after the first scandal, that the famous affair of the *ku* witchcraft took place. The drama opened in this way: a certain Chu Ngan-shi, a leading nobleman of the metropolis, happened to have been arrested on an imperial warrant. In prison he heard that the police would not have succeeded in finding him, for he had hidden himself, had it not been for the assistance given them by the grandee Kung-sun Ho, a minister whose son was Master of the Imperial Stud, and whose wife was a sister of the Empress Wei. That it was Kung who had given him away cheered the imprisoned Chu, because he knew facts about Kung's family which would enable him to ruin it. He is reported to have said with a sinister laugh: 'When I reveal all I know, there will not be bamboo bark enough in the southern mountains for me to write the accusations I have to make against him, nor will the Yie valley supply wood enough for the handcuffs that will be wanted for him and his party.'

The accusation he sent in was that Kung's son had had a love passage with the Imperial Princess Yang-shi, in the course of which he engaged a *wu* priestess to loose against the Emperor an evil spirit, specially bred by her for the purpose. (This breeding of demons was the distinguishing mark of *ku wu*.) In addition, he alleged that Kung's son had caused to be buried images of men in the high road to the Summer Palace, his agents using, as they did so, imprecations and spells. The Emperor's carriage had passed over these venomous *caches*, and it was no doubt their influence that had caused the reported indisposition of His Majesty. So wrote Chu Nganshi, the imprisoned nobleman.

The letter terrified the Emperor, as Chu expected that it would, more especially since he was known to be worried about his health. Kung and his son were immediately arrested, tried and executed. But this was only the prologue of the drama.

In attendance upon the Emperor at the Summer Palace was a certain Chiang Ch'ung, the General in command of the Hunnish Cavalry Division, for at the time to keep the Huns in check, the government had devised means, such as high pay, women, decorations and the like, of attracting numbers of them into the Imperial army, and using them against their own people. Brigaded under Chinese officers, they were a fierce body of men, able to ride down raiders from the steppe, and useful to the Emperor in another way, for they provided him with a corps of foreign mercenaries, who could be relied upon to crush rebels within his dominions.

Their General, Chiang Ch'ung, was a huge man, very hard, for to be General of Hunnish cavalry in the first century B.C. you had to be hard. In his armour, and mounted upon one of the splendid horses which had recently been imported from Ferghana near the Parthian borders, he was a martial figure without peer in Chang-an.

His position, however, was not as secure as it looked. He was on very bad terms with the Empress Wei and her son, the Heir Apparent, Prince Li, who was then thirty-seven years of age. The Emperor was sixty-five and his health was declining. When he should

VII. A BATTLE BETWEEN THE CHINESE AND THE HUNS

VIIIA. A HAN SORCERER

C   B   C

B. A HAN EXORCIST   C. FEMALE MUSICIANS

die—and there were indications that he might not last long—General Chiang could not expect any favour from his successor. He might even lose his life, for the Prince Li was unlikely to forgive him. Now the affair of the *ku* witchcraft seemed to provide him with an opportunity of crushing the Heir Apparent and his mother, the Empress. Evidence given at the trial of the Minister, Kung, and his son, The Master of the Stud, had caused the Emperor to suspect that his whole entourage was plotting to hurt him with sorcery. The charge against the Master of the Stud that he had been favoured by the Princess Imperial was true, but it was the evidence, false and procured under torture, that he had aimed *ku* at the Emperor, which had made his death and his father's a certainty. This was the line to take, concluded General Chiang. In the Emperor's present state of mind and health, he could easily be persuaded to sanction further investigation into the activities of the *wu* priestesses in the capital. These investigations could be made to yield evidence which would incriminate the Empress and the Heir, and so notorious was the Emperor's dread of *ku* sorcery, that he would not look too closely into the methods used to get evidence and could be depended upon to make an end even of his wife and son, should they be incriminated. Had he not, when in the prime of his mental vigour, dismissed his previous Empress and executed his daughter by her on similar grounds? The more General Chiang thought it over, the more convinced he became that a witch-hunt would assure his future. He might hope to obtain the nomination of a new Heir, over whom he had influence. In such happy circumstances he would become the most powerful man in the Empire.

Accordingly, he sought audience with the Emperor. 'The times are dangerous,' he said. 'Sorcery is rife, as the recent trial has disclosed. Numerous officials and courtiers are involved. If Your Majesty allows the matter to rest where it is, these people will continue their nefarious practices. No one knows precisely what is going on, but Your Majesty's health is patently affected. I beseech Your Majesty to authorise an enquiry. Only a drastic investigation will reveal the extent of the danger to which Your Majesty is exposed.' As he had hoped, the Emperor thanked him and sanctioned the investigation. 'I appoint you my Special Commissioner,' he pronounced. 'You have plenary powers. Get to the bottom of it all.'

General Chiang's first step was to ride to Chang-an with some of his Hunnish cavalry and surround the Shang-lin Park which lay without the walls. The city gates were closed and for eleven days a harsh search was pressed in the Park (or what purported to be a search). It was made to appear that the Park was the headquarters of a wu conspiracy. Chiang was assisted by a Hunnish wu, or shaman, whom he instructed to smell out nocturnal places of sacrifice, dig up images, cause spectres to appear and, in order to get direct evidence, to arrest breeders of evil spirits and any other persons, especially officials, whom they caught in the Park, and torture them to obtain allegations against the inhabitants of the Palace. The Hunnish wu carried out his instructions with savage ferocity. Hundreds of people were arrested and in the agony of their torture with red-hot irons said whatever was required of them. In short, Chiang used all the methods which, alas! two millennia later we have become so familiar with. He obtained the evidence he wanted and reported to the Emperor at the Summer Palace.

'Your Majesty,' he said, 'I have faithfully completed the first stage of my investigation. Devilish influences aimed at the Son of Heaven are emanating from the Metropolitan Palace. Have I permission to enter there and push my enquiries even into the women's apartments?' The Emperor gave him the required authorisation, and ordered that the Yellow Gate Officer, Su Wen, should accompany him.

The Empress and the Heir were resident at the time in the Metropolitan Palace, neither having accompanied the Court to the summer residence at Kuan-ch'üan. She, informed of what was happening, had sent a number of urgent letters to the Emperor, but he vouchsafed her no reply. The cruelties inflicted by Chiang had aroused the greatest alarm and indignation; nevertheless not a minister was found brave enough to approach the Emperor and acquaint him with the truth.

When General Chiang made his irruption into the Metropolitan Palace with Su Wen, the Commandant of the Yellow Gate as his adjutant, and his Hunnish *wu* as assisting sorcerer, he went straight to the main hall of audience, had the Dragon Seat removed and ordered his sorcerer to dig. The dreadful ruffian dug and, howling as if he were fighting off spectres, declared the ground to be contaminated with *ku*. Having thus established that under the very seat of Majesty was a nest of devils bred for nefarious purpose, Chiang passed on to the residence occupied by the Heir Apparent. Here he ordered his *wu* to dig again, and this time, screaming as if hallucinated, the grievous steppe shaman took from the ground a wooden doll, the most damning evidence that witchcraft was afoot. Going thence and continuing his search, Chiang entered the Wei-ying Pavilion, the Empress Wei's residence within the Palace, and penetrating into the Pepper Boudoir, so called because the plaster of the walls was mixed with pepper to make them warm and fragrant, he seized correspondence which, he afterwards told the Emperor, proved that, combined with the conspiracy to destroy him by black magic, a further plot existed to call in the Huns from the steppe.

Had Chiang been better advised for his own safety he would have arrested the Empress and the Prince on the spot. But either he was not authorised to do this or he wished to accumulate more proof before he took that drastic step. Certainly he must have held them to be too cowed to strike back. But the Prince had greater resolution than supposed. Indeed, even had he been a man of weaker character than he was to show himself, his situation was so desperate after the discovery of the doll that he had to make a frantic bid for life or else resign himself to death. So now, taking advantage of an opportunity when Chiang, with Su Wen and his *wu*, had moved to another part to arrest and torture in order to squeeze more evidence, the Prince began to consider a counterstroke. He first summoned his Junior Tutor, Shih Teh. 'You shall advise me,' he said.

'They have found this doll under my apartments. Will the Emperor listen to me if I declare my innocence?'

'He will not,' answered Shih Teh. 'You have no means of explaining the doll, for you do not know whether Chiang planted it or some other person. Merely to declare your ignorance will carry no weight.'

'What then do you advise?' enquired the Prince. Shih Teh, who knew that the Prince's ruin involved his own, was in favour of an extreme course. 'Your credentials,' he said, 'are red, the same red as the Emperor's. Send out orders at once supported by your red credentials, and make it appear that the orders originate from the Emperor. In them declare that Chiang and his crew have feloniously entered the Palace and command their arrest.'

The Heir Apparent immediately followed this advice. He drew up the warrant of arrest and sent resolute men to execute it upon Chiang and Su Wen. When Chiang saw the warrant, supported by the red credentials, he thought for a moment that the Emperor had turned against him. But recognising one of the men who bore the warrant as belonging to the Prince's Household, he guessed the stratagem and refused to surrender. The Prince's men, who knew that if they hesitated all was lost, seized him and, in the struggle which ensued, cut him down. Su Wen escaped.

This act by the Heir Apparent amounted to rebellion. His only possible safety now lay in a successful revolt. That night he sent his Chamberlain urgently to the Empress to announce what he had done and to ask her to lend him all the military force at her disposal. 'Have the fighting cars which are in your stables got ready,' he told her. 'Man them with archers. Parade the soldiers of the palace arsenal and such of the Body Guards that are here. In the morning march them out and direct them to join themselves to my forces.' And he issued a proclamation to all the palace officers. 'The General Chiang has revolted. I have decapitated him and have scorched with fire his Hunnish *wu* in Shang-lin Park.'

But to be able to overcome the Imperial troops which he knew would soon be sent against him he must have more help. To obtain this, he sent a message to Jen Ngan, the Inspector General of the Army of the North, to come to his assistance. This Jen Ngan was a personal friend of Ssu-ma Ch'ien's, the famous historian. On receiving the Prince's warrant he decided to wait and see how the revolt went before committing himself. Accordingly he closed the gates of his camp, and dismissed the messenger without a reply. The Prince had also told a partisan called Jü Hen to carry the red credentials to the depot of a Hunnish Cavalry Brigade, calling upon it to march with him. But the Intendant of the Gates and Doors, who had pursued Jü Hen, caught him up as he was reading out the Prince's order and declared his credentials to be bogus. A furious altercation ensued, but Jü Hen was overpowered and immediately decapitated.

The Prince, though without the help of the Army of the North and the brigade of Hunnish cavalry, could not now turn back and, when reinforced by the Empress's fighting-cars, archers, arsenal soldiers and her Guards, he sallied forth from the palace on 4 September 91 B.C., and engaged the Imperial troops in the outer part of the capital, which were commanded by the Lieutenant Chancellor Liu Ch'u-li, a younger brother of the Emperor.

The Lieutenant Chancellor, after hearing, as he did shortly after the event, that General Chiang had been killed and that the Prince was raising forces for a rebellion, should have entered the Palace and nipped the outbreak in the bud. But the Prince, who was very active, had sent soldiers that night to his mansion in an attempt to kill him before he could move. Liu Ch'u-li fled out of a back door with the loss of his seals and so evaded the Prince's men. His chief secretary jumped onto a horse and rode like a madman to the Emperor at Kan-ch'üan. Demanding an immediate audience from the eunuchs at the door, he was announced, called in, and, flinging himself down, reported the turn which events had taken.

'Where is Liu Ch'u-li? What measures has he taken?' demanded the Emperor in a frightening voice.

Wu Battles with Sorcery

The chief secretary beat his forehead on the ground. 'His Highness has not yet presumed to bring out troops,' he replied in an effort to avoid a straight answer.

'What do you say? Not presumed to bring out troops! Then what is he doing?' the Emperor shouted, his anger flaring up.

Shaking, the chief secretary managed to say: 'He was obliged to hide himself, Your Majesty.'

'You mean to tell me,' raged the Emperor, 'that when the capital is in turmoil the Lieutenant Chancellor runs for it!'

'He had to,' submitted the chief Secretary. 'He was beset without warning.' And he described the Prince's attempt to seize him.

'He is a useless man,' cried the Emperor. 'He is totally lacking in any character.' But he was not so furious as to be unimpressed by the danger of the situation and the necessity of cautious action. Presently, writing an order he sealed it. 'Give this to the Lieutenant Chancellor Liu Ch'u-li,' he commanded. The order was to the following effect: 'Build armoured turrets on ox-cars. Do not engage hand to hand at present or you will be overwhelmed before reinforcements arrive. And remember that while there are rewards for catching rebels, there are, of course, also punishments for neglect to do so.' And he directed that to avoid confusion in future the Imperial credentials were to have yellow tassels.

By the time this mandate was delivered to him, Liu Ch'u-li had pulled himself together. He was joined by the Hunnish cavalry, which the Intendant of Gates and Doors galloped to his assistance. And he called to arms the mariners of the river flotilla. So it was that when the Prince sallied from the palace into the city streets on 4 September, he found Liu Ch'u-li tolerably strong and in a mood as desperate as his own, for he knew that failure was court-martial and death.

On entering the city, the Prince forced into his service what ablebodied men he met with. There followed a battle which lasted five days and which was fought with such desperation that, it was said, the moats were red with the blood that flowed into them. In the course of it, the Emperor, in spite of his indisposition, left Kan-ch'uan palace and, at the head of further troops which he called in from the various depots in the metropolitan area, came down to the Chien-chang palace, his new imperial residence, which lay west of the city. From there he steadily reinforced Liu Ch'u-li. This re-inforcement, together with the refusal of the people to side en masse with the rebels, decided the issue. The Prince was defeated and fled southward to the Fu-ang Gate. By this time all the gates were in the hands of the imperial troops. T'ien Jen, the Director of Justice, happened to be at the Fu-ang Gate, and the Prince knew how to persuade him; under cover of night he was allowed to escape out. He spurred eastward to the Hu district on the way to Shan-tung. After covering some hundreds of miles, by when he had lost his few followers in one mishap or another, he arrived alone at a small village. There he concealed himself in the house of a poor man, to whom, after a while, he revealed his identity and who pro-vided for his wants by the sale of shoes. But unable to endure for long the wretchedness of this existence he was tempted to get in touch with an old friend in the town of Hu. This proved his un-doing, for the messenger was stopped, and the letter he carried dis-covered by the police. They hastened to the village and surrounded the Prince's house. When he saw that all was lost, he entered an inner room and hanged himself. The police broke down the door and found him suspended from a rafter. The poor man who be-friended him was killed as they rushed in.

The Empress Wei did not attempt to escape. She remained in the palace during the battle and, on the Prince's defeat, committed suicide. This Empress was referred to further back as a famous singer. Her beginning was of a piece with her end. She was the daughter of a slave in the household of an Imperial Princess, the Emperor's sister. Her singing and dancing so pleased the Emperor that he installed her as a concubine with the rank of Beauty. Her hold over him became such that the then Empress Chen grew alarmed. The witchcraft scandal of 131 B.C. can be explained as an attempt by that Empress to counteract by magic the Lady Wei's influence. The Empress fell and her rival took her place. Thus the Empress Wei owed both her rise and her fall to black magic.

After the Emperor's suppression of the Heir Apparent's attempt to break out of the horrifying net he saw closing about him, there were many punishments. Jen Ngan, the Inspector of the Army of the North, who had neither joined the Prince nor yet acted for the Emperor, was arrested. While under detention he wrote, though in vain, to the historian Ssu-ma Ch'ien, asking him to use his influence to save his life. Ssu-ma Ch'ien's long letter in reply, which will be discussed later, is one of the great documents of the period. The Director of Justice, T'ien Jen, who had allowed the Prince to escape, was cut in two at the waist. Liu Ch'u-li, the Lieutenant Chancellor, suffered the same death, for by an irony of fate he was suspected of breeding *ku* and, in the Emperor's then state of mind, suspicion of that sort was equivalent to a death sentence. Many other persons were executed and a relentless hunt made for all breeders of *ku*. But before the Emperor's death, which occurred four years later, he found out the truth: the Empress and his son had not bred *ku*; General Chiang's case against them had been concocted; the Prince had broken into rebellion from fear. In his grief and rage at this discovery, he exterminated the whole family of General Chiang, and burned on the Red Bridge Su Wen of the Yellow Gate.

A Great Confucian

The name of Ssu-ma Ch'ien, the first historian of the Chinese epoch into which we have been delving, has been mentioned several times. Graded as a Duke, and holding the office of Grand Astrologer, he was one of the great figures of all antiquity, and has never been properly introduced to the English-speaking public. But not to know his story, which is deeply moving, is to be ill placed to view the ancient world in its panorama of East and West. Our education for centuries has been focused upon the Mediterranean, and when we think of the first century B.C. it is the figures of Republican Rome that appear before us as they are enbalmed in Livy's prose. But, though as an artist Ssu-ma Ch'ien is not to be compared with Livy, as a savant he is greater, as a man more arresting; and to be ignorant of his personal drama and the principles it demonstrated is to have an unbalanced view of human history. Moreover, his life has a profound bearing upon the theme which is in process of illustration, namely, the sanity, the nobility, and the earnest virtue of a true follower of the First Holy One. He has come down to us unstylised and directly human, so that, moved as well as edified by the drama that overtook him, we are able to see into the privacy of his heart, that of a great man whom later academic dogma has not turned into an effigy. Moreover, the whirligig of time has briefed us by the experiences of these days to understand his ordeal.

First as to his colossal historical work, the *Shi Chih*, rendered by Chavannes, its sole translator, *Mémoires Historiques*. It is in 130 chapters and covers the period from the Yellow Emperor, whose traditional date is 2697 B.C., and with whom Chinese history makes a start, to the death of the Emperor Wu in 86 B.C. Ssu-ma Ch'ien himself died two or three years later. The method of composition he employed, and which became the accepted way in China to write history, differs from any method ever adopted in Europe.

The book opens with annals, that is to say, a carefully dated narration of the chief events of each reign, not only years, but months and days of the month, being given where possible. These annals are concise and objective; the character of the chief actors is suggested by deft touches; and important public documents, such as Imperial Edicts, are quoted in full. The narrative has the further particularity that, wherever the sources upon which it is founded provide the continuing relation required, they are bodily incorporated, without acknowledgment, comment or discussion, and without any weighing of alternative accounts of the same event. It follows that the sources, being undisclosed, can only be identified where they happen to survive independently, as does, for instance, the classic *Book of History*, which Ssu-ma Ch'ien copies into the early part of his work. The historian's art is thus seen to be, not, as we conceive it, the construction of an ordered synthesis of stated material, but the judicious selection from a mass of unspecified writings of those documents which he judges to be the most authentic, and their incorporation into the mosaic of his history. The objection to this method is that it precludes the working up of the story into a literary form; its merit is that embedded in the text are all sorts of ancient pieces, which in their untouched state give a purer impression of the period than had they been polished by the author. The result has something of the value of a select anthology of documents. While it is the opposite of the calculated work of art, it also differs profoundly from the typical early chronicle, with its neglect of dates, its confused sequences, its contradictions, its credulities and marvels.

After in this way building in his Annals a solid chronological framework, Ssu-ma Ch'ien proceeds to select general subjects of importance and treats them in detailed and lengthy essays, each comparable to a thesis for a doctorate. These amount to a commentary upon the Annals and explain important events or usages which have been stated baldly therein.

The essays are followed by a long series of chapters of a biographical nature, some concerned particularly with the Grand Feudatories, others with prominent or extraordinary individuals, the whole forming a kind of biographical dictionary.

These lives often illustrate the great principles of Confucian conduct. Such was Pein Ho's, a famous worthy of the eighth century B.C. He was a man of rugged honesty, extreme loyalty and superhuman persistence, and deemed it a matter of the utmost importance that the government should admit this to be the case, for otherwise it would be guilty of a lie, would lose its reputation and the support of Heaven. Truth must prevail or ruin would follow. It seems that he held a minor post in the state of Ch'u, the largest of the ten feudal states into which the Chou empire was then divided. One day he dug up a jade, one of those sacrificial jades which were ancient even in the eighth century B.C. For a small official to keep such an object connected with the imperial rites was improper; it was his duty to present it at once to his Duke. Its finding was an event of importance, not because, as a rare antique, it would interest the amateurs as a work of art, but because the coming up from the ground of what had been used in high antiquity by the Emperor or at the altar of Heaven was an auspicious sign, an indication that Heaven was disposed to bless.

Accordingly, Pein Ho, taking the jade, hastened to the Court of the Duke of Ch'u. There he had the same experience which has befallen many who in our time have gone to the Director of the National Gallery with an alleged old Master: the jade on examination by the Duke's experts was declared a forgery.

Pein Ho was convinced that it was not a forgery and protested with indignation against the decision. The language he used was not discreet, and the experts took serious umbrage. The fellow is an impostor, they advised, who has deliberately sought to deceive your Grace, either in the hope of getting a reward or, worse still, with the felonious intent of causing confusion in the sacrifices, for a bogus jade, if used by your Grace, would upset their equilibrium and, so, breed disasters. The Duke was alarmed by this hint of hidden dangers and, since mutilation was the punishment for an attempt to mislead a sovereign, Pein Ho was condemned to lose his left foot.

When sufficiently recovered, he returned home, and, wrapping the jade carefully in silk, put it away in a safe place. Lamed though he was, he continued his avocation, that of a beadle, it is said. Now and then he would inspect the jade and polish it with respectful assiduity. Some years later, news came that the Duke was dead and his son had succeeded. Pein Ho considered what he should do. The jade was genuine; it had been pronounced a fake. He was a loyal man; he had been adjudged an impostor. It was his duty to the state to have both these verdicts set aside. So, taking the jade, he set out for the capital.

Received by the new Duke, he told his story, unwrapped the jade and presented it to him. Again the jade was scrutinised by experts. Again they declared it to be a copy. Pein Ho was arraigned as an incorrigible rogue and sentenced to lose his other foot.

This time, on return to his native town, he was declared unfit for duty and dismissed. Reduced to beggary, he hardly kept alive. But conscious that what he had done was right, he did not sink into utter despondency.

Years passed and again the news was brought that the Duke was dead and a new one appointed. Pein Ho wondered whether it was his duty to go to Court a third time. Having lost two feet, should he expose himself to a further mutilation? He must do so, he decided; he had no option.

His appearance was pitiable as he came before the third Duke, pale, emaciated, propped on crutches. He declared his story, weeping violently; though his grief, he explained, was not due to his mutilation but because a true jade and a true subject had gone unrecognised. The Duke was moved and ordered a fresh scrutiny of the jade. This time it was reported to be a genuine piece. Much affected, the Duke sought to make amends for the grave injustices Pein Ho had suffered. First the jade was installed after a public ceremony, when a style was conferred upon it, by which it would afterwards be known in the records. And the Duke offered to make Pein Ho a Marquis, with a style to perpetuate forever his devotion.

But Pein Ho refused the title on the ground that he would accept no reward for doing his duty, nor compensation for the sufferings incident to its accomplishment. That what had been called false was proved true, provided him with all the satisfaction he required. After this magnificent gesture, he returned quietly home.

Ssu-ma Ch'ien's massive life-work may have been written on bamboo tablets with a stylus. In this method the words, scratched on polished bamboo bark by the stylus, are inked by spreading a wash of black over the whole surface and wiping it off, a device which leaves the ink in the scratches. Or the book may have been written with a brush on paper, for that method was then beginning to come in. Its first publication was the deposit of copies in the Imperial Library. The author was recognised before he died as having accomplished a work till then without parallel. It set the model for all future dynastic histories. A great monument to Confucian culture, it looks backward over the whole of China's classical past, which it joins on to the Han, a dynasty which though it dates from the second century B.C., is the beginning of modern times in China.

In his autobiography, the last chapter of his history, Ssu-ma Ch'ien ascribes the origin of his great work to his father Ssu-ma

A Great Confucian

T'an, who from 140 to 110 B.C. had the grade and office of Duke Grand Astrologer at the Court of the Emperor Wu. Under the Han the departments of astrology and divination had less authority than under the old Empire. The style, Duke Grand Astrologer, sounded impressive, but the bearer no longer stood behind the Son of Heaven as his interpreter of the celestial signs. The office was somewhat of a survival, neither well paid nor influential, though it had some importance, for the Grand Astrologer was responsible for the calendar, and the calendar not only had its modern uses, but might also be described as an agricultural guide, for it indicated the astrologically favourable moments for sowing, ploughing and reaping. But since high policy was no longer discussed with the Grand Astrologer, he was rather an archivist than a minister of state.

Ssu-ma T'an had opportunity for research, for he had the entry to the Imperial Library. It seems to have been the sight of the stacks of ancient records that gave him the idea of the history. Not like a man set to write by order, he was able to fondle the idea for years, as he slowly and methodically sorted the material.

When in 110 B.C. the Emperor Wu made his famous expedition to sacrifice on T'ai Shan, Ssu-ma T'an, as Grand Astrologer, was necessarily of the party. But on reaching Lo-yang, with only a third of the journey accomplished, he became over-tired and fell ill. Obliged to take sick leave, he went to bed and, bitterly disappointed, saw the Imperial train proceed without him. Growing worse, he sent for his son, Ssu-ma Ch'ien, who was in the capital. By the time he arrived, Ssu-ma T'an knew he was dying. His parting admonition was to this effect: 'My son, they asked my advice about the ceremonial which the Son of Heaven will use upon T'ai Shan. As Grand Astrologer I would have had a part to play, which even if minor would have been important. But, alas! I cannot be there; my life is slipping from me. And I have a second cause for distress. My history, for which I have been preparing all these years, is left but an unrealised dream. This is the more particularly unfortunate because my astrological researches have led me to believe that every four or five hundred years there comes a period particularly favourable to savants and that such a period is now at hand. Five hundred years before Confucius, the Duke of Chou composed those poems which we still love to recite; and four hundred years separate us from the great Sage whose teaching is imperishable. As you know, only last year or so they caught a queer animal, which was alleged to be a unicorn, a creature not seen since Confucius's day. All this makes me think that the moment is ripe for the appearance of a man of great talent, whose writings will for ever be indestructible. I had imagined myself destined to be that man, but now, my son, I perceive that you are he. Promise me that you will bring my labours to fruition. On my death, go to the Emperor, acquaint him with the fact and beg him to appoint you Grand Astrologer. When you receive the appointment, you will have all the facilities for continuing my labours. You will find my notes; the books will be to your hand. Go on with my researches, and when they are complete, begin to write and let nothing prevent you from finishing the history.'

This command of his dying father Ssu-ma Ch'ien received kneeling and in tears, and, after protesting his incompetence, promised to obey. It is said that at this time he was thirty-five years of age. His youth had been passed at Lung-men (Dragon Gate) 150 miles north-east of the capital, a country life on the family estate. He showed an early bent for literature and, encouraged by his father, had by heart before he was eleven all the principal classic texts. At the age of twenty he went travelling through the Empire to round off his education by visiting the famous sites of antiquity, his taste for history being already marked. He reached as far south as the present province of Che-kiang, and saw the mountain cave where legend said had died the sainted Emperor Yü; he climbed the Miao-ku-shê mountain to visit the tomb of Hsü Yu, the intractable sage who washed his ears when the sainted Emperor Yao called and offered him the throne; he made a copy of a lapidary inscription in which the Ch'in First Emperor of evil memory had lauded himself and his achievements; he viewed the Mountain of the Nine Doubts, with its nine peaks so confusingly similar that no one could tell which was the real summit; and he went to Ch'ang-sha in the present Hunan, to see the whirlpool forever associated with the name of Ch'ü-yüan, the celebrated Confucian of the fourth century B.C., whose elegy, the *Li Sao* or *Falling into Trouble*, that laments his wrongful exile, is one of the most famous poems in the language and whose story is still recalled annually to every Chinese by the Dragon Boat Festival, held to commemorate his death. In the biographical part of his History, Ssu-ma Ch'ien wrote of him: 'I have read the *Falling into Trouble* and at Ch'ang-sha I saw the whirlpool into which Ch'ü-yüan threw himself; I wept for that man, who was a man.' And he relates his story, its phrasing arranged to demonstrate the Confucian idea of virtue. In 295 B.C. Ch'ü-yüan was ordered into banishment by his relative, the Grand Feudatory of Ch'u state, whom he had served honestly but offended by his frankness. When the sentence was communicated to him, he consulted the Court Diviner in the hope of obtaining guidance in his trouble. Perhaps he had been too rigid; his advice had been too plain spoken; he should have been more pliant; he should have given way. 'Resolve my doubts,' he said to the Diviner. This functionary arranged his augury sticks, wiped his tortoise-shell and enquired what were his Honour's doubts.

'What I am anxious to know,' said Ch'ü-yüan, 'is whether in the wretchedness of my disgrace I shall be able to be constant to my principles. Shall I remain honest or shall I yield to the drift of the world? Shall I hide myself on some peasant's farm or, my resolution wavering, shall I return to Court? Shall I continue to speak frankly at the peril of my life or shall I be weak and prevaricate? The times are topsy-turvy, values are reversed. The wing of the cicada weighs a thousand pounds, the jewelled cup is laid aside for a pot. Shall I be able always to tell right from wrong?'

The Augur laid down his implements, the rods and the tortoise-shell, and replied in the tone of one excusing himself. 'There are things larger than can be measured by the foot, there are insoluble problems, irremediable situations. The tortoise and stalks are no good in your case. I can only advise you to think for yourself.'

When Ch'ü-yüan reached his place of exile near Ch'ang-sha he was lonely and miserable. He tried at first to keep up his spirits, but could not help brooding over his wrongs. As the months passed, he neglected his appearance; his appetite went and he grew very thin. One day out wandering alone by Hsiang river, he was spoken to by a fisherman: 'You have the air of an unfortunate nobleman. Why have you come to this remote spot?'

'Because the world is muddy and I am clear,' replied Ch'ü-yüan bitterly. 'Because others were drunk and I remained sober.'

The fisherman, who was a Taoist, had his answer to this: 'The Sage does not quarrel; he adapts himself. If the world is water, follow its course. If your fellows drink, drink as they do. What is the use of principles and aspirations if, in the end, they land you in banishment?'

'Never, never,' cried Ch'ü-yüan, 'will I sink to that level! I would rather the fish had me than that.'

The fisherman smiled, hoisted his sail and pushed off, humming the country song: 'When the water is clean I wash my clothes in it; when the water is dirty it does to wash my feet.'

It was after this that Ch'ü-yüan threw himself into the whirlpool.

Ssu-ma Ch'ien's travels all over China eventually brought him to Confucius's tomb in Lu, a visit that impressed him deeply. He afterwards wrote of it: 'The hall in Lu where the disciples used formerly to live was later transformed into a memorial chapel in which were placed the Master's clothes, his ceremonial hat, his lute, his carriage and copies of his books, all of which have been carefully preserved there for three hundred and fifty years.' And he goes on, taking the words of an old song: 'His gaze was towards the high mountain, his steps to the wide horizon. And though he failed to reach his goal, he never ceased trying to get there. When first I read his works I thought I could perceive the manner of man he was.

Then later when I went to Lu and saw his chapel with the relics in it, I could not drag myself away. Many are those, even rulers and sages, whose repute has come to an end with their lives. But Confucius, though never more than a plain civilian, has been revered for ten generations. Now everyone in the Middle Kingdom, from the Son of Heaven downwards, who discusses the six liberal arts, is guided by what he wrote and said. That indeed may be called the perfection of sanctity.'

The perfection of sanctity. These words of open admiration, showing that Ssu-ma Ch'ien regarded Confucius as a divine sage, should be contrasted with the guarded manner, not without irony, in which he records the Emperor Wu's journeys from mountain to mountain in search of a revelation. The revelation was already to hand, hints the Grand Astrologer. Confucius's measured doctrine of the mean, his emphasis on upright behaviour, on respect towards parents, on loyalty to friends, his insistence that government must chime with the will of Heaven, and the ruler live for the benefit of his subjects, all this amounted to a revelation, one that insured humane government, a happy home life, honest social intercourse and a humble attitude before the great mysteries of the universe. The Han had the opportunity to translate this revelation into practice, insists Ssu-ma Ch'ien. Under them China was re-united, the old empire was re-created. It remained only to follow the sage's admonitions and the golden age which he had looked back to with such longing would return. That this was Ssu-ma Ch'ien's view, that he himself was essentially a sane, moderate, dignified and humane man, is the measure of his disapproval of his royal master, who was not satisfied with a simple rule of behaviour but dabbled in alchemy, consorted with magicians, became terrified of witches and punished with ferocity.

On his return to the capital from his grand tour, Ssu-ma Ch'ien was given the appointment of secretary in one of the administrative departments. Here he worked quietly, acquiring a practical knowledge of the machinery of government, an experience of value to the future historian. In 111 B.C., the year before his father's death, he was deputed to visit the western frontiers. The Emperor had recently sent military expeditions to tranquillise the tribes living in the region now called Yunnan. Ssu-ma Ch'ien's duty appears to have been connected with the administrative system which the Emperor was seeking to introduce into the tribal areas. It is not known what tribes these were, but one may assume with confidence that some of them were the ancestors of the Shans, Burmese, Karens, Chins and Kachins, who in later centuries migrated into Burma and with whom we have ourselves had so much to do. The vast expanse of hill and mountain between Burma and China is still occupied by many distinct Mongolian peoples, each with their own language, costume, handicrafts and ghosts, and anyone, like myself, who has travelled among their villages, will have seen much of what Ssu-ma Ch'ien saw two thousand years ago, for tribal life is fixed in a conservative rut hardly to be imagined. For example, I have in my possession what is known nowadays as a Karen bronze drum, because it has been made until modern times by the tribe whose present name is Karen. The shape of this drum and the decoration upon it are so similar to those of drums known to date from Han times that only a diligent examination reveals the differences. Ssu-ma Ch'ien journeyed as far westward as Talifu, the last big town on the way to Burma, whither a track, in our time transformed into the Burma Road, existed from the remotest antiquity.

He returned to the capital in 110 B.C. in time, as we have seen, to hasten to his father's death-bed at Lo-yang. The appointment of Duke Grand Astrologer was, as his father had hoped, conferred upon him, when the twenty-seven months of his mourning were over.

Taking over the office, he found there was little routine business and that he had leisure to set about his historical researches in accordance with his father's last wishes. He began compiling his narrative, as he says, 'from the memoirs of past historians and from the archives in the Stone Room and the Iron Cabinet'. In 104 B.C. he was appointed to a commission to correct the calendar. The discrepancy between the true time and the official time had become rather great, because the inter-calary days between solar and lunar time had not been correctly inserted since the beginning of the dynasty, a hundred and two years before. The astronomical and mathematical knowledge of the period sufficed to rectify the error. Indeed, it seems that an ingenious method, thought preferable to intercalary days, was adopted, at least for a time, every day being divided into eighty-one units of time, the eighty-first being an intercalary fraction sufficient to maintain the time exactly true. But it is unnecessary here to probe into such details. Suffice it to say that Ssu-ma Ch'ien distinguished himself on the commission. When it was wound up, he continued his work on the history which was steadily growing under his hand.

But now approached the year 99 B.C. when, at about fifty-six years of age, he was to be involved in a fatal mischance. This had to do with the Huns. On a previous page the Emperor's challenge in 110 B.C. to the Hun High King, the Shan-yü, was touched upon. But the Huns, like the Tartars, their successors on the steppe between Lake Baikal and the Great Wall, presented an insoluble problem. If you defeated them, they retreated into the Gobi. When you withdrew from those inhospitable wastes, in which civilised people could not live, they returned to the attack. The only course was to defeat them again. But the expeditions against them were not always successful. The Emperor had had several set-backs: on two occasions, in 123 and 103 B.C., his commanders had surrendered and in the year 100 B.C. his ambassador, Su Wu, had been detained by the Shan-yü. It was to punish him for this and rescue Su Wu that in 99 B.C. the Emperor fitted out a fresh expedition, the command of which was entrusted to his senior Marshal, Li Kuang-li, who happened to be the brother of the beloved Lady Li, with whose ghost the Emperor had once sought rendezvous. The plan was for Li Kuang-li to march up the road which later on was called the Silk Road, because the silk caravans to Europe were to go that way, and after passing the oasis of Hami to engage the

Huns, who at the moment were near Lake Burkal in that vicinity. These places were over twelve hundred miles west of the capital, so that it was an expedition on a grand scale, very expensive and to which the Emperor attached the greatest importance. The force consisted of 30,000 Hunnish cavalry, under Chinese officers, all mounted archers capable of that most difficult feat, the discharge of their arrows at full gallop, which only men trained from childhood to the saddle and the bow could master.

Before the expedition started, the Emperor was memorialised by a youngish officer called Li-ling, who had been deputed to supervise the lines of communication. This man, whom, as it happened, Ssu-ma Ch'ien had recommended to the Emperor, was the grandson of a celebrated General, who was said to have defeated the Huns in seventy engagements, but in the end had been obliged to commit suicide because in 119 B.C. he was found guilty by a court-martial of disobeying orders. Li-ling, who had inherited his grandfather's ardent temperament, now begged the Emperor to allow him, instead of remaining on lines of communication, to make a diversionary flank attack on the Huns, so as to reduce the pressure which Marshal Li Kuang-li would have to meet. The Emperor said there was no more cavalry available at the moment. To this Li-ling replied that he did not want cavalry; he would carry out the manoeuvre with the five thousand infantrymen under his command. These men, he pointed out, were picked troops. Moreover, they were armed with the improved crossbow, a weapon which outranged the Hun bows and which, by reason of its trigger mechanism, was extremely accurate. They would be more than a match for the Hun cavalry, urged Li-ling, though no infantry had ever been able to withstand it in the past. The Emperor was impressed by these arguments and reflecting that in any case the use of infantry would afford a most interesting military experiment which, if it proved successful, would enable him to modify advantageously his frontier tactics, up to this dependent altogether on cavalry, he sanctioned Li-ling's proposal.

Accordingly, Li-ling moved out of the frontier post on the Great Wall where he had assembled his troops and, leaving the main road for Hami, struck north towards the Gobi and then swung west towards the Hun position, a march which occupied a month. His approach was discovered and the Shan-yü flung thirty thousand horsemen at him. In the battle which ensued Li-ling, thanks to his cross-bows, inflicted a heavy defeat upon the Huns, the first time they had ever been defeated by infantry. (It is interesting to remember that the battle of Carrhae was fought forty-five years later, when the Parthians, whose army was steppe cavalry, defeated Crassus and his Roman foot-soldiers, who had only the usual weapons of the legionary.)

Li-ling, considering that he had now done what he set out to do and effectively drawn off and destroyed an appreciable part of the Shan-yü's army, began his withdrawal to the Great Wall. But the Huns brought up reinforcements and began to harry his retreat. Their attacks became very formidable; when more distant levies arrived, their numbers reached eighty thousand horse. Li-ling, however, managed to keep his men together; the wounded were carried in carts, the moderately wounded pushed them, the slightly wounded fought. His cross-bows prevented the Huns from closing in. But would his reserves of arrows last? He was using them up at a dangerous rate. In an effort to hasten the pace of his retreat, he abandoned his baggage carts when he was within some sixty miles of the frontier. But his pursuers were relentless; he could not shake them off. With only forty miles still to go, he had to enter a narrow valley. The Huns, who were now commanded by the Shan-yü in person, saw their opportunity to finish the affair. Moreover, a captured Chinese officer had informed them that the expected had occurred; the Chinese arrows were exhausted.

The end came in this way. The Huns blocked the exit from the gorge and discharged their arrows from the heights on each side of it; they also rolled down a quantity of great boulders. The Chinese were helpless; they could no longer shoot back. Nevertheless, their discipline was so good that they did not break. A desperate attempt was made to force open the road-block at the end of the gorge; they fought with swords and spears made from axle-trees. But they could not force it.

At last darkness fell and gave them respite. Li-ling called a council of officers. What was to be done? Was there hope of other forces coming to their aid? There was no such hope because, though a relief force to meet them half way on their return had originally been mooted, the arrangement fell through. If, then, no rescue was to be expected, could they fight their way out of the gorge and cover the short distance that lay between them and the Wall? It did not seem possible. In his despair, Li-ling went so far as to say that he would disguise himself and creep alone to the Shan-yü's tent and kill him, but his officers would have nothing of this mad scheme. 'Then there is only one thing to be done,' he cried. 'If the Huns find us here at dawn they will massacre us at their leisure. As an army we must cease to exist; let each soldier as best he can make his way home. As for myself, I will remain, bury the treasure, destroy the banners and as the Huns close in do away with myself.'

'What need for that?' they protested. 'Your conduct of the retreat has covered you with glory. You defeated the Huns in fair battle and only now when your arrows are spent do they obtain the upper hand. We will get you out of this trap. In the darkness there are side paths by which a small body well mounted may escape. The Emperor is fair. He will take account of your first victory to forgive this last defeat. To flee is to be able to fight another day. Honour is not lost. What need is there of suicide?'

'The Emperor will make no allowances,' replied Li-ling bitterly. 'He expects a defeated general to die on the field. If such a one returns home he is court-martialled and executed. My grandfather's seventy victories did not save him from the obligation to commit suicide. And my case is aggravated. I persuaded the Emperor against his first judgment to sanction my manoeuvre. He will never forgive me this disaster.'

A Great Confucian

'He forgave Marshal Li Kuang-li on former occasions,' they reminded him. 'Twice he was worsted by the Huns and did not commit suicide, but the Emperor gave him a chance to re-establish his reputation and here he is now in command of the main army.'

'Everyone knows the explanation of that,' said Li-ling. 'He is the brother of one whom the Emperor madly loved.' But in the end they persuaded him to attempt the escape. 'A good many of our men will get through,' they said confidently. 'When we reach the frontier, we will rally them and march across it in good order, not the whole army that marched out but a sufficient proportion of it to prove we have made a successful fighting withdrawal.'

After orders had been issued to the troops to split into small companies and get out as they could, Li-ling with ten of his most devoted captains made a dash to escape. They found a way through the Hun forces and at dawn were galloping towards the Wall. But their passage had been observed; Hun troopers were in pursuit; they were ridden down, surrounded in a wide circle and told to surrender.

It would have been in keeping with the code which the Emperor expected of his Generals had Li-ling refused to surrender and died riddled with arrows as he made a wild effort to close with the enemy. But he did not do this and gave himself up. It may have been loss of nerve or exhaustion; or perhaps he saw no reason why he should let himself be killed to indulge the Emperor's whim. He had tried to escape and, had he succeeded, would have been obliged to brave the Imperial temper. Now, as he could not escape and so would never see the Emperor again, what was to be gained by seeking to placate him? He had done all that a man could do and his surrender would not trouble his conscience. The Emperor had been too hard on his heroic grandfather and did not deserve a fanatical loyalty from the grandson. And if he had been hard in that case he would be hard in this. Why, therefore, should he go beyond honour and conscience for a man who, over severe, would misjudge him?

All or some of these reasons will have actuated Li-ling when he gave himself up to his pursuers. The meaning of a surrender to the

Huns in the first century B.C. requires explanation. Li-ling's position was not that of a prisoner of war in our sense. The Huns would not merely hold him until the end of hostilities and then send him home. He would never be able to come home, even if the High King should make a lasting peace with the Son of Heaven, for to go home would be to court execution. If the Emperor might have sentenced him to death for losing his army and not dying on the field, he would certainly do so for his surrender. That he could never return meant settling down with the Huns, even taking employment of some kind and being ready to advise when his advice was sought; in fact, it amounted to permanent exile at a barbarian Court. The circumstances of the time turned a plain military surrender into an act almost equivalent to going over to the enemy. For a Han General to surrender was a far more irretrievable act than we understand by the word. He became a renegade.

When the news of the disaster was reported to the Emperor (only three or four hundred out of the army of five thousand reached safety) he assumed that Li-ling had been killed. When he heard of his surrender he became so enraged that he ordered his family to be exterminated.

Before describing how Ssu-ma Ch'ien became involved in this storm, I must refer to a letter of Li-ling's written later from the Hun Court which in its poignancy brings us close to the man and his times. Su Wu, the Ambassador whose detention by the Huns was the cause of the expedition, was its recipient. When Li-ling reached the Shan-yü's court he met Su Wu and the two became friends. Years later Su Wu was able to get back to civilisation and he wrote to Li-ling. Li-ling's reply is the letter that follows.

It begins: 'I have your kind letter, urging me to keep up my spirits, and I thank you for it from my heart. But it is not easy to be cheerful alone in a barbarian land. Indeed, since the day of my surrender I have not known what it is to be carefree. Never to see anyone except a Hun. You know what that means; I need not tell you. Nothing has changed since you left. With the late autumn the steppe is stiff with ice. I hear the moan of the bitter wind as I sit wrapped in furs in my felt tent. They bring me slabs of mutton to eat and pots of whey to wash it down. With nothing to occupy my mind I can only brood, thinking of the man that once I was. And when dark comes, I cannot sleep. I toss and listen to the Hun pipes, to the whinnying of the Hun horses. I was so wretched after you left, with not a soul that I could talk to. In my melancholy I could not stop thinking of my old mother, butchered by the Emperor because of my fault, and my poor wife and child butchered too. I may have been to blame, but that was too cruel. Are they not sorry for me at home? Do they not say the Emperor has been unjust? My good record was never taken into consideration. Condemned in my absence I had no hearing. I suppose some declare I should have put an end to myself. But they do not understand. To have done so would have been an admission of guilt. And I am not guilty, my conscience tells me so. In any case life here is worse than death. That I did not die is my chief crime in their eyes. But why should one defeat mean the end of man, as if there was no such thing as retrieving a failure? Oh, it makes one shed tears of blood! But in spite of all I am glad that I did not commit suicide. I have been treated with too brutal an ingratitude. Why should I have given all to a government that had no scrap of clemency for me? A brave man, who could have done the state great services, is left to die like a dog in exile. Forget me, Su Wu. A thousand miles separate us forever. I shall live out my days here with my Hun wife; our children will sacrifice at my tomb. My very ghost will never return. This letter is my last farewell. Speak of me to my old acquaintances. And you, my friend, may you be happy; take care of yourself; and with your dear family about you let your long exile seem as if it had never been. Think of me no longer—yet, should there be opportunity, write, write to me once again.'

This despairing letter recalls the *Tristia* and the *Pontine Epistles* written by Ovid ninety years later after his banishment to the frontier town of Tomis, the modern Constanza in Rumania, which lies on the edge of the steppe in its western extremity. The Scythians who lived just over the border were, like the Huns, nomad horsemen. In the *Tristia* are sentences which echo Li-ling's lament: 'I cannot sleep, I have no appetite, I have lost much weight, nor in mind am I healthier than in body. . . . When I look at this land, the ways, the dress, the language of the barbarians, when I remember what I am and what I was, I have such a longing for death that I wish the Emperor had executed rather than exiled me. . . . With skins and padded breeches the barbarians keep out the cold. Often their hair tinkles with hanging ice and their beards glisten white with frost. . . . As soon as the river Hister which flows between us and the steppe is frozen, the mounted nomads come riding to the attack, an enemy formidable in horses and bows.'

This brings home to us how the same steppe threatened both the Empires of Rome and the Han and that though those empires were inhabited by men vastly different in manners and appearance, the steppe dwellers were similar east and west. It will occur to the reader at this point to enquire whether the Huns of the Chinese northern marches were the identical nomad people who afterwards invaded Europe. To this question no positive answer can be given, but it seems likely that they were. It is known that they moved westwards in the first century A.D. to lands north of the Caspian. There were Hunnish invasions of India and Persia in the fifth century and the same century saw the rise of Attila to the position of High King of the Huns, his incursions to the walls of Constantinople and Rome, and his forever memorable defeat on the Marne near Chalons. To see in him the successor of the Shan-yü with whom Li-ling resided so long is more than a fancy, and we begin to apprehend the first century B.C. in its world perspective, with Ovid's nostalgia for its western corner of civilisation so like Li-ling's for its eastern.

In his letter to Su Wu Li-ling makes no reference to the fact that he was valiantly defended before the Emperor when the news of his surrender reached Court. But while stay-at-home courtiers sneered at his defeat, and, to curry favour with an angry Emperor, rivals by insinuation made his conduct seem worse, a man stood up for him, not for friendship's sake, as Li-ling was no more than an acquaintance of his, but for principle's, and that man was Ssu-ma Ch'ien. What he said, in open Court, is recorded in his biography written by Pan Ku, and which is chapter 54 of the *History of the Former Han.* It was to this effect: 'Li-ling served his parents with filial piety and was well known among his colleagues as a man of his word. Never one to put comfort before duty, he was always ready to risk his life to repulse any danger threatening the state. Now, because of one failure in the field, our amateur strategists hasten to belittle him in the usual odious manner of their kind. But consider what were his actual achievements. He led five thousand unmounted men into the heart of a mounted enemy's territory and inflicted such a defeat upon them that they did not stay to pick up their wounded. Afterwards, massing the host of their archers from all parts, they followed his withdrawal, but he kept them at bay until, choosing their ground and time, they were able to encircle him. By then his reserves of arrows were exhausted but he fought on, though without hope of aid being sent. None of the famous Generals of the past have done more. That he did not die on the field was because of his longing to wipe out his defeat and show his gratitude for his sovereign's clemency, upon which with clear conscience he dared to count.'

The Emperor was in an exceptionally bad frame of mind because he had lost face. It seems that Li-ling, at the time of his withdrawal when he was beating off the Huns, had sent a special messenger to Court, announcing the successful outcome of the expedition. A banquet was held and the Emperor had been toasted in congratulation by the Marquises and Privy Counsellors. When the news of the disaster reached him, he was the more angered. Now Ssu-ma Ch'ien's speech was little calculated to soothe him. It was too downright; it reflected upon his sense of justice. Moreover, he thought that he detected in it a reference to Marshal Li Kuang-li, a hint that if Li Kuang-li had been a competent officer he would have sent troops to aid Li-ling. This veiled complaint against the brother of Lady Li was too much. In a rage, he replied that Li-ling was a headstrong and foolhardy General who had lost five thousand men and sustained a defeat most injurious to the dynasty's reputation, after having falsely represented his ability to win and thereby overborne the Emperor's prudence. 'It is a criminal offence under the code,' he said, 'to deceive the Emperor or try to do so. You, Ssu-ma Ch'ien, misled me into employing Li-ling by recommending him to my notice, and now, trying to mislead me a second time, would have me excuse him.'

Uttering this, he immediately gave orders that Ssu-ma Ch'ien should be indicted before the courts on that charge.

The criminal code was very harsh, though to be harsh was contrary to the Confucian conception of the humane Emperor, a ruler who governed by kindness and example and ascribed the evil deeds of his subjects to his own lack of virtue. The Sainted Emperors, Yao, Shun and Yü, were supposed to have been so kind that, in lieu of the mutilations, which were the traditional method of punishing crimes in China, they caused convicted criminals only to be symbolically mutilated. Instead of the nose being amputated, a grass cord was worn round the neck; for amputation of the feet, hemp sandals were substituted; in place of castration the wearing of a grey apron; to denote a capital sentence, ochre-red garments were worn. There is, of course, no more foundation for such a legend than for the other amiable stories of the Sainted Triad, but the Han Emperors believed it to be true and were fully aware that a Confucian government should have a mild code. Wu's great-uncle, the Emperor Wen, as we have seen, had abolished mutilations. Wu, however, did not feel that he could manage to govern with such mildness. In June 135 B.C., he had set an essay on this subject to the candidates for official appointments who had been sent up from the districts. Addressing them he said: 'It is recorded that the Sainted Emperors merely portrayed mutilating punishments, but did not use them. Nevertheless, the people committed no crimes, being sufficiently restrained by the pervasive force of the said Emperors' virtue which reached even to birds and beasts. But We have been unable to make Our virtue felt at a distance. Their culture extended to the Four Seas; the constellations produced no comets; the sun and moon were not eclipsed; unicorns and phoenixes were in their suburbs and marches. We have risen early to seek for the springs of their perfection and gone to bed late in order to ponder it. How can We reach the level of Yao and Shun? Answer this question in writing. We Ourselves will read your essays.'

Whatever advice the essays may have contained, the Emperor restored the punishment of mutilation in 119 B.C. To find soldiers for his campaigns against the Huns and the independent kingdoms of the south-west, to get workers to build his palaces, his roads and his embankments, he had to force the people, press his officials and drive his military officers. Such was his excuse for a harsh code. Now Ssu-ma Ch'ien was to experience what it meant, even for a Grandee, to be handed over to the judges for trial.

When an Emperor, as in the present case, was complainant in an indictment, a court of law was no more than a board of punishment, with a duty not to judge guilt but to deliver a sentence. The punishment in the code for misleading the Emperor was castration. Accordingly, Ssu-ma Ch'ien, the Duke Grand Astrologer, the most learned savant of his day, was condemned to be castrated, or, in the euphemism of the period, to proceed to the Silkworm House.

It is true that the code allowed in alternative a fine, but this was so high as to be ruinous for a rich man and far beyond an ordinary man's reach. One cannot ascertain what the figure was, nor, if one could, would it nowadays convey any meaning. Suffice it to say that it was out of all proportion to Ssu-ma Ch'ien's salary as Grand Astrologer, and that, besides his salary, his means were limited. The family estate on which he had spent his youth was worth much less, even if, which is uncertain, he had the power to mortgage it.

In this predicament he turned aside to his friends, hoping that between them they would put up the money. But it seems that they were more terrified by the Emperor's displeasure than obliged by the duty which friendship imposed. That he was entirely deserted in this crisis is unlikely, but that enough help was wanting to save him from mutilation is evident. While in the hands of the police he was roughly handled, and, failing to raise the fine had to go to the Silkworm House and submit himself. The feelings engendered in him by this terrible ordeal, his sufferings, the motives that prevented him from committing suicide and the reflections that enabled him to endure the ignominy attaching to such a punishment, are revealed in a letter which he wrote in 91 B.C., eight years later. Before considering this letter, it should be recorded that on recovering from the mutilation he was offered the appointment of Chief Clerk of the Palace, which was equivalent to that of Imperial Private Secretary, and was a post available only for eunuchs. He accepted it. All confidential papers and edicts passed through his hands and he had opportunities of tendering advice like a Privy Counsellor. He was enabled to continue his History and finished, or practically finished, it before his death, in the year 86 B.C. when he was sixty-nine.

And now to examine his letter of 91 B.C., one of the great documents of the Han period, as I have already declared it to be. It was addressed to Jen Ngan, the Inspector General of the Army of the North, who, it will be recalled, fell under grave suspicion of wavering in his allegiance at the time of the witchcraft scandal of that year and who, on his arrest after the flight of the Heir Apparent and the suicide of the Empress Wei, wrote to Ssu-ma Ch'ien, who was an old friend, in the hope that as Chief Clerk of the Palace and continually at the Emperor's side he would be able effectively to intercede for him. 'It is your duty now to do what the upright ministers of the old empire were wont to do,' he said, and called upon him to act again like a Confucian worthy regardless of all else but truth and right, as eight years before he had acted in support of Li-ling. Ssu-ma Ch'ien thought the matter over and in due course replied in these terms: 'Some little time has elapsed since you were good enough to address me a letter in which you drew my attention to your predicament and reminded me that loyalty in friendship and the support of worth are great principles and were honoured in antiquity. Perhaps you suspect that I have made no move to aid you because I am afraid of public opinion. If so, you are mistaken, for such conduct could never be mine. All my life I have looked up to classic example. But now I am like an ancient discarded horse; I have a body that is degraded, a presence that soils. The mere fact of my proposing any action renders it unacceptable; for me to try and help a friend in fact does him harm. I am cut off from life and in my solitude am a broken man.

'I wish I could make my meaning clearer. Since my virility has been taken from me, I can never be accepted as a man of honour, no matter how high my character, how splendid my talents. To attempt to act as such would only expose me to the added shame of ridicule.

'I should have replied more promptly to your letter. I had just returned from a tour eastwards in the Emperor's suite and found a mass of papers awaiting my attention. Each day was too short for me to have leisure to visit you; indeed, I was so overwhelmed with work that this moment is the first I have had to write at the length which the subject demands. Weeks, months, have passed; it will soon be spring and I must be ready to go on tour again with the Emperor. Any hour now I may suddenly hear that the irrevocable has happened and that I have put off speaking for you until too late. Your spirit will have departed on its long road and will bear towards me an eternal resentment. I know that I have wanted in duty by leaving your letter so long unanswered. Do not, I beg, reproach me; let me further explain my thought.'

In the next paragraph of this heartrending letter Ssu-ma Ch'ien insists that to be punished by castration is the greatest possible disgrace that any man can suffer, for he is lowered to the level of a

IX. THE PRINCESS OF COLOURED CLOUDS
(see page 118)

eunuch, a class regarded as more contemptible than any other. Even Confucius, he says, when he saw the Grand Feudatory, the Duke of Wei, go out driving with a eunuch, left the state in disgust. The humblest people, he goes on, do not like it when their petitions to the Emperor have to pass through the hands of eunuchs. Yet Jen Ngan, one of the most distinguished military officers in the Empire, seeks to make use of this same disreputable intermediary.

'Formerly,' the letter continues, 'I was a Grandee of the Third Rank. I was not expected to give my advice until those of the higher ranks had spoken. That I spoke out of my turn when I made my appeal on behalf of Li-ling and, in a manner too assured and frank, invoked the grand principles of justice, was the fault for which I was punished. If, speaking as a Grandee, what I advanced was held excessive, how can I now, no better than a servant who sweeps the floor, raise my head and declare what should or should not be done?

'Let me set out more fully the circumstances which brought me to my present wretchedness; they are not easy to grasp without a knowledge of my temperament. In youth I was always impatient of control and, paying for my inability to submit to rule, was not popular with my seniors when I grew up. My appointment as Duke Grand Astrologer was solely due to the regard in which my father was held by the Emperor. A member of his suite, I tried to please him and, striving to be modest and reverential, devoted my energies to the tasks which he laid upon me. But my character would not let me maintain this role of self-effacement. I could not help blurting out my admiration for Li-ling, and so destroyed in a moment a reputation for prudence which years of restraint had succeeded in building up. The fact was that he had qualities of an admirable sort. Not that he was an intimate friend of mine. Though we were both attached to the Palace, our duties did not bring us into close touch, for he was a soldier and I was a civilian. I do not think we ever dined together or that we frequented the

same places of amusement. But all I saw of his character delighted
me: honest in money matters, just to his dependents, respectful to
his superiors, reverential at the rites. When I heard him belittled,
run down after his defeat, I could not keep silence, I had to protest.
But I was too carried away and spoke without tact. I so wanted the
Emperor to know the truth, which should have cheered him in his
distress; Li-ling's deeds, far from bringing discredit, crowned the
Imperial arms with glory. But I was unable to convey my meaning
with adequate clearness. His Majesty did not follow my argument,
suspected me of slandering Marshal Li Kuang-li, and thought my
defence of Li-ling was a sophism. You were present when the
judges pronounced sentence. You knew I was too poor to pay the
fine. What was your opinion of my conduct? In submitting to
mutilation, did I behave with propriety or should I have taken the
other course that was open to me? Did I act as becomes a man?'

So Ssu-ma Ch'ien comes to the question of suicide. Should I
have taken my life rather than allow myself to be shamed for ever?
he asks in effect. And this question, raised in reply to the letter of
a man also threatened with a humiliating punishment, takes on the
double meaning: should not you, Jen Ngan, commit suicide rather
than expose yourself to a similar disgrace? The implication is that
Jen Ngan has no alternative but to do so, though the advice remains
veiled in accordance with the literary conventions of the period.
And to the counter-question—if suicide is better than a dishonour-
ing punishment, why did not I, Ssu-ma Ch'ien, kill myself rather
than submit to castration, the most dishonourable of all punishments?—an answer is given.

After declaring that what a man of mind and character should
most strive to avoid is outrage to his dignity and to his reason, he
describes what may happen to such a man if he allows himself to
be taken into custody (and means it to be inferred that he is speaking of his own bitter experience): 'They bind you hand and foot;
they put the wooden collar on you and the chains; they torture you,
they beat you, they throw you into a dungeon. In such a situation,

when you see the gaoler you abjectly touch the ground with your forehead. At the mere sight of his underlings you are seized with a terror in which your reason takes flight and your self-respect is mortally hurt. Such ignominy can never be wiped away.'

In his next paragraph he cites the cases of eight eminent personages of the past, who because they did not commit suicide suffered abominably at the hands of their gaolers. How tiresome a paradox would it be had they maintained that they had not been degraded! he exclaims. And he goes on, his argument always that Jen Ngan has no course open to him but to take his life, and that, indeed, he has delayed too long: 'Moreover, if a man does not make up his mind fast enough, if he has let himself be outraged little by little until things go so far that he is beaten with whips and sticks, is it not too late, has he not already lost his dignity? All of us love life and have a horror of death; we desire to spare our parents and our families the grief they are bound to suffer at our going. But men who put dignity and reason[1] first cannot allow themselves such feelings.'

Having argued that suicide for Jen Ngan is the only way out, Ssu-ma Ch'ien begins to explain why he himself did not take that way.

'Do not think that I held back because of my parents; my parents are dead. Nor believe I desired to spare my wife and children; when I spoke out for Li-ling, I proved that truth and justice had first place in my heart. Nor yet think that my nerve failed me. There are occasions when even the most brave perceive that to die is less urgent than to live. Furthermore, to say that a brave man is ready to die and a coward not so, is too simple. There have been timid men who, carried away by a great cause, have accomplished prodigies. Why, even the offspring of slaves, servants and concubines have been known to commit suicide in a situation that appeared unbearable. No, no, it was not cowardice. I had a special

[1]The word reason here and above has the sense of the even and calm mind of a man who is master of himself.

reason for living. If I allowed myself to be dragged in the dust, to go down into the smoke, it was because I could not bear to contemplate my inmost thought remaining unexpressed, could not bear to leave the world with my great enterprise unfinished. Many, many are the rich and powerful whose celebrity has been quenched by death; oblivion can be circumvented only by merit the most extraordinary.'

By this Ssu-ma Ch'ien means that an immortal name is so high an aspiration, for nor riches nor power can encompass it, that every ignominy, every humiliation may be borne if thereby the winning of it is made possible. Had he not submitted to castration, but committed suicide, he could not have finished his *History*.

And he develops these thoughts as follows: 'I am not the first to have had in mind the creation of a great literary work when he was in trouble. Ch'ü-yüan composed his well-named *Falling into Trouble* after he had been driven from Court in disgrace; and others, too, some who had had their feet cut off and some who were blinded, left to posterity writings that forever will proclaim their quality. I will not fall behind these examples. I have confidence in what I have written. The ancient traditions which were scattered and lost I have collected and set in order; I have sifted the evidence for the principal events; I have found out the reason for triumphs and disasters; in my hundred and thirty chapters I have indited all that concerns heaven and earth from the Yellow Emperor until today. But before I had finished I was overtaken by this atrocious mishap; and, because to abandon my task would have filled me with inextinguishable regret, I underwent the most terrible of punishments with equanimity. As soon as I have put the last touches to my manuscript I will deposit it in the Imperial Archives, so that it will be transmitted to those capable of appreciating its quality and will be spread thereafter through every town. When that happens, when even in the village schools it is read, then I shall have washed away the stain of my disgrace. Had I suffered ten thousand humiliations to attain this end, they would not have been too much.'

A Great Confucian

With this fervent declaration of faith in the value of his *History*, Ssu-ma Ch'ien ends his letter to Jen Ngan. Its weighty argument, which while expressing to perfection the Confucian standpoint also transcends it, for it is as cogent today as when it was penned, does not seem to have convinced the man to whom it was addressed. Jen Ngan did not commit suicide. His reasons we do not know, for we have no information except the brutal statement that he was cut in two at the waist, a form of execution traditionally supposed to have been effected by means of a heavy blade, hinged at one end and forced down by leverage applied to the other.

Ssu-ma Ch'ien's belief in the permanence of his History was fully justified. Every subsequent historian was and still is obliged to go to it for the whole Chinese classical period, that is for the legendary epoch of the Yellow Emperor and Yao and Shun, the Hsia Dynasty (2205–1766 B.C.), the Shang Dynasty (1766–1122 B.C.), the Chou Dynasty (1122–253 B.C.) and the Ch'in Dynasty (255–206 B.C.), as well as the Han Dynasty up to and including the reign of the Emperor Wu. The period from the death of Confucius in the fifth century B.C. to the establishment of Confucianism as the state cult in the second century B.C. is the most important in Chinese history. During those centuries China, as we understand the term, came into existence. The size was about the same as it is today; the language was so similar that the present literary language hardly differs from it, a phenomenon as strange as if the Italians still wrote in classical Latin; the system of government then established was not changed until the founding of the Republic in this century; the various schools of political and moral philosophy continued century by century to be debated; and art, anchored to the classical forms and the theory of calligraphic line, provided the foundation for all that follows. In short, it may be said without undue paradox that, except for the introduction of Buddhism between the first and third century A.D., nothing of first importance happened in China after the periods covered by Ssu-ma

Ch'ien's *History*. Pursuing the paradox, one may declare that where he stopped, China stopped, and that, in consequence, everything necessary to the understanding of Chinese civilisation is contained in his book. Furthermore, not only is the History a most extensive and irreplaceable historical document, but it also created for the future what it described of the past. In detailed narrative it revealed ancient China to be the prototype of all that was desirable. Since this view of antiquity was accepted by the Chinese, it can be argued that the *History*, in providing a main source of information about antiquity, afforded the precedents necessary to sanction the subsequent Chinese way of life.

That the author of this *History*, so extraordinary both by its scholarship and its influence, should in addition to his labours of the study have had to solve a problem of personal conduct involving life and death, honour and disgrace, makes it difficult to find a parallel to his story. Though dramatic it does not lend itself to drama nor has it inspired any great biography. Nevertheless, it has survived and its present redaction here, inadequate though it is, is proof of its power still to move us.

For this book it has the further particular relevancy that it illustrates the opposition between the Confucian and Taoist points of view. Of Ssu-ma Ch'ien the Taoist would have said that he was too stubborn, too opinionated in spite of his good heart. Instead of trying to do the impossible and impose his conceptions of justice and right on the sort of men he met at Court, he should have lived in retirement and, undisturbed by mundane interruptions, have given his whole attention to his *History*. Sages lived in gardens or on mountains, refused to see ordinary people, never meddled in public affairs and under no circumstances accepted government appointments, or titles. To do any of these things was to seek trouble. Ssu-ma Ch'ien had done them all and so was the cause of his own misfortunes. His right course would have been to resign rather than battle on behalf of Li-ling, no matter what were the rights of the case, just as Confucius, instead of offering unwanted advice and services to the Grand Feudatories, should have with-drawn from the world, and so become a real sage.

To this argument the Confucian reply was that resignation was too easy, a life of retirement too pleasant and too selfish. A man of eminent qualities should struggle against opposition and not antici-pate that by a passive example he could overcome active wrong. Though he could not hope to command worldly success, for that depended on circumstances beyond his control, he should continue to strive, whether it was his or not, never forgetting that he was master of his own mind and that true greatness is to take with equanimity what may come.

8

Wu Finds a New Earth and Opens a Way to Heaven

The orthodox Confucian view of the frontier problem has been stated: if the Emperor's virtue were sufficient, there would be no problem, because the barbarians would come and submit voluntarily. The conception is beautifully put by Mencius, where he is speaking of the founder of the Shang Dynasty (1766 B.C.), who shared with the older Yao, Shun and Yü the reputation of being a Saviour King. 'When the Emperor T'ang advanced towards the East, the barbarians of the West were jealous; when he advanced towards the South, the barbarians of the North were jealous. They said: "Why did he not advance upon us first?" Everywhere the people turned their gaze towards him, as men gaze towards a rainbow in days of drought.'

This Confucian standpoint was not entirely fanciful. The virtue of the Chinese, using that term in the widest sense, had enabled them when, a savage tribe themselves, they had first settled in the basin of the Yellow River, to evolve a way of life superior to that of the other tribes, a civilisation which these, out of admiration, copied, until China proper expanded from being the Middle Kingdom, the area between the Yellow River and the Yang-tse, into what it now is. But virtue is compounded of many ingredients, in-

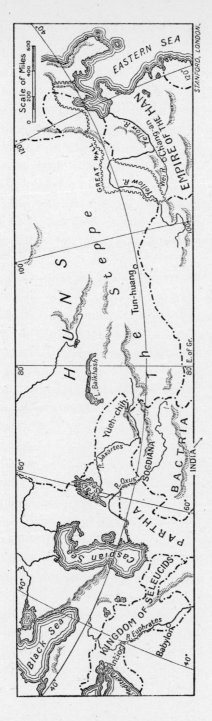

THE HAN EMPIRE AND THE HELLENISED WEST IN SECOND CENTURY B.C.

cluding prudence, for without that preservative it cannot survive; and part of prudence is to be practical. Though the Confucian dogmatists had a case, commonsense at least dictated that if the spectacle of virtue were insufficient to keep the barbarians quiet, other methods would have to be applied or they would burst in and that would be the end of the Chinese and their Confucianism. The Master himself was not such a fool as to think otherwise. When one day a disciple of his was criticising the famous politician Kuan Chung of the seventh century B.C. who had thrown back an invasion of the hill tribes, he remarked: 'Were it not for Kuan Chung we might now be wearing our hair loose and folding our clothes to the left.'

At that time it was hill tribes who endangered the existence of the small Chinese state, tribes whose territory afterwards became the outer provinces of China. On the north these tribes lay between the Gobi Desert and the Middle Kingdom. When by the third century B.C. they had been absorbed, the enlarged Chinese state was brought face to face with the far more formidable denizens of the steppe. These people were of various stocks. In antiquity they are said to have been Indo-European. By the third century the Huns, a Turkish speaking horde, were in position; later, in the thirteenth century A.D., the Tartars, Mongolian speaking, came in; and, four centuries afterwards, the Manchus, Tungus speaking and connected with the reindeer people of the sub-arctic tundras of Siberia. These last two steppe people conquered China and in the latter case Confucius's remark about hair came true, though in an inverted manner, for the Manchus obliged the Chinese to wear pigtails. Besides these two major barbarian conquests there were many others, and, though the Chinese had no dark age as long as Europe's after its barbarian invasions, for they always civilised their barbarians much quicker, an invasion from the steppe was always a dreadful catastrophe. The knowledge that such a fate threatened perpetually was never absent from the minds of Chinese rulers. The nomads had to be kept out somehow, by virtue, by treaties, by the Wall, or, failing all else, by carrying war into the steppe, a desperate undertaking since no final victory would be won in a country that had no end.

The early Emperors of the Han were very civil to the Hun Shan-yü. The first of the line sent him an Imperial princess; the third presented him with food and clothing. A letter from this Emperor is extant. It begins: 'We respectfully trust that the Great Captain is well. We have respectfully received two horses which the Great Captain forwarded to us.' And goes on to beg him to live quietly in his own country. 'Let us forget bygone troubles in a sincere desire to cement an enduring friendship. The rulers of old never broke their treaties. May you remember this, Great Captain.' So wrote the Emperor Wen, the appeaser.

But the Huns were not amenable to arguments of this kind. They continually raided the frontier, killing and looting, and in the winter of 167/6 B.C., during the mild reign of this same Emperor, were so bold as to enter the metropolitan province and burn one of the Imperial palaces. They were beaten off with difficulty.

The Emperor Wu spent a great deal more on the army than had his predecessors and, being much stronger than were they, abandoned appeasement and a defensive policy for offensive operations. A glimpse of him has already been given in this connection when in 111 B.C. he passed through the Great Wall, mounted the Shan-yü's terrace and challenged him to fight.[1] We have also seen in more detail the disaster which overtook his General, Li-ling, in 99 B.C. These were, however, mere episodes in a struggle which lasted the whole of his reign without a decision, for the Huns could not be decisively defeated. It was in the course of his efforts to corner the Shan-yü, that Wu made the discoveries named at the head of this chapter.

While it was useless to drive straight into the Hun's territory, for they retreated into the endless North, it struck him that their right flank might be turned if he could ally himself with other

[1]See page 113.

nomads lying to the west of them. To effect this he sent in 138 B.C. Chang Ch'ien, one of the most tenacious and intrepid explorers who ever lived, to get in touch with a nomad tribe known to the Chinese as the Yüeh Chi, who were probably of Indo-European stock. Proceeding due west from the capital, Chang Ch'ien made his way along the corridor which exists between the north of Tibet and the steppe, and after travelling two thousand miles through deserts, oases, and over high passes, emerged from the belt of savagery which sealed off China and found himself in regions where there were towns, mansions, law, coinage, and the other amenities of civilisation. He had arrived in that part of the world which we know as Sogdiana, Bactria, Parthia, and the N.W. frontier of India.

We are more familiar with the names of these countries and their principal towns than we might be expected to be, did they not occur in a resounding passage of *Paradise Regained*, one often committed to memory in youth and which, if read in maturity, makes on some so profound an impression with its rolling cadences that insensibility thereto is held more than any other lack to brand a man a barbarian. The Adversary and the Saviour are in colloquy upon the mount. They look north-eastwards across the Euphrates towards the country which used to be the Persia of Darius before Alexander overwhelmed it in 333 B.C., and which became on his death the Greek kingdom of the Seleucids. At the time of the vision it was Parthia, ruled by nomads who had come down from the steppe in 250 B.C., and had adopted the Greek civilisation which obtained there. The Adversary in splendid language, which also shows a very exact historical knowledge, draws the Saviour's attention to their various cities, Bactra, Hecatompylos, Seleucia, Susa, and uses Artaxata, Teredon, Ctesiphon, to form a great line of English blank verse. Mustered at the third of these cities and issuing from its gates, is the Parthian host, for the King is marching to the aid of Sogdiana, a former Greek kingdom between the Oxus and the Jaxartes, which has been attacked by wild nomads from the steppe. The vast array is composed chiefly of horse-archers, for the Parthians, though they had become hellenised, retained the nomad tactics and equipment of the steppe, which had enabled them to defeat the Macedonian phalanx of the Greek Seleucids and destroy the Roman legions at Carrhae in 53 B.C. The classical nomad tactics are given in the lines:

> *How quick they wheeled, and flying behind them shot*
> *Sharp sleet of arrowy showers against the face*
> *Of their pursuers, and overcame by flight.*

And the Parthians' later development of the heavy cuirassier is noticed, the mailed lancer, mounted on the powerful horse bred in the plains of Media south of the Caspian, who charged when the archers had forced or induced the opposing infantry to break formation. At the conclusion of the description, the most memorable ever penned of a civilised steppe army marching against the wild steppe, comes the comparison which lifts the whole into the realm of the high baroque, lines which must be quoted, for the reader will not be cheated of them, and, were I to omit them, would put my book aside to get the other:

> *Such forces met not, nor so wide a camp,*
> *When Agrican, with all his northern powers,*
> *Beseiged Albracca, as romances tell,*
> *The city of Gallaphrone, from thence to win,*
> *The fairest of her sex, Angelica,*
> *His daughter, sought by many prowest knights,*
> *Both Paynim and the peers of Charlemain:*
> *Such and so numerous was their chivalry.*

Agrican was a Shan-yü of the steppe and Gallaphrone was Emperor of China. Angelica, his daughter, after innumerable adventures, retires heartsick to the castle of Albracca within her father's domain. Thither coming the Shan-yü Agrican to take her for love, he besieges the castle, but is slain in single combat by Orlando, who has galloped to her rescue. So does the steppe figure in the epic romance of Europe. The reader of this book is well equipped to savour the paradox. Let him open his Bojardo and his Ariosto. They will give him a sense of largeness, of vast interminglings of East and West. Orlando, the Roland, who fell at Roncesvalles 'sounding terribly his horn after the dolorous rout when Charlemain lost the sainted emprise',[1] to be infatuated with the Son of Heaven's daughter and to deliver her from the Shan yü, what elbow-room, what fine disregard of fact, what abandoned imagination, what a flight for giants!

Yet, the sober truth we are about to relate in this chapter of the intermingling of East and West is hardly less extravagant than the adventures of *la bella Angelica*.

The Emperor Wu's emissary, as we have said, burst through the crust of the sinic world in his search for the Yüeh-chi, and found them installed in the north part of the Greek kingdom of Bactria, into which they had been driven by the pressure which the Huns were exerting on the steppe. As the Emperor Wu sent several more missions between 138 and 100 B.C., whose members visited Parthia, Bactria and India, he will have gradually accumulated enough information to give him some notion of the new earth he had discovered. But he cannot have learned all we know. What is here to be given will be the whole story in outline. It will reveal how, in this remote corner, almost exactly equidistant from Rome and Ch'ang-an, events of a very queer nature were brewing, destined to become a threat to Confucianism.

First as to the Greek overseas empire, to the edge of which Chang Ch'ien had strayed. The following pointers are offered on this vast subject. In 480 B.C., approximately the year of Confucius' death, Xerxes, King of Persia, not only the strongest sovereign of the orient but of the whole world at that date, tried to take Greece, the heart of western civilisation, and failed. In 334 B.C., when Mencius was 38 years of age, Alexander, the pupil of Aristotle, at the head

[1]Dante's *Inferno*, Canto XXXI, i, 16.

of his Macedonians, who were hellenised barbarians living north of the Greek city states which had been obliged to acknowledge them as their overlords, invaded Persia, as the leader of western civilisation, and seized the whole of the Persian Empire, which included Egypt, Syria, Asia Minor, Bactria, Sogdiana and Afghanistan to the Indus. This was a conquest of the civilised world, except for the nascent republic of Rome, the Hindu kingdoms of India, and the Grand Feudatories of the Chou dynasty in China. All else on the globe was savagery. The result of the transference of the government of this great and fecund area from Persian to Macedonian hands was the introduction thereto of the miraculous heritage of Greece in literature, painting, philosophy, sculpture, architecture and politics. As Greek thought already enjoyed a prodigious reputation, the inhabitants of the Persian realms hellenised themselves as fast and as thoroughly as they could under the direction of Alexander's successor Kings, the Seleucids in Syria and the Ptolemies in Egypt. The inhabitants of Athens, Corinth, Thebes and the other Greek cities whose ancestors, during the lifetime of Confucius and in the century after his death, had created the glittering life and art we still adore, were poor, but now began to enjoy, as it were, the deferred foreign royalties on the books of Aeschylus, Sophocles, Plato and the rest, so that any Greek who could write a drama, spin a philosophical commentary, compose a copy of verses, or edit a classic, was sure of a lucrative appointment in Asia, at the Court of Antioch or Alexandria, or in one of the very numerous Greek-named cities with democratic constitutions, which were built all over the East, as far as Sogdiana and the Indus, with their theatres, colonnades, temples, libraries, and where Greek architects, sculptors, painters and engravers were no less welcome. Here such Greeks lived in far greater comfort than ever they or their ancestors had at home, and though few of them had creative genius and could do more than work in the tradition, they had such a wonderful tradition, such personal cleverness and such an appreciative following, that they were able to make a new Greece overseas, less fresh and profound than the old, but more luxurious, opulent and sensational. An enthusiastic audience saluted with frantic applause the austere masks of the classical masters. Every inhabitant of this great Asian realm, who had any pretentions to gentility and culture, wanted to learn Greek, read the Greek classics, dispute in the Greek way and adopt the Greek life of the theatre, the temple, the market place and the assembly. This spectacle of Greece enjoying a cosmopolitan celebrity was watched with admiring eyes by rustic Rome.

While, in this way, the whole world, with the exceptions aforesaid, had gone Greek, the Nanda power in the Gangetic plain gave place to the Maurya Dynasty, and in 274 B.C. Asoka came to the throne, his capital at Patna, which is in the vicinity of Buddh Gaya, the spot where the Buddha had found enlightenment. The Buddha's dates being 560–480 B.C., he was thirty-five years older than Aeschylus, who was born in 525 B.C., and was the exact contemporary of Confucius, who died in 479 B.C. If Confucius was a remarkable man, the Buddha may be claimed to have been as remarkable. In many respects he was the opposite of the other. Thus, while Confucius' main ambition was to get into government employ, the Buddha's first precaution was to get out of it. As the heir-apparent of a respectable state he was well placed to be a philosopher King. But he preferred what Confucius would have condemned and left the Court to live as a hermit, just as if he were a Taoist. His meditations led him to certain conclusions, which he described as his enlightenment. These were of two sorts, philosophical and ethical. In the first, starting from the premise that life was evil, and that endless rebirths were a fact, the latter a Hindu dogma of great antiquity, he declared that the rebirths could be made to cease if desire for life and all that it afforded were eliminated, for without such desire there could be no personality. With the obliteration of personality, a state of bliss was reached.

While such speculations as these would have seemed to Confucius of no value, he would have agreed with the Buddha's ethical con-

XIA. KING EUCRATIDES

B. KING DIODOTOS   C. KING MENANDER

(see pages 182-185)

XII. THE GRECO-BUDDHIST RELIQUARY OF BIMARAN

clusions which enjoined the same practical right behaviour as he did. Confucius always wanted a ruler who would give official backing to his ideas about right conduct, but had to wait three hundred years for the Han Founder. The Buddha did not seek for any such ruler, but one was accorded two hundred years later in the person of the aforementioned Asoka,[1] who, declaring his admiration for the Buddhist ethic, set up a humane government, whose officials were instructed to provide free medical attention, a kind jail administration, poor relief, old age pensions, amenities for travellers and animal hospitals, while they admonished the people to be dutiful to parents, kind to children and servants, charitable and tolerant. Asoka's frontier policy was in the same vein; he renounced war as a method of settling disputes, and in a proclamation addressed to the border tribes he told them not to be afraid of him, for his heartfelt desire was to be good to them. That this was pure Confucianism shows how applicable to all the world were the teachings of the Sage.

On the numerous stone pillars that Asoka set up were long inscriptions in which he lectured the people in a fatherly tone, and to some extent took them into his confidence, explaining how he had been touched to believe in the Buddha's conception of right conduct by the shock he had sustained in the early years of his reign by seeing with his own eyes the miseries he had inflicted on the Kalinga state to the south of him, by making war on it. But he did not refer to the speculative side of the Buddha's teaching nor invite the people, who from time immemorial had believed in their Hindu deities, to abandon them in favour of the Buddha. Did he then regard the Buddha, as Wu did Confucius, as no more than a sage? (The Buddha himself claimed no more; Confucius did not claim as much.) The question may be answered in the following way. During the two hundred years that had elapsed between the Buddha's death and Asoka's reign, the Master's disciples had com-

---

[1]His reign was contemporary with the rise of the Ch'in power, inspired by Lord Shang's ideas, the exact opposite of Buddhism as of Confucianism.

posed many books about him, and their followers, becoming
numerous, certainly believed already that he was more than a man.
Had he not discovered the secret of how to avoid being born again?
No man had ever discovered that before. Where was he? What was
the blissful state of non-personality in which he existed? These
were mysterious and entrancing questions. Many people were occupied in trying to answer them. In the process, the Buddha became
less human, more divine. The division between a great sage and a
deity is not easy to define, for a great sage acquires supernatural
powers. There can be, I imagine, little doubt that Asoka, despite
any reference to these matters in his inscriptions, the absence of
any sculptured representation of the Buddha on his pillars, and the
fact that he encouraged the people to worship the Hindu gods and
respect their priests, regarded the person whose moral doctrines he
propagated as supernaturally endowed. The large number of votive
shrines he is reputed to have erected to him throughout his dominion is proof of this. In short, by 250 B.C. the Buddha had begun
to discard the trappings of mortality, which Confucius had not, nor
ever did, in spite of the existence of temples dedicated to him.

Such was Asoka, a very different person from the Emperor Wu.
Having the Buddha, he was under no necessity to go round the
sacred mountains of India, supplicating Heaven to reassure him.
He had all the assurance he required. Buddhism had become a
divine revelation; the particularity of Confucianism was that its
Heaven had never vouchsafed a revelation.

Asoka's realm marching with that of the Greek Seleucids (his predecessor had pushed the frontier from the Indus to central Afghanistan), there was diplomatic, commercial and intellectual intercourse between the two.[1] For instance, his pillars with their inscriptions, reliefs and animal sculptures in the round, were inspired
by models to be found in the Greek lands, some of them pre-
Greek, being Assyrian, Persian and Egyptian. From these his artists

---

[1] In the reign of Asoka's father, the Greek envoy Megasthenes stayed some months
in Patna. His despatches are lost, though quotations from them are preserved.

wrought a magistral Indian synthesis. His are the earliest Indian stone sculptures that have come down to us, since we do not possess any Hindu sculpture of the earlier periods. Such art must have existed, though perhaps only in perishable materials, and it will have included representations of the human figure, for the Hindu deities, angels and tutelary spirits were legion. Nevertheless, Asoka did not draw upon that source to advertise the Buddha and his circle. Nor did he draw upon the vast store of Greek figure sculpture which was to be found in the utmost profusion in the hellenised East. For this extraordinary restraint he had his reasons, though they are difficult to state. Evidently, the vogue among Buddhists was to represent their Master only by symbols, such as the Wheel of the Law, because they wished to be different from the Hindus with their images. Moreover, his *paraninvana*, as his passage from life into the freedom of non-personality was termed, was a great mystery, the contemplation of which left one confused about his identity, so that to give him the appearance of the identity which it had been his object to discard might be inappropriate. And there was the further consideration: the Buddha, after all, had been an atheist, for the truth had not come to him from calling upon any god; that he himself should now be represented as a mere god would be a paradox. It was therefore more proper to suggest him by symbol.

Asoka had no feeling of inferiority *vis-à-vis* the Seleucid kingdom beyond his frontiers. Though he made use of a few of its art forms as they suited his purposes, he was not dazzled by its lavish display of philosophies, literature, mythology, politics. On the contrary, he thought that he knew truths which it was his duty as a humane man to make available to the Greeks. Accordingly, he despatched several missions, composed of Buddhist monks, to Antioch of the Seleucids, to Alexandria of the Ptolemies, and to Macedonia itself. The Seleucid Kings, Antiochus Soter and Antiochus Theos, who were Asoka's contemporaries, were noted for their interest in oriental ideas. At this time, for instance, a Chaldean called Berosus published in Greek the history and mythology of Babylon taken from the cuneiform records. In Egypt, too, a Greek history of Egypt had been translated from the hieroglyphics for Ptolemy Philadephus. The Hebrew Pentateuch in Greek also dates from this time. The Greeks of the dispersion were highly sophisticated; as they believed in nothing in particular, they were always on the look-out for something new to believe in. They had been fascinated, for instance, by oriental astrology. Like us still, they associated the East with marvels. How Alexander at Peshawar tried, through an interpreter, to get the Indian ascetics to tell him their secrets is a typical story.

But in spite of these predisposing circumstances, the Greeks do not seem to have been much interested in Asoka's Buddhist envoys. We cannot tell precisely why, but may guess that what the visiting monks had to say was not sensational enough. If the lectures they gave were similar to those which Asoka gave his subjects on the pillars, they will have been concerned exclusively with moral behaviour, both for private individuals and the state as a whole, a subject which for two and a half millennia the Chinese have found quite absorbing, but which to the Greeks, in the decadence following their classic period, would have seemed intolerably wearisome. Had the monks been able to announce that India had found a Saviour, a new deity more powerful than any of the old, kinder and sweeter, who promised eternal happiness, redemption, paradise, who had performed miracles, conversed with Heaven, who knew the last secrets of the Elixir, and who, for men of intellect, had a metaphysic to prove his transcendence, then, indeed, we may be sure, the envoys would have had a great reception. Their writings would have been translated into Greek and been read everywhere Greek was understood. Buddhism might have become the religion of the whole West. But this did not happen. The envoys did not present the Buddha in that guise, for he was not yet conceived of thus, being still half way between sage and deity. His moralities fell as flat as would have those of Confucius, had the Master's dicta, as preserved in the *Analects*, been circulated among the Greek cognoscenti.

This brings us to the next episode in the surprising story. In 250 B.C. when Asoka had been fifteen years on the throne, the Parthians, who were kinsmen of the Scythians at whose doorstep the wretched Ovid was to languish, began to move down from the steppe in the vicinity of the Sea of Aral, being pressed like the Yüeh-chi by the Huns, and, crossing the Jaxartes and the Oxus, in due course broke into the territory of the Seleucids westwards of Afghanistan, and drove on south, under their leader Arsaces, to Hecatompylos, and the heart of old Persia, Persepolis. They did not, however, enter the mountainous country to the East where lay the Greek states of Sogdiana and Bactria which then were vice-royalties under the Seleucids. In the part of the Seleucid territory which they occupied they founded a kingdom. Like most nomads who conquered sedentary peoples, they immediately came under the influence of the higher civilisation which they had overthrown. Adopting everything they found, the government machinery, the coinage and the way of life, they became as Greekophil as the local population. On their coins was the legend: 'the King of Kings, Arsaces, the just, the illustrious, the beneficent, the friend of the Greeks.' That they even came to appreciate Greek classical tragedy is proved by the following well-known story.

When the Roman millionaire, Crassus, who at the time was sixty, though he looked more, was taken by the Parthians after his defeat at Carrhae, his head was cut off and carried by special messenger to the capital, Seleucia. On the messenger's arrival, King Orodes, the reigning monarch, happened to be at the theatre, watching the *Bacchae* of Euripides. The messenger, not sure whether, even with his trophy and news of victory, he could interrupt a command performance of a Greek classic, hesitated to burst into the presence. The actor, who was taking the female part of Agave, then had a brilliant idea. He would announce the victory from the stage by making use of Crassus' head. Behind the scenes, the

Theban women were supposed at the moment to be tearing to pieces the unfortunate King Pentheus, and in a moment Agave had to come in, bearing aloft the mask which represented the King's severed head. Grasping the Roman's instead, the player made his entry. His action was perhaps not quite in keeping with classical decorum, but it was certainly dramatic. Somehow, the word was passed round whose head it was and that the Roman legions had been annihilated. It is impossible to imagine a more telling curtain. One is glad to know that King Orodes immediately had a talent carried up and presented to the resourceful tragedian. In the Victorian era this story shocked Mommsen, the Roman historian, very much. How times have changed! We find it so droll.

The Parthian empire lasted from 250 B.C. to 220 A.D., the Han from 206 B.C. to 220 A.D. The history of the latter we know in the minutest detail through the labours of the great historians, Ssu-ma Ch'ien and Pan Ku. Of Parthian history we are largely ignorant, because the Greeks did not write it. Nevertheless, we possess an excellent portrait of nearly every Parthian King, thanks to the Greek artists they employed at their mint. But no portraits of Han Emperors survive, for they did not stamp them on their coins, nor carve them in stone, and their painted likenesses have perished. So we shall never know what Wu looked like. The Greek capacity and desire to make likenesses of men and women far exceeded that of any other nation of antiquity. This is the key to the sequel to which we are advancing.

The effect of the Parthian irruption from the steppe in 250 B.C. was, as stated, to drive a wedge between the western part of the Seleucid kingdom and the Bactria–Sogdiana viceroyalties on the east. Cut off from the home government in this way, the Bactrian Greeks established shortly afterwards a kingship under Diodotos, their Viceroy, who claimed to be a descendant of Alexander. It is important to remark that in Bactria there happened to be some of the very best Greek artists, as one may perceive by looking, for instance, at a gold stater of Diodotos, a most melting portrait,

and Opens a Way to Heaven

with a beautifully modelled naked boy on the obverse. When
Chang Ch'ien, Wu's emissary, reached Bactria about 130 B.C., he
found, as has been reported, that the steppe Yüeh-chi were occupy-
ing the northern part of it. In fact, the Bactrian Kings—it was a
King Demetrius—had moved their capital southwards sixty years
earlier, and the Yüeh-chi, no longer nomads, were already becoming hellenised. Demetrius had moved south, partly because of
pressure both from the Parthians and the steppe, and partly because, after Asoka's death in 237 B.C., the Maurya Empire had
broken up and, as no paramount power took its place, Afghanistan
and the Punjab, which lay adjacent to Bactria and had known Greek
rule in the early days of the Seleucids, were left without a master.
What more natural than that King Demetrius should descend and
assume that mastery, more particularly since Alexander, his ancestor, had campaigned there and his name was still uttered with
wonder and admiration, as, indeed, it still is in rural parts of that
land? He started south in 190 B.C. and, passing through Afghanistan, took possession of the Punjab without difficulty, as there
was no central power to oppose him. But in 175 B.C. a certain
Eucratides rebelled with the result that he was able to seize half of
Demetrius's territory. What Chang Ch'ien actually found in 130
B.C. was the house of Eucratides ruling southern Bactria, the Kabul
valley and India to the Jhelum, with the house of Demetrius in the
Punjab, his capital at Sialkot.

In short, the Greeks, with the whole apparatus of hellenism behind them, had moved into Buddhist India. During the century
which had elapsed since the death of Asoka and the end of his dynasty, Buddhism, though it had ceased to guide any imperial overlord, for none existed, continued to develop as a religion. A myth,
which was to turn the Buddha fully into a divine Saviour, was
building up. This was far more to the taste of the Greeks than
what Asoka's missionaries had had to say, and they were now
brought into close contact with it.

The reader who is unfamiliar with the hellenism of the dispersal

183

may be surprised at my insistence that the later Greeks were on the look out for a Saviour. On the contrary, he may urge, later Greek thought was dominated by the doctrines of the Stoics, the Cynics, and the Epicureans, the famous Three Schools founded in the fourth and third centuries B.C., which, gathering up the fruits of the wide speculations of the fifth century, sought in their various ways to indicate to rational man how to govern himself without resort to mythology. For instance, the Stoics, like the Confucians, posited a divine purpose and declared that if man lived a life which was practically wise, human and beneficent, he would be forwarding that purpose and not all the world's apparent evil need cause him to despair or deviate from virtuous conduct. Epicurus went further, declaring that man, if to stoic virtue he added affection, could not only stave off evil and supernatural fears, but be actively happy. 'Reason is the god within us,' declared the Cynics, 'and that suffices a man.'

But, in fact, these magnificent efforts to steady man by reason in the face of death, catastrophe, pain and the other evils of common existence, did not suffice the later Greeks. The old gods of Olympus had been explained away, but there were other deities, of whom Asia had knowledge, other supernal beings, refuges, saviours, other mysteries, ways of communicating with heaven, other succouring voices, other transcendent paths. And just as the Emperor Wu, not satisfied with, insufficiently comforted by, his Confucianism, so like what the Stoics taught, went in search of the Fortunate Isles, seeking the elixir, of all imaginations the most entrancing, for without submission to death's hand and the unnerving passage to paradise, you became, in life and full daylight sense of being, as endowed as any god, deathless and invincible, so, too, those Greeks, and there were many as they became more orientalised, for whom the virtuous path, brave reason, simple pleasures, the wry smile of the Three Schools were too stiff and called for too calm a courage, sought for salvation in supernatural assurances. The religious archives of Babylon, old Egypt, hoary Judaea were ransacked; ancient mystery cults were refurbished, new ones discovered. Syria had an encyclopaedia of marvels. Every endowment that a god made flesh should possess was tabulated, his state in heaven, how he should announce his coming down, how he should be born, the signs that should accompany it, his precocious wisdom, the miracles of his maturity, the sacrifice of himself, his promise of salvation.

When, therefore, I write of the Greeks arriving in India in the second century B.C. with all the apparatus of hellenism, I should be understood to mean in particular that along with their purely Greek craftsmanship in sculpture and glyptics they brought a thorough acquaintance with current near-eastern revelation. They had already equipped all sorts of transcendent beings and divine kings, supplying not only the representations in stone or metal required to propagate these epiphanies, but also the literary expression for the same. Now in India they were to find a fresh subject for their skill as sculptors and narrators in the person of the Buddha, already created a high divinity by the Indians, but not fully fitted out to conquer Asia.

The exact date when the Greeks began to turn their attention to Buddhism cannot be stated. No doubt they had heard of it before they moved south from Bactria. Asoka's missionaries in the third century B.C. will have assured that. Whether by 130 B.C., the year of Chang Ch'ien's arrival in those parts, any of them had become Buddhists is impossible to say, but that they had begun to interest themselves in the religion is certain. Proof of this is the extant dialogue between the Indo-Greek King Menander (170–150 B.C.) and a Buddhist philosopher, preserved in a Pali book called the *Milindapanha*.

With the turn into the first century A.D. they began actively to advance the Buddhist religion. Part of this subvention took the form of providing an iconography of the Buddha. As has been pointed out, King Asoka of India made no images of the founder of the religion which he turned into a state cult. The Greeks, with their enormous experience of figure sculpture of all kinds, were

well qualified to evolve a suitable form, and it was natural for them
to do so. It is well to remember here that during the period we have
been traversing, Rome gradually rose to paramountcy in the Mediterranean and, sixteen years before Chang Ch'ien reached the Greek
kingdoms, the Romans had reduced Greece to the condition of a
Roman province. The Greek style evolved gradually into the Greco-
Roman. This modification of style became felt even on the con-
fines of the Greek world, particularly after the conquest in 66 B.C.
of the Seleucids by Pompey. And it was this evolved style that the
Greeks in India employed to represent the Buddha in stone. Quan-
tities of this statuary have survived, though some experts declare
that none of it so far unearthed is earlier than the first century A.D.
As, however, the Greek governments came to an end before that,
being overwhelmed about 50 B.C. by the Yüeh-chi, who, now
called Kushans, pressed after them into India, it would follow, if
the experts are right, that the statuary, which we have, was made
during the Kushan overlordship. Strictly speaking, therefore, these
carvings, known as the Ghandāra style, were not made in the Greek
kingdoms but by the hellenised barbarians that followed them, and
so were an expression of the Greek genius at second hand.

With these reservations in mind, which cannot affect the main
statement that the Greeks invented an iconography for the Buddha
(for even if the Greek government had fallen, the Greek artists
were still there, and the government, if not Greek by race, was
Greek by culture), we may proceed to examine their achievement
more closely. The Buddha is represented as a Greek god or deified
king. The Greeks did not invent the deified king, because that was
a long-established eastern conception. Alexander, after conquering
Persia, allowed himself to be hailed as a god, the god who had
overthrown the god, Darius. The Seleucids were glad to accept the
same flattering ascription. Their titles declare this; for instance,
Antiochus Soter, the Saviour, and Antiochus Epiphanes, the god
made manifest. The Ptolemies were not behindhand; in 271 B.C.
Ptolemy Philadephus proclaimed himself a god and ordained how

he was to be worshipped. We know how later the Caesars made the same arrangements. The Greeks tried to give this extravagance an air of reasonableness by arguing that they were merely continuing an old practice; the gods of their classical mythology were, in real fact, they declared, deified rulers, and had become gods because while men they had virtuously used their power, not to oppress but to help their fellows, for to love and succour humanity was the most divine of virtues, as the Stoics themselves had always insisted (though never, of course, in so vulgar a connection). For the Greeks to represent the Buddha as a deified king was, therefore, a normal application of their current ideas. They dressed him in the Greco-Roman costume of the period, which in the statues that we possess is a toga. No doubt the immemorial robe of the Indian ascetics, including the Buddhist monks, had a resemblance to the Greco-Roman outdoor mantle. What the Greeks did was to tidy this oriental robe, arrange its folds and govern its fall by the graceful artifices of their canon. But though the Buddha was dressed up as a Greek god-king, he was given an oriental face, the face that belonged to the Punjab. His poses and gestures, together with certain appurtenances, were also Indian. Thus, he is provided with the eye of wisdom in the centre of his forehead, the mount of wisdom on the top of his head, some of the gestures called hand mudras, and, if seated, was in the posture associated with Indian meditation, the legs crossed under him, the right foot curled on to the opposite thigh, a position impossible for a European. That this was a popular innovation is proved by the fact that it was soon copied by the indigenous schools of Buddhist sculpture outside the Greek area of the north-west, for instance, at Bharhut and Sanchi in central India, which were in existence in the second century B.C., and later at Amarāvati in the south. In sum, though experts may argue as to the precise date of extant specimens of the Greco-Roman carved figures of the Buddha, it is established beyond question that this art was brought into existence by the Greeks, working particularly in the region of Ghandāra round Peshawar, at the time when their culture was dominant there; that it created the first sculptured image of the Buddha; that these images were meant to be worshipped; that the Buddhists in other parts of India soon afterwards abandoned the practice of denoting their Founder by symbols and showed him as a god after the Greek model; and that this Greco-Roman representation was the prototype of all his subsequent myriad images throughout Asia as far east as Japan. So, just as the Greeks used their art to manifest Mithras, one of the Saviours thrown up at this time in Syria, just as they also supplied in due course the Christians with an iconography, which served as a model for future Christian art, they also supplied, with the magnificent impartiality of supreme talent, all Asia with a vehicle for the propagation of its saviour religion, the new Buddhism, called afterwards the Mahayana, in which the Buddha figures, not as a sage, or god, but as Almighty God.

This is the moment to clear up a point. I have spoken of the Indian indigenous sculpture which, in the period under reference, is to be seen only in Buddhist monuments, as at Sanchi, Barhut and Amarāvati. This indigenous sculpture, whose earliest extant specimens date from Asoka's pillars of the third century B.C., represents a sculptural movement parallel and contemporary with the development of sculpture in the regions between India and Greece. It may be called the same kind of sculpture, not hieratic like the Egyptian and Assyrian, but human or naturalistic. Having this common ground with hellenic sculpture, it evolved in an analogous canon of articulated rhythm and proportion and created an ideal beauty, similar to our own. But its mood is different. It is wilder, sweeter, more tranced, than we know, more daring, more elemental, more ultimate, more pagan, thereby partaking more grandly of the divine, the unknown puissance that rolls through all things. This great Hindu art was so rooted in the soil and climate of India and its beliefs, that it could not migrate like those of other religions. Its influence outside its own region has been limited to the early Indian colonies. But Greco-Roman art was essentially cosmopolitan and allied with the new Buddhism, which I am about to describe, the religion of a Saviour, ready and eager to succour all mankind, spread to the vast expanses and millions of China along the route first opened by Chang Ch'ien.

In describing what this new Buddhism was like, which demanded a Greek image of its founder, we have simultaneously to consider whether the Greeks, besides being its sculptors, were also in part its mythographers. In short, did they help to conceive this saviour religion called the Mahayana, as they helped to conceive Mithraism and Christianity? The new earth which Wu found was the Greco-Roman world; was the new saviour to whom he opened the road into China to some extent a Greek saviour? Did the Greeks help to send a saviour to the East as well as to the West? The answer would seem to be that just as Judaism and Hellenism evolved the Christian mythology, so Hinduism and Hellenism evolved the Mahayanist. One is led to this view by the mere enumeration of its principal elements. The Buddha, a real eremite teacher of four centuries earlier, has become a sumptuous transcendent being. The first scene of his mythical biography is laid in Heaven. There he is seen in an assembly of the gods, to whom he announces, as their master, his approaching descent to earth in order to save mankind from the sorrows of life. The wife of a certain king is selected for his mother. It should be noted that he is represented, not as the son of God, but as superior to all gods and therefore as the perfection of sapience or God.

The next scene is the immaculate conception by his selected mother, who in a dream sees a white elephant with six tusks enter her right side. The white elephant is, as it were, an emanation of the Buddha himself; he has come down from Heaven in that form.

In scene three is the virgin birth. His mother standing in a garden is delivered of the Buddha, who issues from her right hip without causing a wound.

Next the Brahman hermit sage Asita visits the infant and hails him as a saviour, foretelling his greatness; an anecdote recalling what is related in our books of John the Baptist.

The mother dies and immediately is born in heaven, a sort of assumption. The Buddha as a boy astonishes his teachers by his intuitive knowledge of philosophy. When he grows up, his unhappiness at the world's pain causes him to leave his father's palace and go wandering as an ascetic to find the cause of sorrow and how to save mankind from its dominion. During a meditation he is tempted by Mara, a devil, who tries to lure him back to the world by a parade of lovely women. At last his meditations yield him knowledge of the truth and he perceives the cause and prevention of human suffering. The Four Kings bring him gifts of bowls, as it were a visit of Magi. Thereafter he begins his mission to men, resolved to show them the way of salvation. Five disciples to whom he first teaches his gospel accompany him as he goes preaching through the villages and converting the people. He has a favourite disciple called Ananda. He performs miracles. A light radiates from him. At the age of eighty when he feels death approaching he is tempted to use his supernatural powers to defy death and live on, but he does not do so, as he holds it to be his duty to die. Death comes in the painful form of a fatal attack of dysentery. After his death, he prepared for those who believed in him a wonderful paradise and showed how all might reach it. He develops later into one member of a Trinity. A second coming is also foretold.

No one knows exactly how this story came into existence. But that it had been largely formulated about the initial date of our era is probable. It has the appearance of a hellenistic story which has also Hindu elements and is made to fit round the main facts of the real Buddha's life, facts like his birth in a royal house, his renunciation of his heirdom, and his life as an itinerant sage. It may have been built up slowly between the death of Alexander and the first century B.C. by the Indians under influences from the Seleucid kingdom, and it may owe its final form to some particular writer unknown during the Greek rule of north-west India. It was never believed by an important section of Indian Buddhists, known afterwards as the Hinayanists, who flatly regarded it as an invention, and declared to be the truth their version of the Buddha's life which, though it contains a degree of mythology, is in comparison a modest elaboration of his actual biography.

But it was the Mahayana, the fictional form with the Buddha as deified saviour, that was to conquer, rather than the historical, because the Eastern world demanded a saviour. By the time, some centuries later, when Indians decided to have nothing further to do with Buddhism either in its fictional or original form, and returned wholly to their ancient Hindu mythology, the Mahayana was firmly set in China and the surrounding countries, while the Hinayana had a precarious hold only on the one island of Ceylon.

As I have said further back, Wu could only have known a part of this extraordinary story. The reports that he had from Chang Ch'ien and the other emissaries he sent to the western regions could assure him of the existence of the new earth, a new earth which should have caused him to abate his claim to be Lord of the World, but did not, nor ever did abate that claim, which was maintained by his successors till 1912 A.D. But the news that, four hundred years before his time, a saviour had lived in India, a transcendent deity higher than the gods, a being who had come down to earth and made a revelation, assuring mankind of redemption from sorrow and of a certain home in a paradise of bliss, that intelligence, I think, he will not have received, though for him, weary and discomforted by his fruitless search for a voice, a sign, a guarantee of immortality, it would have been joyful tidings. Nevertheless, if not carried by his emissaries, the news was to come down the very road which they had opened. The new mythology became with time infinitely more complex, with its heavenly hosts, angels, presences, its multiplication of Buddhas, mystical bodies, recess within recess, sphere upon sphere, and particularly its lovely conception of the Boddhisatva, the supernal saint who, to succour the world, delays his own entry into the void, the void that is sweeter than even the bliss of paradise. Behind this mythology was constructed a metaphysic. And here again the question arises—had Greek thought a hand also in this?

The metaphysic of the Mahayana took its rise in the first century A.D. and developed until the fifth. Its four great philosophers are Asvaghosha, Nagarjuna, Asanga and Vasubandhu. The system of thought they developed is excessively obstruse and a lifetime might be spent in disentangling its intricacies. But its object can be simply stated. This was to explain how a man might apprehend the state of Buddhahood, i.e. divinity, by himself entering it and experiencing the sensation of an absolute union with the divine, a union in which this and that, the subject and the object, the individual and God, coalesced so that all duality melted into an overwhelming realisation of a oneness, which was truth. This condition, in which the ego disappeared, was called the Void, but was equally the Plenitude, being the essential nature of things or Suchness, an absolute that was both the substance and the processus of all things. In terms of this kind was described the Nirvana into which the Buddha originally was supposed to have withdrawn, the mysterious state of non-personality, the state which seemed like nothingness, since all things had disappeared, but which was really all things, for nothingness had disappeared. The attainment of this state of mind was equivalent to attaining the powers of the Elixir, for to be sensible of such ultimates was to be invincible in the face of all earthly vicissitudes. Nevertheless, it is insisted, such powers have no existence in the temporal or phenomenal sense. But the very non-existence of their existence is proof that they exist, for apparent existence is unreal, and unapparent real. Therefore, the answer to the question—where did the Buddha come from?—is, nowhere; the answer to the question—where did the Buddha go to?—is, nowhere; for he never moved from where he always was, which is where all men are, though they do not know it. Thus everyone is already in Nirvana, whether they perceive it or not, though to per-

INDO - GREEK BUDDHA.
FROM SWAT VALLEY.   1ST CENTURY A.D.

XIII. A BUDDHA IN GHANDĀRA STYLE
(*see page 186*)

XIV. A BODDISATTVA IN EARLY CHINESE STYLE

ceive it is the supreme aim; and again, stranger still, since the Buddha came from nowhere and went nowhere, he never came, for he was always there. And inasmuch as he never came, he never existed, for his existence is not existence, nor yet non-existence, but the transcendence of both. The Buddha had therefore not disappeared, for he had never appeared; he was not anywhere, because he was nowhere, but his nowhere was everywhere, though his everywhere was otherwhere.

Now, persons acquainted with the classical Hindu metaphysic of the Atman, the ultimate identity of the soul with deity, will perceive that the Buddhist metaphysic, which was evolved when the other was already ancient, is in essence no more than the restatement of that theory in Buddhist terms. But why were the Indians, at the moment when they did so, prompted to make that restatement? An arguable reply is that the Greeks were then engaged in formulating a similar metaphysic, though in Platonic terms. The Greek speculations culminated in the third century A.D. with the philosophy of Plotinus. The object of his metaphysic was precisely the same as the Mahayanists', namely the statement of what was the meaning of an absolute oneness with the divine. Of him, his disciple, Porphyry, in his *Vita Plotini*, writes: 'It happened to this extraordinary man, who constantly was engaged in reaching toward the divine, by the force of his own thought and by employing the means explained by Plato in his Symposium, that there actually was vouchsafed a vision of that God who, without phenomenal appearance, exists beyond understanding. His whole aim and goal was to draw near God and be made One. And he attained that goal four times, I think, while I was living with him, not merely by being in a state of mind that admitted of such a possibility, but actually, though in an actuality that transcends expression in words.'[1]

[1]Compare a quotation from the *Aeneads* of Plotinus with one from Asvaghosha's *Awakening of Faith*. Plotinus: 'Each being contains in itself the whole intelligible world. Therefore All is everywhere. Each is then all, and All is each. Man as he now is has ceased to be All. But when he ceases to be an individual, he raises himself again and penetrates the whole world.' Asvaghosha: 'He who has attained

The centre of neo-Platonic philosophy was Alexandria, incorporated by 30 B.C. in the Roman Empire. The inhabitants of that Empire not only traded with India in the first century A.D., but had settlements along her coasts as the British had afterwards in the seventeenth century. The university of Alexandria was the most famous on earth. When that university was throbbing with neo-Platonic speculations, we can be sure that the whole hellenised east, wherever men of letters of whatever race were gathered, followed with intense interest what was there being debated. As has been stated, the hellenised Kushans ruled at this time as far as the Punjab. And it was precisely in this region that the Mahayana metaphysic arose. That its speculations had their source in the discussions aroused in philosophic circles by the transcendental debates at Alexandria's university seems the natural corollary of the iconographical and mythological promptings from the same Greek lands. So we may say that the Greeks not only helped to create a popular representation of the new Asian saviour and supplied a store of marvels for use in his biography, but also set the Indians in the half-Greek Kushan state speculating upon his nature as the Absolute and how communion might be had with him at those altitudes of mind.[1]

to the radiance of the highest unitive Knowledge will be able to realise the perfect unity of all sentient beings with the Primordial Mind, the Clear Light of the Void. In that pure Absolute there is no dualism, neither shadow of difference. All sentient beings, if only they were able to realise it, are already in Nirvana, the Void that is the Plenitude. The Mind's pure essence is Highest Perfect Wisdom.'

[1] The thesis here is that Greek thought in its Eurasian guise of Hellenism was a tremendous ferment, which stimulated Asiatic thought hardly less than it did European.

9

The First Holy One Wins Out

So equipped to appeal to all conditions of men from the highest to the lowest, the saviour was sent off on his journey to China, where there had never been a saviour, but only a heaven unrevealed and a cult, the aim of which was to demonstrate, not how to get to heaven, but how to behave on earth, not how to become God, but how to be a gentleman. Rumours preceded the Buddha's coming. They were passed from mouth to mouth up that long long road from Afghanistan, over the Oxus and the Jaxartes, to the present Samarkand and Tashkent, which turns east to go by the oases of Kucha and Turfan to Hami and Tun-huang, and thence through the Great Wall to Lan-chow, and so to Ch'ang-an, a stretch of about three-thousand miles. Perhaps it was these rumours which caused Ming, the Bright, an Emperor of the later Han, whose capital was Lo-yang, to dream in 65 A.D. that an important god existed in the west, and to send envoys to bring his books for the perusal of the Son of Heaven, a rather confusing conjuncture of ideas. They were brought on a white horse, and two Indian monks (residents, it is thought, of the already converted border country, for otherwise they could not have known Chinese) translated them from the Sanskrit in which all Mahayana texts were written. This preliminary Imperial interest in a new deity is not to be thought of as a conversion but should be compared with

Wu's installation at headquarters of mediums through whom spoke country divinities. The Buddha, a foreign divinity with a great reputation and a literature at his back, was a Court novelty at this stage. Those outside the Imperial circle knew nothing about him and the Confucian littérateurs smiled, as we have observed them to smile at Wu's meddling with the supernatural. But the new faith had made a lodgment; it proved more than a passing Court fashion, and in course of time became a religion in the full western sense, a copious revelation far different from the cautious deism of the Confucians and less of a fairytale than popular Taoism. Its sweetness appealed greatly to the general population, ground down in misery by the troubles which followed the fall of the Han dynasty in 221 A.D., an age of insecurity and confusion which lasted for four hundred years until the country was united again under the T'ang dynasty in 618 A.D. That long period, with its invasions from the steppe and internal revolutions, so-called dynasty after dynasty following with such rapidity that fourteen of them are counted in the time, has been compared to the Dark Ages in Europe when the Greco-Roman spark was barely alight in Constantinople and the remainder of the empire was plunged in night. In that night the promises of Christ were the great consolation; gradually the barbarians were converted and when the medieval period began the western world, except Denmark and Scandinavia, was Christian.[1] Though the Chinese dark age was not as stygian as was the corresponding period in Europe, for south China was never invaded by the nomads, nevertheless civilisation had a terrible set-back. The imperial library at Lo-yang, in its collection of classical literature comparable to the Alexandrine library, was burnt; the examination system was disrupted and the civil service, the body synonymous with culture, had not the security, the peace of mind or the authority to make itself felt as heretofore. Small wonder that

[1]Like the hill tribes on the sinic periphery, these barbarian countries came late into the fold, the Danes being Christianised in the ninth, Norway in the eleventh and Sweden only in the twelfth century.

multitudes, so distracted and insecure, turned to the smiling faces of the Boddhisatvas and yearned for the paradise over which they presided.

A few citations will illustrate the nature of this period. In A.D. 311 the Huns captured Lo-yang, the then capital, the occasion when the library was burnt. The reigning Emperor Huai, who by a curious twist of fate was a descendant of the family of the historian Ssu-ma Ch'ien, was taken prisoner and carried to the Shan-yü, who made him his butler. On New Year's day, 313, when the fallen Emperor was pouring out wine for the guests, some spectators moved by pity wept. The same day the Shan-yü put him to death. His successor, Min, who had managed to maintain himself for five years at Ch'ang-an, the old capital to the westward, was beseiged by the Huns in 316. Provisions gave out and one day they served him for dinner with a bowl of soup made of the sour paste used for leaven. He burst out crying and said: 'If we have got to this, it were better to give up and perhaps save the people.' Many of his officers in despair committed suicide. Deciding to surrender, he got into a small carriage without bothering to put on Court dress and, as there were no horses or oxen left, desired his servants to draw him to the Hun camp. He was sent prisoner to the Shan-yü, where he succeeded his deceased predecessor in the office of butler. Shortly afterwards he too was despatched.

These events, which yielded all the north of China to the Huns and obliged the Imperial Court to set up its capital at Nanking on the Yang-tse, four hundred and fifty miles to the south-east, sufficiently indicate the political background, though they amount, of course, only to a peep at the tribulations of this sorrowful era. With the Court went the Confucian hierarchy, and a state of affairs developed which may be summarised by saying that the Court, though continuing an interest in the Mahayana which it had maintained on and off since its first introduction, did not abandon the Confucian state rituals and the study of the classics, while the people became predominantly Buddhist, that is to say, they looked to the Buddha as to a saviour while continuing to respect Confucius as a sage.[1] In the north the Hun invaders, lying on the road from India, eventually became more fervent Buddhists than did the Chinese.

What was going to happen in this curious conjuncture when the state cult of deism and Confucian conduct was still maintained in the face of a Buddhist revelation, now accepted by millions? The very year that the Emperor Huai was serving as the Shan-yü's butler, the Emperor Constantine saw the luminous cross in the sky, with its inscription 'By this conquer', and decided to replace the state cult of Emperor worship with the mythology which the Greeks had sent westwards. Was there to be a Chinese Constantine? In this comparison it must be borne in mind that, while the Chinese state cult was a dignified deism, the Roman was a much coarser, stupider thing, in spite of the interpretation given to it in the second century by the Emperor Marcus Aurelius.

The answer is that a sort of Chinese Constantine did appear in the person of Liang Wu Ti, who ruled the south from A.D. 502 to 549. In a poem of his which is extant[2] he relates how he grew up as a student of the Confucian classics and as a young man read the books of the Taoists. Not till he was fifty-four did he turn to the Buddhist texts. 'That revelation made me forget all the rest,' he says, 'as the rise of the sun dims the stars of night. At last I had what I so much desired.' At the time of his conversion he had been on the throne fifteen years. Thereafter, he made the capital of the empire a great centre for Buddhist study, building monasteries, inviting foreign monks, supervising translations and composing liturgies. On the practical side he did all he could to humanise the administration by softening the law, remitting death sentences,

---

[1] The conversion of the populace to Buddhism meant that they looked less to country gods than before, though they continued in the Confucian rite of ancestor worship.

[2] c.f. translation by Wieger on p. 164 of his *China through the Ages*.

giving largely to the poor and burying the outcast dead. The royal hunting park was converted into a refuge for animals; he allowed no professional singers or actresses in the palace; and abolished forced labour on imperial buildings. In appearance he was handsome; his manners were perfect; his heart was warm; his disposition mild. Growing older he became more ascetic, ate only one meal a day, and that of vegetables, abolished animal sacrifices at the Imperial rites, and on three occasions took the Robe and lived awhile in a monastery. In short, his was a conversion of the most emotional sort.

He was beloved by all, even by the Confucian Grandees, for his scholarship was ample, his calligraphy elegant, his prosody faultless, his filial piety tender. As often as he entered a monastery these sober gentlemen contrived to induce him to leave it; when he would have renounced his style as Son of Heaven they knew how to dissuade him from this course; nor did they allow him to neglect the imperial sacrifice to Heaven at the Winter Solstice. They carried on, in fact—the hallmark of the first-class civil servant.

The end of his life was clouded by a disaster which put his otherworldliness to the extreme test. In 549 a rebel General, Ho Ching, took the capital after a terrible siege. The Emperor, now eighty-six years old, was worn out and in bed when he received the news of the city's fall. Presently Ho Ching entered his room and sat down. Calm and polite, the Emperor observed: 'The campaign has been long and exacting. I fear that your Excellency must be very tired.' This caused General Ho to break into a perspiration. Later, when he had recovered his aplomb, he appointed himself Regent and so bullied the Emperor that he refused to eat and died.

His death caused widespread grief. Later, the Confucianists canonised him under the style, the Bright Master, a paradox since he came near to establishing the Mahayana as a state religion, but the strongest proof of the universal affection in which he was held. His resemblance to Constantine will be seen not to have been very close. He embraced a saviour religion and, supported by the bulk of his subjects, strove to substitute it for the ancient cult, but he had none of Constantine's practical ability.

During the remainder of the sixth century Buddhism continued to increase in strength. Eminent Chinese monks visited India to obtain first-hand information and no less eminent Indian missionaries arrived in China. A catalogue of the period lists no less than 2,257 Buddhist works. The top of this religious tide was reached in 601. The Sui Emperor Wen, of a family which had managed like so many others in the long period of chaos to seize power (in this case, though precariously, over the whole of China[1]), caused enquiry to be made into the proportion of Buddhists to the total population and was informed that the entire population was now Buddhist. Accordingly, he closed, as useless, all the Confucian schools with the exception of the Imperial Academy, whose pupils, however, were restricted to seventy, just enough to maintain the cadre of annalists.[2] A contemporary observer would have been justified in holding that Confucius' day was over, that having reigned seven hundred years from the time when Wu had installed him, a revealed religion was now preferred to his counsels. But such an observer would have been wrong. What happened in Europe did not happen in China.

The year 618 marks the beginning of the T'ang dynasty, the first real universal dynasty since the fall of the Han in 221, and which endured for three hundred years. China's dark age was over. A brilliant renaissance was at hand, a classical renaissance, a Confucian renaissance, a restoration of the old values, a return to the First Holy One.

The inaugurator of this period was a very great man, known posthumously as T'ai Tsung. 'Wu Ti,' he remarked sarcastically one day early in his reign of the saintly Liang Emperor, 'preached Buddhism so successfully to his officers that they were unable to

[1]The short Sui Dynasty (581–618) which preceded the great T'ang.
[2]This action was later described by Confucian writers as no less atrocious than the Burning of the Books by the First Divine August One.

mount their horses to defend him against the rebels.' This showed the way his mind was working. He had not the smallest intention of continuing the Buddhist policy of the Sui Emperor Wen. He was Son of Heaven, the representative of the unknown God on earth. The Confucian system would be restored in its entirety, the ritual sacrifices, *The Four Books*, *The Five Classics*, the examination system, the Imperial University, the Civil Service, all carefully modelled upon Han precedent. Beneath the official cult there would be toleration for private creeds, no one sect being favoured more than another, nor any allowed to be a nuisance. T'ai Tsung was the Julian the Apostate of China, but a successful Julian, for his restoration of the empire's ancient cult was final. The Confucian hierarchy regained all its previous power. Never was it seriously threatened by Buddhism again. Occasionally later Emperors dallied with the religion, but were always pulled up by official remonstrances.

In the course of his policy of toleration under Confucianism for all creeds, T'ai Tsung had a strange confrontation. He came face to face with the other great saviour religion, the one which the Greeks had helped to equip and to send westwards from the hellenised lands, a religion more human and tragic than Buddhism, the religion of Christ. After its triumphs in the west, its recognition by Constantine and its exposition by the three great Fathers, St. Jerome in his *Treatises*, St. Chrysostom in his *Commentaries*, and St. Augustine in his *De Civitate Dei*, all capital events of the fourth and fifth centuries, it turned east and followed, by the same road, the Mahayana into China, arriving at Ch'ang-an, again the capital, in the eighth year of the reign of T'ai Tsung. The cause of this astonishing journey is one of the curiosities of Christian theology, tolerably well known, but whose relation here, placed opposite to what has gone before, will yield one of those vistas, which show us in a flash where we are.

Heresy and schism, grave sins from which, in the Litany, we used to ask God to preserve us, though now they trouble us no more, having long ceased to have urgent meaning, were the sins that brought Christianity to the notice of the Son of Heaven. How this happened can be stated with brevity. In 431 when Nestorius was Patriarch of Constantinople, that is to say head of the Greek Church, and Cyril was Bishop of Alexandria, the Bishop convened a Council at Ephesus to try Nestorius on a charge of heresy. The Patriarch had tampered with the mythology, perhaps with the notion of making it more credible, for he had declared that Mary, the Blessed Virgin, could not be truly called the Mother of God, for her Son was evidently a human being, even though his nature was divine. This was said to amount to a declaration that there were two persons in Christ, and accordingly the Patriarch Nestorius was convicted of heresy. In result, the Christains of Syria took Nestorius' side, for he was a native of that part of the world; they affirmed that his gloss on the mythology could not bear the meaning attributed to it and that his views were as orthodox as his opponents'. In their dudgeon, they broke off relations with the home authorities, elected their own Patriarch and carried on as before, having no idea that they had ceased to be Christians. In that, however, they were in error, for the Council of the Church adjudged them all heretics and dubbed them Nestorians. Since the Council had the legal right to adjudge them so, they were heretics, no matter how fervently they declared their orthodoxy. But their predicament in no way affected their prosperity. They flourished exceedingly and since expansion westwards was impossible they spread eastwards, founding dioceses by permission in Persia, now no longer Parthian, for Artaxerxes had overthrown that alien rule in 226 and restored the pre-Seleucid royal family of Darius and the religion of Zoroaster. From Persia, whose north-eastern boundary was on the Oxus, the way was open to China, and the Syrian Christians took it. In 635 one of their ecclesiastics named Ruben, transliterated Alopen by the Chinese, arrived in Ch'ang-an and petitioned the Emperor T'ai Tsung for permission to found a diocese.

His application was referred to the department concerned and in due course he was required to submit his books for inspection, in case they contained what was seditious or improper. When they were translated and examined they were found to be harmless and a rescript was drawn up for the Imperial seal. This rescript has come down to us and is to the following effect: 'Countries have their own religions as they have their own sages to expound them. Alopen, evidently a priest of good character, has brought images and books from the Roman domain. We have found on examination that his doctrines are pacific and have a very creditable perspicuity in respect to the moral principles they inculcate, being logical and without vagueness. There is no objection to Alopen propagating them here. The Office of Works will build in the I-ning ward a monastery large enough to house twenty-one inmates.'

In this way the Emperor allotted to Christianity a place under Confucianism. Its moral teaching was innocuous; its other-worldly promises there was no need to discuss. Since this was precisely his attitude to Buddhism, we have the spectacle of this Emperor turning an indifferent eye on two saviours, a denial which makes him unique in history. How unbelievable it would have seemed to Wu, crying from mountain to mountain, that the day would come when a successor, offered salvation by a pair of divine personages, both of them unique and absolute, would coolly brush their revelations aside, as with a chilling condescension he commended their moralities!

This is no place to assuage the reader's curiosity about the subsequent history in China of Nestorian Christianity, though it is a drama with many surprises. For instance, the religion spread far more widely than in later centuries did its orthodox version or the more drastic heresy, Protestantism, for a Christian church was built in every prefecture. The dioceses, under a Patriarch at Bagdad, were linked to Syria, and the whole Church, under twenty Metropolitans, amounted to a larger ecclesiastical organisation than the Greek Church. But in two centuries and a half the branch in

China was shrivelled, the desiccation later spreading to the trunk in Mesopotamia, until now, except for a rabble at Mosul and a few impoverished black rustics in Malabar, nothing remains of this community, which sought to bring the whole of Asia under Christ. In all its curious history perhaps the revenge taken upon the Malabar remnant by the Goanese Inquisition in 1630 is dramatically the most complete, for the faithful descendants of the vanguard of the evangile in further Asia, fallen into the power of the Roman successors of their old Greek rivals, were seized and burnt for a heresy which by that time was of twelve hundred years' standing.

The T'ang was an era of great intellectual curiosity and with toleration extended to all religions there was much discussion of the various systems. In addition to the saviour religions of Christianity and Buddhism (several Mahayanist forms existed of the second) there entered two more religions, one being Zoroastrianism, the religion of pre-Greek Persia, whose central figure was also deity made flesh, and the other Manichaeism, a creed compounded by a Persian called Mani in the third century A.D. from Zoroastrian, Christian and Semitic elements, syncretised into a gnosis of mystical knowledge which gave an up-to-date explanation of the existence of good and evil. After Mani's crucifixion by the Magians in 276 as a false prophet, his religion spread both east and west, for besides obtaining a following as far as China, particularly in the northern territories, and along the Silk Road through the oases, it had its Mediterranean communities, the young St. Augustine being a Manichaean, as, much later, were the Albigenses of France.[1] When one adds the religion of Islam (Mohammed died in 632 A.D.) and that of the Jews, both of which also reached T'ang China, one counts six religions: the two saviour religions, three theisms with prophets, and Zoroastrianism, less easy to define so sharply. We have thus the spectacle of irruption after irruption of neareastern revelations beating against the citadel of Confucian deism.

[1] The most recent work on this subject is *The Medieval Manichee* by Steven Runciman, an exhaustive treatise.

The First Holy One Wins Out

The Mahayana was by far the most dangerous assailant, because it was adaptable to Chinese taste and submitted itself to a sinification so complete that it seemed in time no more foreign to the Chinese than does Christianity to us for analogous reasons. That naturalisation enabled it to reside permanently in China, when the other near-eastern religions failed to maintain their first lodgment, either disappearing altogether in the face of government displeasure, or dwindling to the position of obscure sects.

After the deposition of Buddhism by T'ai Tsung from the high position it attained under Liang Wu Ti and the Sui Emperor Wen, it renewed from time to time its efforts to win back first place at Court. But the Confucian watchdogs were always on guard and growled when they thought the occasion required it. In the ninth century such an occasion arose and brought out in defence of the canon, the great Han Yü, then Metropolitan Viceroy. This celebrity was known as the Prince of Literature; it was already becoming the fashion to wash the hands in rose-water before opening his books. All sorts of stories were told about him, of which the most amusing is that relating to Chia Tao, an obscure poet. One day this Chia Tao was out for his usual stroll, his habit being to compose as he walked. He would be quite oblivious of his surroundings, his eyes on the ground or raised to the sky, beating the rhythm with his walking stick. On this particular occasion, after he had gone some distance and composed a very engaging poem, he wondered whether the word 'push' would not be better than the 'knock' which he had used. Push or knock, that was the question, and was a difficult question to settle, for both effected a neat antithesis. Much afflicted by the problem, he began to push and knock with his stick, seeking to get the feel of the words. While so engaged, he turned a corner, and knocked over a man all in a second. The man was a porter in the front shafts of a sedan chair, and when he fell he dropped the chair, which struck the ground with a nasty jolt. The curtains were drawn back and there looked out a gentleman. 'What is the meaning of this?' he demanded angrily of the porter, who had picked himself up. 'Sir,' said the porter, 'this man attacked me', and he pointed accusingly at Chia Tao. 'How do you mean, attacked you?' asked the gentleman testily. 'He ran at me with a stick and hit me', explained the porter, mimicking Chia Tao's efforts to get his poem right. Four of the gentleman's attendants, who had been walking behind the sedan, now stepped forward and seized the poet. 'We saw it all,' said one of them, a clerk, 'the fellow deliberately gave the porter a knock with intent, no doubt, to rob your Excellency in the confusion of the moment.'

At this awkward conjuncture Chia Tao recognised his Excellency be no less than Han Yü, Metropolitan Viceroy and famous stylist, travelling in little state though certainly that great man. Far from alarming, this reassured him. Though little used to conversing with high dignitaries, he knew quite well how to talk to a man of letters.

'Sir,' he began, 'I am a poor scholar and poet,' an opening that at once made a favourable impression. He continued: 'I most humbly apologise for striking your porter, but assure you I was not encompassing a robbery but trying to settle a point of prosody.'

Han Yü's frown was now quite gone. 'Prosody,' he said, savouring the word on his tongue, as if it were choice wine, 'ha-ha, prosody, that is interesting. You shall pose for me, if you please, your problem.' And he leaned forward with animation.

'Your Excellency is very kind,' said Chia Tao, 'and, indeed, there is no one in the wide world to whom I would rather submit it than to yourself.' And he quoted the verse he had composed, first with the word 'knock' and then with the word 'push'. 'When I tell you,' he went on, 'that at a loss to decide between the two words I was walking along knocking and pushing, and so, by mischance, upset your porter, you will understand and pardon me.'

'Say no more about the porter,' said Han Yü. 'The important thing is to decide which word.'

The First Holy One Wins Out

'Your Excellency, I am certain, can settle that,' submitted Chia Tao, his face expressing boundless admiration.

'I will settle it,' Han Yü assured him, 'but first I must know what is your opinion.'

'The word "knock", I conceive, is correct,' replied Chia Tao, 'and that it is so I became aware in the act of knocking down your footman.'

'You are right,' exclaimed Han Yü, 'perfectly right. "Knock" is the word, and that you should have been in doubt until you had put it to the test I consider an interesting literary event.' And he added feelingly: 'You are poor, you say?'

'Very poor,' murmured Chia Tao, with a sad look at his cotton robe.

'In that case I take you under my protection. Mount beside me and we will continue the conversation.' And he made room for him in the sedan.

This tremendous Confucian celebrity in 819 addressed a memorial to the Emperor Hsien Tsung, who had succumbed to the fascination of the Buddhist saviour. It was the matter of a relic, of a bone, which the Emperor wanted to bring into the palace. Religious relics have, indeed, been multiplied in the Western Church, but in the Eastern their multiplication has been far greater because of the Buddha's many former births, both as a man and as an animal, any particle of which metempsychoses is equally holy and to be venerated. In this case, however, it was the Buddha's own finger bone, though which phalange is not stated, nor of which finger, nor of which hand. That it was a celebrated bone is certain, for the monks of the Fa Men Ssu monastery held it to be their greatest treasure. The Emperor would have liked to keep it in the palace, for he believed that its possession would lengthen his life, but, not able to get the Abbot to part with it permanently, he induced him to lend it for three days. The plan was to carry it in splendid procession from the monastery, and later exhibit it to the public, the occasion to be one of general rejoicings. When things had gone so

207

far, Han Yü made his protest, in a style so pure and with a senti-
ment so correct that it was hailed and still is held a Confucian
masterpiece of prose.

'The ancients, more especially the Sainted Emperors, Yao, Shun
and Yü, knew nothing of the Buddha, but this had no effect
on their longevity, which was immense', he began. 'The first
Emperor to have to do with him was Ming of the later Han, who,
prompted by a dream, sent for his books, though it served him
little, for he died in middle life, and after him were only short
reigns and rebellions.

'During these troubled times', contined Han Yü, 'Buddhism
spread, and the more it spread the more troubled became the times.
How useless it was as a prop, how broken as a support, was demonstrated by the pathetic misadventures of Wu Ti, the Liang Emperor, who three times entered a monastery, and three times was
prevailed upon to return to his duties. In spite of this devotion to
Buddha, and in spite of the ascetic diet he lived on and the ex-
aggerated kindness he showed to animals, he was harassed in old
age by the rebel Ho Ching and having lost his capital died of
starvation. What an incompetent deity the Buddha must be, if he
could not better requite his worshipper!

'At the coming of the T'ang', the memorial went on 'the Emperor
T'ai Tsung and his father, on whom the son had bestowed the title of
Kao-tzu, Eminent Founder, though he himself was the real Founder,
an act of true filial piety, contemplated the radical suppression of
Buddhism, but advised by ministers of limited capacity, whose
knowledge of the classics was lamentably weak, these two great
ones did no more than dethrone it from high places and, after, toler-
ated its practice by the masses.

'On Your Majesty's accession', Han Yü then declares, 'it was
anticipated that the Founders' original decision to extirpate Buddhism would be implemented and their subsequent dangerous indul-
gence be rescinded. To this hope colour was at first lent by Your
Majesty's Edict refusing to sanction the construction of more

XV. A GHANDĀRA STYLE HEAD OF A BUDDHA

(*see page 186*)

XVI. PORTRAIT OF THE EMPEROR WEN OF THE SUI DYNASTY
(*see page 200*)

monasteries, and limiting the number of candidates for holy orders. Alas! these anticipations were doomed to disappointment. Far from suppressing the religion, it seems that the Court proposes directly to patronise it. A party of priests have Your Majesty's instructions to carry in procession to the palace the Buddha-bone preserved in the Fa Men Ssu monastery, which ceremony Your Majesty has arranged to view from the top of one of the palace towers. Idiotic though your humble servant is,' pursues Han Yü, 'he is not so devoid of propriety as to believe that Your Majesty is seeking any personal advantage, but rather at this time of plenty and prosperity is moved to indulge the common people. But how can Your Majesty, without losing face, be mixed up in such a piece of preposterous mummery? For Your Majesty to watch the procession will be interpreted as an act of worship. The sight of the Son of Heaven looking on while the Buddha-bone is carried past, will excite the public, drive it frantic. A wave of morbid extravagances will result, the cauterising of heads, fingers burnt with incense, clothes sold to buy offerings, good money flung away, along with an empty market, the temples crammed and fanatics slicing themselves in a frenzy. And all for what? For a barbarian, because Buddha was no more than that. He could not speak a word of Chinese. His clothes were of some savage indecorous cut. Stupidly ignorant of the writings of antiquity, he had never heard of Yao or Shun. His teachings run counter to the maxims of the sages, for oblivious of the claims of filial piety and of devotion to the state, he abandoned his father and his public duties to roam about like a common vagabond. Suppose, for the sake of argument, that this said Buddha, sent as an emissary by his King, had come to the capital with presents for Your Majesty. The proper procedure is laid down for such a case. Your Majesty would have granted him audience in due course, admonished him to behave with suitable propriety, and, after giving him an official dinner, and bestowing upon him a suit of clothes, more proper than those in which he had come, would have sent him home under an escort, with orders to prevent him from speaking to the people.[1] How different from the correctness of this procedure are Your Majesty's present arrangements! A bone of this barbarian, who died twelve hundred years ago and is now, one surmises, wholly decomposed, is to enter the precincts, with a ceremony appropriate were the elixir itself to be installed. Relevant here is the First Holy One's dictum: "Respect, but keep your distance from, transcendent beings." Though a bone of this sort cannot possibly do good, has Your Majesty reflected that it may do harm, that there are such things as evil influences, against which the ancients took care to protect themselves? But Your Majesty now, without any precautions, proposes to house an object, anyhow disgusting, which may give rise to emanations of a noxious character. How strange that none of the censors, not a single official, has done his duty and given warning as he should, and that it has remained for this insignificant memorialist to come forward in defence of Your Majesty's person!' And Han Yü concludes: 'Speaking with deep consciousness of his limited attainments, your servant implores that this bone be burnt, or reduced to powder and flung in the river, an act which, far from antagonising the public, will impress it by the demonstration of Your Majesty's power over the supernatural. As to any danger of Buddha's revenge, your memorialist will be happy to support in his own person all misfortunes that may accrue. Submitted, trembling, for the Benign Consideration.'

In this capital document of Confucian rationalism the reader will note that the great Han Yü does not altogether exclude the possibility of the bone being the vehicle of an evil spirit, bred perhaps by malcontents as *ku* spirits were bred. It may be that he gave this hint only to frighten the Emperor without himself believing in magic. But the presence of the sentence should give us pause nor allow us to exaggerate the mental toughness of a T'ang intellectual.

[1]This was precisely the procedure adopted by the Chinese more than a thousand years later when Lord Macartney came as Envoy from England. See my *The Great Within*.

The First Holy One Wins Out

After all, the date is only 819, when the best Europe could show was uncouth old Charlemagne. China, of course, was buzzing with evil spirits, who seemed to demonstrate their power as unmistakably as demonry spoke through our witches. It is, therefore, more correct to regard Confucianism, in this aspect of its thought, as standing for reason in a world of occult dangers, rather than as a narrow rationalism for which such dangers were an illusion. In Han Yü's last sentence, however, he makes it plain that he personally is not afraid of an offended saviour; he does not believe the Buddha can hurt him. But it is one thing for a person to hold that those who trust their reason are trusting what mankind has found to be its best shield, and another for him to declare that reason can give the whole explanation of experience. Confucian thought did not make that claim. Divinity existed, a divinity undefinable but which must be held in respect, a divinity which had never vouchsafed a revelation. The saviours and prophets who declared themselves emanations of divinity or its mouthpieces, were demented persons, no matter how respectable might be the ethics they preached, and to follow them, believe in them, pray to them, depend on them, instead of upon reason, the only divine thing certainly known, was to become demented, to put salvation before conduct, to prefer rejection of the world to sane behaviour in it, and so to endanger the stability of society, thus precipitating the worst catastrophe that could overtake men, the anarchy that meant no food and security. Good government, stable government, that was the most important thing on earth, humane government with its concomitants of loyalty, fairness, sanity, obedience, respect, moderation, without extravagance, without eccentricity, with sense and with clarity. Men with that ideal could feel that they had sight of the heavenly way, because it was against reason to think that way could be otherwise, and since it must surely be thus, to live so was to chime with the will of heaven. That was all a man could know and all he needed to know. Such was the body of thought behind Han Yü's letter.

On receipt of it, the Emperor immediately transferred him from his appointment as Metropolitan Viceroy to a district charge in the far south,[1] a fate similar to that which has overtaken so many officials, from remote antiquity to the present day, who have given advice which was unpalatable. One is glad to know, however, that he was recalled within two years by the next Emperor, and again promoted to high rank. On his death in 824 he was canonised and his tablet placed in the Confucian Temple, a sort of Pantheon for the worthies of the Empire.

Although Han Yü failed to prevent the Emperor Hsien Tsung from bringing the Buddha-bone into the palace, it may be said that his protest, which, as is evident from his canonisation, had official backing, was conclusive. In 843 the Emperor Wu Tsung decided on drastic action against all foreign religions, for monks and nuns had so increased as to be a monstrous nuisance. Under his measures, which took the form of a dissolution of religious houses, the secularisation of their inmates and the confiscation of their property to the state, Christianity and Manicheism came to an end,[2] but Buddhism, which was allowed as many as thirty monks in each city, survived. The restrictions against it were lifted later on and it became as widespread as before, but it had lost face, its vogue with the Court was over for ever; the Civil Service had conquered, the First Holy One had won out. From this date, along with Taoism, in its form as a popular religion, it entered upon a gradual decay, which after lasting a millenium is still going on. Both religions grew more and more popular, less and less respectable; fewer persons of education found them interesting or stimulating, till they became vast repositories of magic and fairytale, in the case of Taoism a sort of pilgrims' pleasance, typified by T'ai Shan as it is today.[3]

[1]It was there that he wrote his famous letter to the crocodile, which is still often quoted.

[2]The reader can judge from this early history of Christianity in China what little chance the Jesuits and other missionaries had when they came a thousand years later to convert the Emperor and his subjects.

[3]Christianity escaped this fate because the western masses became better educated than the eastern.

The First Holy One Wins Out

This statement refers only to popular Chinese Buddhism and Taoism, to the ceremonies, rites, processions, magic, alchemy, etc. that drew the people to the temples. The transcendent speculations of these systems[1] continued to inspire privately thinkers and artists of all kinds. In both systems was the mystical aspiration towards union with the divine, an aspiration which, rising far above denominational mythologies, is common to all mystics everywhere. There is a great literature in China and Japan devoted to this transcendence. It even interested for a time certain types of Confucian mind, for a group of neo-Confucian littérateurs of the twelfth century composed a syncretism, called the Li philosophy, in which elements of Buddhist and Taoist metaphysics have their place, and are brought into line with Confucian deism. In their explorations of these regions of the mind, Buddhism and Taoism remain living forces, not only in China but throughout the world. Some modern thinkers regard a deism with such a mystical background as the universal religion of civilised mankind, the only religion that reason can accept. But mystical apprehensions, even in the elementary form felt by artists, are experienced by few.

During the twelfth century, when the Li philosophy was being developed, the more orthodox intellect of the country was engaged on the re-editing of the Confucian canon, and the systematic interpretation of conflicting passages. Textual difficulties were cleared up and the whole made yet more coherent and compact. The philosopher Chu-hsi (1130-1200) is the great name associated with this final elucidation of the classical texts.

In the fourteenth century, however, when the Chinese had got rid of the nomad dynasty called the Mongol or Yuan, which had given them the great Kublai Khan in whose reign (1260-1294) the empire was in closer touch with the west than in any time of its history, they decided to shut themselves off from the rest of the world. Behind this barrier against outside ideas, Confucianism

[1]Christianity, of course, inspired the same kind of transcendent thought. For many it has become a mystical deism.

turned into a lifeless dogma. A system which, in its essence, was one of compromise and moderation, grew so narrow and rigid that it lost all flexibility and became a clog to the acquisition of new knowledge, an obscurantism instead of a liberal education, to the great detriment of the government which, by failing to adapt itself to events, particularly the expansion into Asia of the west, prepared its downfall.[1]

By the nineteenth century the later Ch'ing Emperors were expressing themselves in a Confucian patter that had ceased to mean anything. The paradox developed that the philosophy of life, which had enabled Chinese civilisation to survive by being reasonable in the face of unreason, fossilised until it grew into a caricature of reason. This was not due to any inherent unsuitability of the classics to inspire new ideas, but to the extreme academicism of the educated class. Poor Confucius was mummified. There reigned a conservatism inconceivably dense. An ignorance and ineptitude prevailed only possible among academic intellectuals completely blind to the outside world. Neither the Court nor the bureaucracy would hear of any change, and they were strong enough to prevent reformers from getting into power. A revolution was inevitable, but was delayed until 1912, when at last the Ch'ing dynasty was overthrown.

Before putting down this book, readers will want to know the answers to two questions. What happened to Confucius in the revolution of 1912 and what is his position today in China? And they will want the answers to be short, for to delay the finish after a gallop over two and a half millenniums would be intolerable. In a sentence then, the revolution damaged Confucius as much as did the First Divine August One, but he recovered his position as quickly as on the former occasion.

This time the classics were not burnt; they were drowned. The abolition of the imperial system and the establishment of a republic opened China to the torrent of western culture. In the light of

[1] See the detailed exposition of this in my *The Great Within* and *Foreign Mud*.

world ideas Confucianism with its ancient language and Sainted Emperors suddenly appeared antedeluvian, an extraordinary anachronism. What a white elephant of an institution had the nation been keeping up all those centuries! In the first flush of realisation, study of the classics was banned in schools; Confucius became a figure of fun; and a host of new writers abondoned the literary language to write western style novels, plays and poems in the spoken language, and to translate the European classics. As a result, intellectual China grew to be like a suburb of London, New York and Paris; it echoed what was said in those capitals, and in Moscow.

But this period of juvenile admiration passed. After a time the novelties of European thought became less intoxicating. Armed with a new critical acumen, the more balanced minds looked again at the sources of their own culture, and perceived that Confucius was, in fact, a very great man; that his ideas, freed from the scholastic interpretations which armies of bookworms had given them over centuries, were fresh and vital; and that his teaching in general was not only suited to modern men, but was indispensable to them. Far from being a rigid old conservative, he would, they reflected, have supported the 1912 revolution, for one of his cardinal doctrines was that the people were justified in overthrowing an evil government. The virtues on which he insisted were the great virtues; all his thought was pervaded by sanity and sweetness. There followed a revulsion of feeling; they had wronged their Sage; he was truly their First Holy One. They saw him now in a wider perspective as one of the transcendent talents of world history. His books were restored to the curriculum. The modern student, however, studies him in a modern way along with the great minds of other lands. But this does not reduce, it increases, his stature. More intelligently understood, he emerges still more gigantic.

31st August, 1947

Notes on Authorities

I HAVE indicated in the text the sources as they are used. Chapters Eight and Nine rest upon general reading and the facts they adduce are common knowledge. The stories scattered about the text are summarised in Giles's *Chinese Biographical Dictionary*, and I have rendered them to the best of my ability, not as history, but as anecdotes. The original Chinese sources upon which the book rests are, in chief, Chavannes's partial translation of Ssu-ma Ch'ien and on volumes I and II of Homer Dubs's translation of Pan Ku, the rest of the translation not having been published. I append for the convenience of the reader details of these authorities and of the principal other original sources I used in translation, and the names of the books in which original sources in translation form part of the contents.

Les Mémoires Historiques de Se-ma Ts'ien. Eduard Chavannes, 1895, Vols. 1, 2, 3(ii) and 5.

The History of the Former Han Dynasty by Pan Ku, translated by Homer H. Dubs, 1938, Vols. 1 and 2.

The Religious System of China. J. J. M. De Groot, 1907, Vols. 5 and 6.

China throughout the Ages. Dr. Leo Wieger, 1928.

The Book of Lord Shang translated, with introduction and notes, by Dr. J. L. Duyvendak.

The Chinese Classics, The Book of History translated by James Legge, 1865.

The Book of Songs translated by Arthur Waley, 1937.

The Analects of Confucius translated by Arthur Waley, 1938.

Three Ways of Thought in Ancient China. Arthur Waley, 1939.

Notes on Authorities

The Book of Mencius (abridged in *Wisdom of East* Series) translated by
Lionel Giles, 1942.
The Great Learning and the Mean-in-Action. E. R. Hughes, 1942.
Gems of Chinese Literature. Lionel Giles, 1922.
Chinese Biographical Dictionary. Lionel Giles.

LEADING DATES

	B.C.
The Yellow Emperor	2697
Emperor Yao	2357
Emperor Shun	2255
Hsia Dynasty	2205–1766
Emperor Yü	2200
Shang Dynasty	1766–1122
Chou Dynasty	1122–253
Buddha	560–480
Confucius	550–479
Aeschylus	525–456
Xerxes expedition against Greece defeated	480
Plato	427–347
Aristotle	385–322
Mencius	372–290
Lord Shang died	338
Alexander overwhelmed Persia	333
King Asoka reigns	274–237
Duke of Ch'in extinguished Chou Empire	253
Parthian Empire	250 B.C.–A.D. 220
Hannibal	247–183 B.C.
Ch'in Dynasty	221–206 B.C.
Han Dynasty	206 B.C.–A.D. 220
Emperor Kao-tzu (born 246 B.C.) reigns	202–195 B.C.
Establishment of Greek rule in India	190 B.C.
Emperor Wen reigns	180–157 B.C.

Notes on Authorities

King Menander reigns	170–150 B.C.
Ssu-ma Ch'ien	145–86 B.C.
Emperor Wu (born 156 B.C.) reigns	141–88 B.C.
Julius Caesar	100–44 B.C.
Pompey conquered Seleucids	66 B.C.
Livy	59 B.C.–A.D. 17
Battle of Carrhae	53 B.C.
End of Greek rule in India	50 B.C.
Alexandria incorporated in Roman Empire	30 B.C.
	A.D.
Buddhism reached China	65
Six Dynasties	220–589
Mani crucified	276
Huns capture Lo-yang and the Emperor Huai	311
Huns capture Ch'ang-an and the Emperor Min	316
Council at Ephesus and beginning of Nestorian Church	431
Liang Wu Ti (born 463) reigns	502–549
Sui Dynasty	581–618
Emperor Wen closes Confucian schools	601
T'ang Dynasty	618–906
Mohammed died	632
Christianity brought to China	635
Emperor Wu Tsung dissolves the Buddhist, Christian and Manichaean religious houses	843
Sung Dynasty	960–1279
Chu-hsi re-edits the Confucian canon	1170
Yuan Dynasty	1206–1368
Kublai Khan, Emperor of China	1260–1294
Ming Dynasty	1368–1644
Ch'ing Dynasty	1644–1912

Notes on Illustrations

Plate I (page 80)—Attempted assassination of Ch'in Shih Huang-ti, the First Divine August One. This is a rubbing from a bas-relief inside one of the tombs of the Wu family which are situated ten miles south of the city of Chia-hsiang in Shantung (this family had no connection with the Emperor Wu). The walls of the tomb are covered with bas-reliefs of this kind. Though they date from the later Han period, the second century A.D., they are thought to give a tolerably exact impression of the costumes, carriages, horses, etc., of the earlier Han, for they were not original compositions but were copied from pictures, probably the sort we call old masters. The illustration here records an episode not mentioned in my text, but to be found in Ssu-ma Ch'ien's *History*.

A certain Ching K'o was sent by the Prince of Yen to kill the Divine August One. This was in 227 B.C., while he was still King of Ch'in. To be sure of getting audience the assassin brought the head of a rebel General in a lacquer box as a credential. In the picture one sees the box half open at the base of a pillar, with the top of the General's head sticking out of it. No one moment is selected, but the story is telescoped into one depiction. To the right of the pillar is the future First Emperor holding a jade disque in his left hand, and starting backwards. His right sleeve has been cut off and is falling to the ground. Ching K'o, with his hair streaming and his hands up, has been seized by the royal physician; a man behind is beckoning for help. Lodged in the wooden pillar is Ching K'o's sword with which, after the miss that only cut the sleeve, he had aimed a second stroke and missed again. A guard rushes in on the right. The assassin's colleague lies on the ground, as if he had been hit on the head or had fainted.

Modern art has made us familiar with the convention of simultaneity, and we do not find this picture old-fashioned or difficult to understand. Indeed, it appeals to us for various reasons. The composition is tight, the figures, particularly the struggling group, are conventionalised into a dynamic pattern, the line is extremely vigorous and the character or state of mind of each of the parties is cleverly particularised. This is the Han style, vigorous, direct and daring, very different from the later style whose conventions are more naturalistic and whose mood is more elegant and languid.

Plate II (page 81)—From the same series of bas-reliefs. In the top picture a personage with fly whisk and his coachman are driving in a Han chariot which has a roof like an umbrella and solid wheels. (The Han also had carriages shaped rather like hansom cabs with spoked wheels for town use, and a pair of horses). With no springs and on a rough road the chariot must have been torture to travel in. The shafts are like a kind of yoke, but there are also traces. The horse itself is a remarkably fine animal. The Emperor Wu was told by Chang Ch'ien, his famous explorer who reached the Greek kingdoms, that while passing through Ferghana, to the North of Bactria, he had seen splendid horses there, some kind of Persian breed related to the Arab. The Chinese horses at the time were more like ponies. The news excited the Emperor and he sent Li Kuang-li, the brother of the loved Lady Li, to try to get some. Considerable force had to be used, as the King of Ferghana did not want to part with any of his horses, but eventually Li Kuang-li returned with a thousand in the spring of 101 B.C. They were given the title of Heavenly Horses. They had the peculiarity that their sweat was red like blood, an effect supposed then to have been the result of a harmful emanation but believed now to have been due to some parasitic insect which caused small haemorrhages. All the horses in the bas-reliefs are this new kind.

They were high spirited and great stayers. (See Appendix V, Volume II, of Dubs' edition of Pan Ku's *History of Former Han*).

The lower picture in Plate II is a detail of a large composition in which the horse and chariot above are also included. A visit to a sovereign is portrayed, some legendary sovereign, perhaps the Queen of the West, but as the figures are contemporary it shows what a visit by a subordinate King to the Han Emperor was like. Taking it in that sense, we see two men kowtowing to the Emperor. They are announcing the arrival of the subordinate King and his wife, who are seen entering behind. The Emperor on his throne signs with complacent dignity to the King to approach. The King's face displays a mixture of fear and respect, the correct ritual expression for such an occasion. In the complete composition there is an upper storey to the pillared hall of audience shown in the detail, with a room full of people seated. The roof is also shown, a roof whose architectural features are similar but plainer than those of Chinese buildings of later ages. On the top of it phoenixes are perching, an extremely auspicious sign. At the door of the audience hall is a tree to which is tethered the visiting King's horse after being unharnessed from his chariot. In a lower register one sees the procession including the aforesaid chariot on the way to the palace.

Plates III and IV (pages 96 and 97)—These are from early twelfth-century (Sung) paintings on silk by the celebrated artist Chao Po-Chu, which are now in the Boston Museum, and once were in the private collection of the Ming fifteenth-century Emperor Hsüan-tê. Plate III depicts the standards of Hsiang Yü as he marches over the passes to the Ch'in capital, Hsien-yang, against Liu, Lord of P'ei, the future Eminent Founder of the Han. The picture is an example of how the Chinese in a great landscape period of painting treated an historical subject. The tremendously wild country dividing the Ch'in state from Wei is romantically suggested with precipices, pine trees, waterfalls, and towering peaks. A strong wind is fluttering the banners.

Notes on Illustrations

Plate IV shows part of the First Divine August One's palace in his capital of Hsien-yang, with the future Eminent Founder standing at the door with his suite. It is early morning and the mountain mists have not cleared away. Hsiang Yü is not far off; indeed, the standards in the foreground may represent his van. The future Eminent Founder stands at the top of the steps awaiting his rival. A scene of some sort, the meaning of which is not clear to me, is being enacted in front of him. That a famous painter should about 1100 A.D. paint two pictures of what had happened thirteen hundred years before shows how green romance had kept the story of the struggle between the two great protagonists for the throne of China.

Plate V (page 112)—A Han war drum (reproduced from Plate 27 in the catalogue of Chinese bronzes in the Berlin Museum). This, however, is not an object of Chinese art, but was made by the hill tribes to the westward who were conquered by the Emperor Wu. As stated in the text (page 147) these drums have continued until today to be made by the hill tribe known as the Karens, with little or no change in design. The one in my possession (17″ high and 24″ diameter) if hung by cords from the loops at the side, emits a dull boom on being struck which may be heard at a great distance. In the quiet of the Karen hills their note will carry from one hill-top village to another. In the centre is a twelve-pointed star, which is surrounded by sixteen concentric circles. Each circle contains a distinct formal design, hatched or corded or in spirals or derived from animal, bird or fish forms. Round the edge are tree frogs. That the hill tribes should have continued to make these drums without change for two milleniums suggests that their clothes, houses and utensils are today exactly as they were in Wu's time.

Plate VI (page 113)—The Emperor Wen of Han. A portrait generally ascribed to Yen Li-pên (seventh century A.D.) who painted a series of imperial portraits called the Scroll of the Thirteen Emperors, now in the Museum of Fine Arts, Boston. They must all be imaginary, unless he had previous portraits on which

222

Notes on Illustrations

to found them, which is possible. Wen is given a kind, rather stupid, face.

Plate VII (page 128)—A battle between the Chinese and the Huns. This is one of the inscribed slabs found on the hill called Hsiao T'ang Shan in Shantung, twenty miles north-west of Feich'eng. The slab is about two-hundred years earlier than the bas-reliefs of the Wu tombs and dates from the reign of the Emperor Wu's immediate successors. It is not a copy of an old picture, like the bas-reliefs, but is the creation of a contemporary artist of little skill in composition, though with a lively sense of draughtsmanship. It succeeds in conveying a good deal of information about a battle with the Huns. On the left side is the Chinese cavalry, consisting of lancers and mounted bowmen, the latter perhaps Hunnish mercenaries. To the right are the Hun, mounted bowmen with peaked caps as worn by the Scythians and fur coats; at their back are foot archers. Below is a hunting scene with dogs, deer, a bear being attacked by a man with a spear, and an archer standing in a cart drawn by a bullock and shooting at some kind of wild cattle.

Plate VIII (page 129)—The terracotta objects on this plate are among the Han tomb figures preserved in the British Museum, and are reproduced by the courtesy of the Keeper of Oriental Antiquities, Mr. Basil Grey. The top figure is a sorcerer. We may suppose that he is a minor practitioner of the black art and that the magnificent Luan Ta and other Masters of the Heavenly Way were more curiously robed. The rigid pose and the intense expression on the face indicate that he is engaged in a conjuration. He is in semi-trance, and is if about to cry out with the voice of the spirit.

The standing figure in the lower plate is an exorcist and carries a broom. His duty is not to raise spirits but to get rid of them; some sort of ritual sweeping with a broom was part of exorcism. It may be that when the T'ai Kung swept the path for his son, the Kao-tzu (pages 90 and 91), there was also in the act a symbolical

223

sweeping away of evil spirits. The expression of the exorcist should be noted. His eyes are staring fearfully as if he saw an evil spirit, and he has a sort of pout on his lips which suggests that though he is afraid he is also brave: he knows that he is face to face with the powers of darkness but has the strength of character to beat them off. The two seated women may be musicians, not court musicians or entertainers, but the mediums who assist at an occult ritual by clapping the hands and reciting spells with gestures, sometimes using cymbals and tiny bells. The rapt expression on their faces, which shows them to be in semi-trance, is very different from the sorcerer's expression. His has a concentration of effort, as if he were bringing forth, but they are relaxed and dreaming.

The men who made these figures were not skilled artists but, like children, they knew how to put expression into their models. As time went on Chinese tomb figures became more articulated and naturalistic, qualities depending on skill and knowledge, but they are less expressive and monumental. At the present moment we admire the early sculptures more than the late, because expression and monumentality appeal to us more than skilled articulation. A present-day critic speaking of the sorcerer, would say that though there is no realised physical relationship between the parts, which do not hinge into each other, there is a formal relationship which has the essential sculptural qualities that are lacking in a purely naturalistic representation. The Han figures here illustrated are not, however, sophisticated in this advanced sense; their effect is achieved by primitive artistic intuition, a state of mind which we cannot altogether recapture.

Plate IX (page 160)—The Princess of Coloured Clouds (Pi-hsia Yüan-chün), also called The Holy Mother (Shēng-mu), a fifteenth-century (Ming) grey limestone sculpture (about 18″ high) in the Art Institute, Chicago, and reproduced by their permission.

On page 118 at the end of the description of T'ai Shan is mentioned the Palace of the Princess which lies near the summit. In that temple was a statue of the Princess of Coloured Clouds, because she was the tutelary goddess of the holy mountain, and I assume the sculpture reproduced here to be its head. How it reached Chicago I do not know, nor do I know her story. But in the East, tutelary goddesses of mountains are generally women who either became during their lifetime the wife of a heavenly spirit and lived on a mount, or whose spirit after death haunted a mount for some other reason. The hat worn by the Princess of Coloured Clouds consists of a tight-fitting cap, like that of a university mortar-board, with a tall crown round which are arranged three pheasants. On page 114 is mention of the descent of heavenly spirits in the form of pheasants. No doubt, the pheasants on Her Highness's hat are symbolical of such a descent. Mr. Ludwig Bachhofer in his *A Short History of Chinese Art* (1946) is of the opinion that the sculpture is fifteenth century and is a masterpiece of the period. The goddess is represented as a beautiful girl with a smouldering eye and a disdainful mouth, but she is essentially a divine personage.

Plate X (page 161)—Scholars collating texts, an eleventh-century (Sung) painting, artist unknown, in the Museum of Fine Arts, Boston, by the courtesy of whose Director it is reproduced here. It is supposed to record a particular event six centuries earlier (556 A.D.) when at the order of Wen-hsuan of the Northern Ch'i Dynasty, a local dynasty twenty-five years before the unification of China under the Sui Dynasty (581 A.D.), the Confucian Erudites were commissioned to collate classical texts for the benefit of the Heir Apparent. It can be taken, however, to show any commission of scholars collating texts in summer. The subject is treated in the most humane manner. There are ample refreshments, two pretty waitresses, a boy pulling off one of the scholar's boots, an attendant with a fan, and another bringing a scroll. As only one scholar only is writing, the picture may be said to represent the lunch interval. The genial, rather playful, air also suggests this. With the dais, the scrolls in their long boxes, and the black bands

Notes on Illustrations

worn by the scholars, the grouping is strengthened. The painting admirably catches the spirit of Confucianism at its best.

Plate XI (page 176)—Three Greek Kings of India. The top portrait is of Eucratides (175 B.C.) who was King of part of Bactria, of Afghanistan and the Punjab to the Jhelum river (page 183). It is taken, by permission, from one of his coins in the British Museum, though to make the portrait more striking it is enlarged and the coin edge is left out. As may be observed, Eucratides was not a pure Greek. He looks very much like what nowadays is called an Eurasian. Except for the fish-plume, his helmet is identical with a Curson topee, a pith helmet associated with Lord Curson and which, after his Viceroyalty, became fashionable for all Europeans in India. For the present writer, who once possessed a Curson topee, it is astonishing to see King Eucratides wearing one. The hat bridges two milleniums in a flash.

The bottom left-hand coin is of Diodotos, the Greek Viceroy of Bactria, who after the Parthian invasion of Persia in about 250 B.C., declared himself King of Bactria. He claimed to be a direct descendant of Alexander the Great (page 182) and is shown as a pure Greek type. The coins of Diodotos are of the greatest beauty. On some of them he has the title of Soter, the saviour, copied from the Seleucid style but which he deserved since he prevented the Parthians from overrunning the Greeks of Bactria.

On the bottom right-hand is the coin of King Menander (150 B.C.) on which is written in Greek characters *Menander Basileus Soter*, Menander King Saviour (page 185). Menander was the most famous of the Greek Kings and, though the full extent of it is unknown, his kingdom seems to have extended some distance down the Ganges. He was reigning at the time of Chang Ch'ien, the explorer's, visit. Though apparently a Buddhist and much liked by Indians, who on his death distributed, (Plutarch, *Praec. reip. ger.* 28, 6) his ashes among all the towns of his realm (as Ghandi's have been in our time), Menander looks Greek.

Plate XII (page 177)—The Gold Reliquary found in the

Buddhist stupa at Bimaran, which lies between Kabul and Jelalabad in Afghanistan. This unique casket is in the British Museum, whose authorities date its burial in the stupa as early first century A.D. (A stupa is a kind of mound, surrounded by a balustrade, under which relics of the Buddha were buried, and worshipped by circumnambulation of the mound). If its date is as early as 25 A.D., it was made during the lifetime of Christ. It is the work of a Greek jeweller living under the Kushan Kings, who succeeded the Greek Kings in about 50 B.C. (page 186). In the top photograph the Buddha is in the centre, his hand raised in the *abhya mudra*, the gesture bestowing peace. He is dressed in a toga. To his right is Indra, to his left Brahma, the two chief Hindu divinities, who bow in token that they recognise him as higher than the gods. (The figure in the centre of the lower left aspect is the donor, the man who paid for the casket.) Were it not for the faces, which are of an Indian cast of feature, the figures, the gestures, the architecture and the general conception strongly resemble a Christian casket in Romanesque style. The figure of Indra in particular looks like the Apostle Peter. In this work the Greeks in India seem to anticipate the course of their art in the Christian West. (Throughout I use the word Greek to mean the heirs of classical Greece, who include the Romans and, later, all the nations of once barbarous Europe.) The representation of Buddha on the reliquary, contemporary with the first sculptures of him in the Ghandāra region, the same in which the reliquary was found, indicates the direction, from the iconographical point of view, in which Buddhist art was to develop. The reliquary therefore anticipates important elements in the course of both western and eastern religious art.

Plate XIII (page 192)—An Indo-Greek Ghandāra sculpture of the Buddha from the British Museum, and dated first century A.D. Often this Ghandāra type of Buddha is empty and vulgar, but this sculpture, which is about a foot high, has charm. It represents an Indian dressed as a Roman gentleman of the period, the bulge on the top of the head and the eye of wisdom in the forehead, both marks of the Buddha's divinity, being treated with such discretion that they do not lessen the naturalistic effect. Figures such as these were made in north-west India in the first century A.D. to meet the demand for an image of the new Saviour. The same demand was also felt in central India beyond the hellenised Kushan state, and Indian artists, too, began to make figures of the Buddha as a personage in a robe. Having taken the general idea of a sculptured Buddha from the Greeks, or thinking of it themselves about the same time, they developed it in an Indian manner (see page 188). While the Ghandāra style never penetrated into India, it travelled into the oases en route for China, being modified and developed as it went.

Plate XIV (page 193) shows a Boddisattva or more particularly the Buddha of the future) in the Metropolitan Museum, New York. It is Chinese and has the date 477 A.D. engraved on it. (See Ludwig Bachhoffer's *A Short History of Chinese Art*: plate 59 and pages 64–66 of text.) It is reproduced here (by permission) as illustrating the spread of the Greek iconography of the Buddha to China via the oases on the Silk Road, first opened by Chang Ch'ien, Wu's explorer. This statue, as Mr. Bachhoffer shows, is copied from the style prevailing at the time in the Kucha oasis, a state on the Silk Road. Kucha had received its art from Ghandāra, but had modified the classical style to suit the only medium available, namely a mixture of mud, dung and straw. As in the fifth century Kucha was looked upon by the Chinese as an important centre of Buddhist iconography, they copied its Buddhas. The illustration is of such a copy. In the early caves of Tun-huang at the Chinese end of the Silk Road the same early type of Ghandāra-Kuchean-Chinese Buddhist sculpture is seen. It was not until the next century, the sixth, that the Chinese, having digested the Greek influences emanating from Ghandāra, began to create a truly Chinese style. Plate XIII thus illustrates the source from which the Chinese evolved their national representations of the Buddha in the Sui, T'ang, and Sung periods (sixth to thirteenth centuries).

Notes on Illustrations

Plate XV (page 208)—Stone head of a Buddha of the Boddis-attva type, British Museum, labelled Ghandāra School second century. This sculpture may be described in lay terms as the type portrait of an Afghan of that date, done according to the canons of Greco-Roman art. It has none of the spirituality of the great Indian and later Chinese faces of deities, being essentially a naturalistic type-form. It falls far behind the head of the Princess of Coloured Clouds which is that both of a human and divine personage. There is no divinity in this head. It was the body which the Greeks knew how to make half divine. How to articulate it was rather their message than how to give the face expression.

Plate XVI (page 209)—The Emperor Wen of the Sui Dynasty (581 A.D.) (see page 200) by Yen Li-pen, to be distinguished from the portrait of the Emperor Wen of the Han (179 B.C.) by the same artist. His extraordinary mortar-board hat will be noticed.

Index

Aeschylus, 175, 176
Agrican, 173
Albigenses, 204
Alexander the Great, 64, 174, 180, 183, 186, 190
Alexandria, 194
Alopen (Ruben), 202
Amarāvati, 187
Analects, 11, refers Duke of Chou, 24; 26; extracts from, 27
Angelica, 173, 174
Annals of Lu (Spring and Autumn), 16, 17
Ariosto, 174
Aristotle, 174
Arsaces, King of Parthia, 181
Artaxerxes, 202
Asanga, 192
Asoka, Emperor of India, 176, 177, 178, 180, 183, 185, 188
Asvaghosha, 192, 193 n(1)
Attila, High King of the Huns, 155
Augustine, Saint, 204

Bactria, 172, 174, 181, 182
Baikal, Lake, 113
Berosus, 180
Bharhut, 187
Bojardo, 174
Book of Changes, The, 16, 17
Book of History, The, 16, 17; contents, 18; Metal-bound coffer story, 21 et seq.; 63, 87, 93, 138
Book of Rites, The, 16, 17
Book of Songs, The, 16, 17; refers Duke of Chou; 24, 63, 93

Buddha, 11, 176, 177; rise of Buddhism, 178; 179, 183; Greek iconography, 185, 187; Mahayana, 188; Mahayana myth, 189, 190; Hinayana, 191; Mahayana, 191; Mahayana metaphysic, 192, 193; and Confucianism, 185; arrival of Buddhism in China, 195; conversion of Liang Wu Ti, 198; and Sui Emperor, 200; and Emperor Hsien Tsung, 207; Han Yü's letter, 207 seq.; deposition of, 212
Burma, 125
Burning of the Books, 63, 100

Carrhae, Battle of, 150, 173, 181
Ch'ang-an (Han capital), 89, 174, 195, 197, 202
Chang Ch'ien (explorer), 172, 174, 183, 185 189, 191
Chang Chih-ho, 33
Ch'ang Sha, 144, 145
Ch'ao Fu (Taoist hermit), 41 seq.
Chao Liang, denunciation of Yang, 58
Chao Wang (magician), 103, 104-105
Charlemagne, 174
Chaung Tzu Book, 33, 34, 39, 40, 47
Ch'en, Empress, 108, 126, 135
Chia Tao (poet), 205 seq.
Chiang Ch'ung (General in charge Hunnish Cavalry Division), 128, 129; search for sorcerors, 130, 131; death of, 132; 136
Ch'iao, Mount, 115
Chien-Chang (Palace), 122, 135

231

Index

Chih (Bandit), 34 *seq.*

Ch'in, Duke of, continues Yang's realist policy, 60; becomes Emperor, 61; (*see* Divine August One)

Ch'in, state of (capital Hsien-yang), strategic position, 50; 53

Ch'ing Dynasty, 214

Chou Bronzes, 102, 110

Chou, Duke of, and Metal-bound Coffer, 21 *seq*; founds Lu's ducal house, 24, 143

Chou Dynasty, 12; capital at Lo-yang, 14; outline of history, 48; 56; extent of Empire fourth century B.C., 60

Christ, 11

Christianity (Nestorianism), 201, history of Nestorians, 202; later history, 203, 204

Chu-Hsi, 213

Chu Ngan-Shi (complainant in *ku* witchcraft case), 127

Ch'u, state of, 50, 72, 78, 79, 80, 82, 139

Ch'ü-Yüan (Confucian poet), 144, 145, 164

Confucianism, discussed, 48, 49; threatened by Ch'in policy, 56; burning of the books, 62, 63; eclipse of, 64; discussed, 88; Confucian civil service begun, 94; 97; Confucian measures of Emperor Wen, 98; Emperor Wu and, 99 *seq.*; 166, 167, 168; and Buddhism, 195; and Liang Wu Ti, 199; and Sui Emperor, 200; and Han Yü, 207–211; system discussed, 211; triumph of, 212; dessication of, 214; overthrow and revival, 215

Confucius (The First Holy One): not a divinity, 11; date, 12; definition of his status, 12; study of past, 14; connection with classics, 15; biographical details, death and burial at Lu, 16; dreams of Duke of Chou, 21; description of in *Analects*, 27–29; elements of his system, 30, 31;

colloquy with Lao Tzu, 33; colloquy with bandit, 34 *seq.*; 56, 62, 63, 88; Eminent Founder sacrifices at tomb, 94; 97; his tomb, Ssu-ma Ch'ien's visit to, 145, 146; on foreign policy, 170; 176, 180, 210; after history, 214, 215

Constantine, Emperor, 198

Crassus, 181

Cyril, Bishop of Alexandria, 202

Dante, 174 *n*(1)

Darius, 172

Demetrius, King of Bactria, 183

Diodotos, 182

Divine August One (First Emperor Ch'in Dynasty), accession, 61; death of, 64; hears of emanation, 70; his treasures, 74, 75; his tomb, 78; on T'ai Shan, 116; 143

Doctrine of the Mean, The, 26

Emanations, 70, 71, 75

Eminent Founder (alias Liu, Lord of P'ei, King of Han, first Han Emperor, called Kao-tzu), 64; birth and early years, 66; fortune told by Lü, 68; his appearance, 70; becomes bandit, 71; becomes Lord of P'ei, 73; takes Ch'in capital (Hsien-yang), 74; flees from Hsien-yang, 77; becomes King of Han, 79; wounded by Hsiang Yü, 81; overthrows Hsiang Yü, 83–86; becomes first Han Emperor (Kao-tzu), 87; banquet, 89; moves capital to Ch'ang-an, 89; invents court ceremonial, 92, 93; founds Confucian civil service, 94; visits P'ei, 95 *seq.*; wounded, 96; death, 97

Eucratides, 183

Euripides, 181

Fa Men Ssu Monastery, 207, 209

Feng, 66, 74, 94, 96

Fêng (ancient sacrificial ritual), 115, 116, 117, 119

Index

Filial Piety, 24; story of Tseng Ts'an, 24; story of Chun Yü, 25; Mao Jung story, 25; Han Po Yü story, 25
First Holy One, *see* Confucius
Five Classics, The, 15; contents, 16, 17
Fortunate Isles, 103, 105, 106, 111, 122
Four Books, The, 15; contents of, 26

Ghandāra, 186, 187
Grand Feudatories, 12, 14, 48, 49
Great Learning, The, 26
Great Wall, 62, 63, 65
Greece, 174, 175, sculpture, 179
Greek Philosophers, 12 *n*(1), 48, 184
Greeks, 175, 176, 180, 181, 183; Buddhist sculpture and, 185–188; and Mahayana, 189, 190, 193

Hami (oasis), 148, 150, 195
Han Dynasty, 64
Han, King of, and First Emperor of, *see* Eminent Founder
Han Yü (littérateur), 205 *seq.*, 212
Hannibal, 88
Ho Ching (rebel general), 199, 208
Hsia Dynasty, 14
Hsiang Yü, 73, 74, 75; supper to Eminent Founder, 76, 77; occupies Hsien-yang, 77; becomes King Lord Protector, 79; defeat and death, 82 *seq.*
Hsien Tsung, Emperor, 207
Hsien-yang (capital of Ch'in), 70
Hsü Yu (Taoist hermit), 40, 45 *seq.*, 143
Hu, town of, 135
Huai, Emperor, 197
Hughes, E. R., 26
Hui (brother of bandit Chih), 34 *seq.*
Huns, 113, 128, 148, 150 *seq.*; in Europe, 155; 170, 171, 197
Huxley, Aldous, 32

Immortals (Taoist genii), 105, 106, 109, 111, 114
India, 172; sculpture, 177, 179; art, 188

Jen Ngan (Inspector General), 133, 136; letter to Ssu-ma Ch'ien, 159; Ssu-ma Ch'ien's reply, 160 *seq.*
Jü Hen, 133
Julian the Apostate, 201

Kan-ch'üan (summer palace), 126, 133, 135
Kao-Tzu, Emperor, Han Dynasty, *see* Eminent Founder
Kou Shih (town), 114
Ku (breeding of demons), 125; witchcraft case, 127 *seq.*; end of case, 136; 210
Kublai Khan, 213
K'ung Fu-Tzu, *see* Confucius and p. 11 *n*(1)
Kung-Sun Ch'ing (magician), 114 *seq.*
Kung-Sun Ho, 127, 128
Kushans (Yüeh-Chi), 186, 194

Lao Tzu (The Venerable Sir), 33
Liang Wu Ti, 198 *seq.*, 208
Li Kuang-Li, General (brother to Lady Li), 148, 152, 156, 162
Li, Lady, apparition of, 103, 104; 157
Li-Ling, 149 *seq.*, 160, 161, 162, 163
Li Philosophy, 213
Li, Prince (Heir to Emperor Wu), 128, 131, 133–135
Li Shao-Chun (magician), 101–103
Li Ssu, minister of Ch'in, memorial about the destruction of classics, 62, 63
Liu, *see* Eminent Founder
Liu Ch'u-Li (Chancellor), 133, 136
Livy, 137
Lo-yang, Chou capital, 14; becomes first Han capital, 87; 142, 195; library at, 196; 197
Lu, 14, 66, 85, 86
Lü (father-in-law to the Eminent Founder), 68, 69
Lü, Empress, 69, 71, 81, 87, 96
Luan Ta (magician), 105–112

Mani, 11, 204, 212

Index

Menander, King, 185
Mencius, 11 *n*(1); *Works of Mencius*, 26; Second Holy One, 26; 30, 99, 168, 174
Miao-Ku-Shê, Taoist mountain, 40, 143
Milton, 172, 173
Min, Emperor, 197
Ming, Emperor of later Han, 195
Mithras, 188
Mohammed, 11
Mommsen, 182
Mu, Duke, 58

Nagarjuna, 192
Nan-Yüeh (Canton), 112, 113
Nine Virtues, 20

Orlando, 173, 174
Orodes, King of Parthia, 181, 182
Ovid, 154, 155, 181

Pan Ku (author of *History of Former Han*), 66; 68, 73, 82, 112; opinion of Wu, 123
Parthia, 172, 173, 181, 182
P'ei, 33, 66, 72, visit to by Eminent Founder, 95
P'ei, Lord of, *see* Eminent Founder
Pein Ho, story of, 139 *seq.*
P'eng-Ch'eng (Hsiang Yü's capital), 80
Pentateuch, 180
Persia, 175, 202
Plato, 193
Plotinus, 193
Ptolemies, 175, 179, 186
Punjab, 183

Rome, 176, 186

Sainted Emperors (Yao, Shun, Yü), 12, 38, 80, 110, 119, 157, 158, 168, 208
Sanchi, 187
Scipio Africanus, 88
Seleucids, 172, 173, 175, 178, 179, 186, 190

Shan-Yü (King of the Huns), 113, 148, 150, 173, 197
Shang Dynasty, 14, 21
Shang, Lord, *see* Yang
Shang-Lin Park, 130, 132
Shantung, 101, 103, 105, 110
Shih Huang Ti, first Emperor Ch'in Dynasty, *see* Divine August One
Shih Teh (Tutor to Prince Li), 131
Shun, Emperor, 14, appointment of, 19; 20, 27
Sogdiana, 172, 181, 182
Ssu-Ma Ch'ien (historian): biography of Confucius, 16, 28; biography of Yang (Lord Shang), 50; scene from biography of Yang, 58; 62; description of Hsiang Yü's end, 82 *seq.*; character of Hsiang Yü, 85; 109, 113; opinion of Wu, 123; 132, 136, 137; his *History*, 138; *History*, how written, 141, 142; starts his travels, 143; visits Confucius' tomb, 145; admiration for Confucius, 146; visit to Yunnan, 147; appointed Duke Grand Astrologer, 147; defends Li-ling, 156; condemnation of, 158; becomes Chief Clerk of Palace, 159; death, 159; letter to Jen Ngan, 159 *seq.*; his *History*, 165, 166; 197
Ssu-ma T'an (father of Ssu-ma Ch'ien), 142
Su Wen (Commandant of Yellow Gate), 130, 131, escape of, 132; 136
Su Wu (Ambassador), 148, 153, 154
Sung-kao, Mount, 116, 120

T'ai Kung (Revered Parent), 79, 81, 87, 90; becomes Grand Emperor, 91; 92, 94
T'ai-shan, sacred mountain, 34, 111, 115; description of, 117, 118; inscription on, 121; 122, 142, 212
T'ai Tsung, Emperor, 200, 201, 202, and Nestorianism, 203, 208
T'ang (Founder of Shang), his speech, 21

234

Index

T'ang Dynasty, 200, 204

Taoism, definition, 32, 33; a quietist philosophy, 39; fable of Yao, 40 *seq.*; as a magical system, 47; 99, 166, 167, 212, 213

T'ien Jen (Director of Justice—partisan of Prince Li), 135, 136

Ting (The Venerable), 116, 119

Tsui (Hsiang Yü's horse), 83 *seq.*

Tung, Great Excellency: advises Eminent Founder, 79

Universal Father, *see* Confucius

University, founded by Wu, 100

Vasubandhu, 192

Venerable Sir, *see* Lao Tzu

Waley, Arthur, 11 *n*(2) and (3), 27, 104

Wei, Empress, 108, 126, 127, 128, 131, 132; death of, 135

Wei River, 50, 59

Wei, state of, 50; Chancellor of, 50 *seq.*; 161

Wen, Emperor (fourth sovereign of Han Dynasty), 98, 157, 171

Wen, Emperor (Sui Dynasty), 200, 201

Wu, Emperor (sixth sovereign of Han Dynasty): measures establishing Confucianism, 99, 100; interest in popular Taoism, 101; dealings with Li Shao-chun, Chao Wang, Luan Ta, 101 *seq.*; as military leader, 112, 113; and Kung-sun Ch'ing, 114; hears voice on Sung-kao, 116; sacrifices on T'ai Shan, 119, 120; kills coachman, 120; and sorcery, 126 *seq.*; sanctions witchcraft investigation, 130; the fight with Prince Li, 134; 146, 148, 149; and Li-ling, 152, 153; and Ssu-ma Ch'ien, 156–158; 171; sends Chang Ch'ien west, 172; 182, 184, 191

Wu (occult priesthood), 125; priestess, 126, 127

Wu Tsung, Emperor, dissolution of religious houses, 212

Wu Wang (Founder of Chou), 21

Xerxes, 174

Yang (alias Lord Shang), at Wei, 50, 52; leaves for Ch'in, 53; Commander-in-Chief and made Lord, 57; becomes Chancellor, 58; flight of, and death, 59; triumph of his ideas, 61; reversal of ideas, 64; 87, 100, 177 *n*(1)

Yang-shi, Princess, 128

Yao, Emperor, 14, character, 18; resignation to Shun, 18; 20; Taoist fable, 40 *seq.*; 143

Yellow Emperor, 14; tomb of, 115; 138, 164

Yellow River, 168

Yi, minister, advice to Yü, 20

Yü, Emperor: appointment of, 19; meeting with criminal, 20; 21, 60, 143

Yu (Hsiang Yü's Beauty), 82 *seq.*

Yu Wang (Emperor), 12

Yüeh Chi, 172, 174, 181, 183

Zoroaster, 202, 204